Neil L Parsons
6-57

G57

Copyright © 2024 by Moving Missouri Forward, (C4)

All rights reserved, including the right to reproduce this work in any form whatsoever without permission in writing from the publisher, except for brief passages in connection with a review. For information, please write:

The Donning Company Publishers
731 South Brunswick Street
Brookfield, MO 64628

Laurie Cupp, General Manager
Dennis Paalhar, Production Supervisor
Anne Burns, Editor
Terry Epps, Graphic Designer
Katie Gardner, Marketing and Project Coordinator

Dennis Paalhar, Project Director

ISBN: 978-1-68184-363-6

Names: Jones, James K., 1968- author.
Title: No turnin' back : G57, Michael L. Parson / James Jones.
Other titles: G57, Michael L. Parson
Description: Brookfield : The Donning Company Publishers, 2024. | Summary: "This book details the story of Michael L. Parson from a meager beginning in the small town of Wheatland, Missouri, in Hickory County to the highest political office in the State of Missouri"-- Provided by publisher.
Identifiers: LCCN 2024000247 | ISBN 9781681843636 (hardcover)
Subjects: LCSH: Parson, Michael L., 1955- | Governors--Missouri--Biography. | Politicians--Missouri--Biography. | Missouri--Politics and government--1951-
Classification: LCC F470 .J664 2024 | DDC 977.8/04092 [B]--dc23/eng/20240108
LC record available at https://lccn.loc.gov/2024000247

Printed in the United States of America at Walsworth

Governor and First Lady Parson showed their excitement and gratitude as they acknowledged the crowd after Governor Parson was sworn-in at the 2021 Missouri Bicentennial Inauguration.

No turnin' Back
G57
Michael L. Parson

Contents

Special Governor Parson Thank You to Loyal Friends and Allies . . . 6

Chapter 1 10
The Hickory County Way: Growing Up—Early Years

"Victor and Hellen raised their boys to understand that you could not put a price on always helping your neighbor, treating people fairly, and valuing hard work."

Chapter 2 22
Know When to Say When: Growing Up—Teenage Years

"Sometimes, silence is the biggest convictor."

Chapter 3 34
Making a Man Out of Him: Military Service (1975–1981)

"I need someone with a pair of balls to step forward."

Chapter 4 48
Playing to His Strengths: Law Enforcement and Turning Wrenches (1982–1992)

"He was not only a loyal customer, but also a loyal friend."

Chapter 5 58
Coming Together: Marriage, Family, and Fatherhood

"He could tell most thought he had outkicked his coverage being with Teresa."

Chapter 6 78
Creating a Winning Culture: Life as the Sheriff of Polk County (1993–2004)

"When I first became sheriff, it was like the floodgates opened."

Chapter 7 90
The Bus Has Only One Driver: Life as a Missouri State Representative (2005–2010)

"He was playing chess when others were playing checkers."

CHAPTER 8. 106
Blessed by an Unexpected Turn of Events: Life as a Missouri State Senator (2011–2016)

> "He had two options – respond with bitterness or respond with kindness."

CHAPTER 9. 194
Taking Its Toll: Life as the Forty-seventh Missouri Lieutenant Governor (2017–2018)

> "Now you said there was good and bad news, what is the bad news?"

CHAPTER 10 202
He Answers the Call: Whirlwind Transition from Lieutenant Governor to Governor (2018)

> "All of the sudden you realize that this is one of those moments in history that you are a part of."

CHAPTER 11. 216
Open for Business: Governor Completes His Term (2018–2020)

> "If everything was a priority, nothing was a priority."

CHAPTER 12. 252
Appropriate Reaction: Governor Earns Four More Years

> "Parson Works for Missouri! It is not just a tagline. It is my dad!"

CHAPTER 13. 266
Making the Right Call: Life as Missouri Governor, Stories from Behind the Scenes

> "Everything he has ever done has prepared him for where he is."

CHAPTER 14. 284
Made His Mark: Legacy of Governor Parson

> "He was poised to leave the Office and State in a better place than he found it."

A Governor Parson Thank You to Two Special Team Members . . .294
Appendix. 298
About the Author. 304

Special Governor Parson
Thank You to Loyal Friends and Allies

Governor Parson has been blessed by many people during his tenure as the fifty-seventh governor of the Great State of Missouri. There is no way Governor Parson can effectively express his thanks to all those that deserve it. During his years as governor, the Lord put three individuals in his life that were with him all the way. These three individuals proved to be valuable allies during his journey and ultimately became great friends. Their influence was not just to Mike Parson the governor but rather Mike Parson the man. These people provided encouragement, support, and inspiration to the governor while being examples of the spirit of this great state. Governor Parson will be forever grateful.

David Steward
World Wide Technology, Founder and Chairman

Governor Parson considers Mr. Steward to be a dear friend and an unwavering encourager of him and the truth. When communicating with Mr. Steward, the conversation is always dominated by God and Jesus. He believes God's word does not return void (Isaiah 55:11). He believes if one shares the word of God with people with the same intended spirit and intention, the power of the Holy Spirit will do what it says it will do. He believes for out of the abundance of heart the mouth will speak (Matthew 12:34). Mr. Steward believes the most important role of leaders is to meet the spiritual needs of people. He felt there was no time in Missouri history it was more evident than when COVID impacted the state. Missourians were in fear, in doubt, and troubled about what was happening around them. The only trust Mr. Steward knows is found in the Lord (Psalm 91:2). During that time, Mr. Steward remembers constantly sharing the Word of God with Governor Parson. Mr. Steward considers Governor Parson to be a friend based on the fact they are brothers in Christ. It was no accident God placed these two men near one another to grow up in west-central Missouri. They both grew up in a time of segregation, but grace and the "fruit of the Spirit" (Galatians 5:22-23) brought them together. Mr. Steward considers both him and Governor Parson to have developed strength through experience. He sees himself and the governor being the same but different. The similarity is they both grew up extremely poor. The difference is one is black and the other is white. Both men understand hard work has no color. Mr. Steward and Governor Parson have a relatable connection. Both men watched their parents selflessly give of themselves and now they have the awesome responsibility to honor them. Mr. Steward is proud to call the governor his dear friend and a brother in Christ.

David Steward led the way on stage at the 2023 NASCAR Cup Series race at World Wide Technology Raceway.

Johnny Morris
Bass Pro Shops, Founder

Governor Parson considers Mr. Morris to be a friend with a giving heart who loves Missouri and preserving the natural qualities that make Missouri great. Mr. Morris overflows with positivity. He always circles back to the fact adversity and challenge create opportunity. He finds the best in everyone and everything. When summarizing the features he observes in Governor Parson, Mr. Morris compared those characteristics of the governor to those of his hero in life: his father! There may be no greater compliment in the world. Mr. Morris does not think of Governor Parson as a politician. He considers Governor Parson to be someone who truly loves Missouri, who also maintains a compass of common sense with moral character and strong values. In these times, Mr. Morris feels common sense is a rare trait. Faith, family, and country are critically important to the governor. He appreciates the passion, enthusiasm, and loyalty Governor Parson demonstrates in everything he does for Missouri. Both Mr. Morris and Governor Parson came from modest beginnings but placed their compass heading on making a positive difference for others. He is not above anyone. Some politicians are motivated by personal ego and others are motivated by the possibility of making a positive difference. He loves that the governor understands his role is much bigger than himself. He appreciates his passion for the outdoors and conservation. When it comes to adversity, Mr. Morris admires the governor's leadership during the pandemic. Being a positive man, Mr. Morris concluded no matter how tough that period was it did two great things. It strengthened the family unit and forced people outdoors. Mr. Morris is grateful their compass headings brought them together in life.

Johnny Morris hosted Governor Parson at the kickoff for the "2021 Johnny Morris Bass Pro Shops U.S. Open National Bass Fishing Amateur Team Championships."

Michael Ketchmark
Ketchmark and McCreight P.C., Partner Owner and Attorney

Governor Parson considers Mr. Ketchmark to be a friend with a strong commitment to assisting people through difficult and challenging times. Mr. Ketchmark believes the governor to be the kindest and the most-humble person of power he has ever known. It is not uncommon for Mr. Ketchmark to have a phone conversation with Governor Parson while he is on a tractor on his farm on a Saturday morning. The dialogue is most often just about family and life. He feels the governor never misses an opportunity to show kindness to others. Mr. Ketchmark learned from his father that one judges a man's character not by the way he treats the people above him but rather by the way he treats the people below him. He considers Governor Parson to be a model person and champion for all the people of Missouri. It doesn't matter who they are, whether they can do something for him or not, Governor Parson is going to treat them with dignity and respect. When he is no longer governor, there will be a giant void in the soul of Missouri. It will be filled, but that individual will have huge shoes to fill. Mr. Ketchmark believes Governor Parson to be worthy of everything he has ever achieved and more. His positive influence on Missouri will last forever. Mr. Ketchmark feels his life is better because he got to know the governor. He concluded the governor has made him a better man, a better husband, and a better father, and he has made Missouri a better state. Mr. Ketchmark is glad he can call the governor a dear friend.

Michael and Susan Ketchmark joined Governor and First Lady Parson at a Convoy of Hope event in Puerto Rico.

THANK YOU TO LOYAL FRIENDS AND ALLIES

Victor and Hellen Parson pictured with their four sons.

Chapter 1

The Hickory County Way
Growing Up—Early Years

"Victor and Hellen raised their boys to understand that you could not put a price on always helping your neighbor, treating people fairly, and valuing hard work."

"It's time," Hellen Parson told her husband, Victor, at their farmhouse in Hickory County near Wheatland, Missouri. This was a first ever experience for the Parson family. In a few hours, their fourth child would be born. They were not sure if it was going to be a boy or a girl, but they knew this would be the first of their four children to be born in a hospital. Victor did not delay. Hellen grabbed the essentials, and they loaded in the truck for the fifty-mile drive to Clinton.

Later that day, Hellen and Victor welcomed a son, Michael Lynn Parson. Victor and Hellen were pretty certain their fourth child would be their last, but what they did not know was the unprecedented journey this young man named Mike was about to embark on. He would prove over his lifetime to be born with a purpose for a purpose. "Not in a million years" would Victor and Hellen have thought they were taking home the fifty-seventh governor of Missouri, but they were. This young man would defy the odds during his lifetime and indeed make the impossible become possible. From the moment he was born, this small-town farm boy from Hickory County was on the move, and there was no turnin' back.

Victor and Hellen both grew up in Hickory County, and Hickory County living was all they knew. They united in marriage when Hellen was just sixteen years old. They moved often in the early years of their marriage but never left the friendly confines of Hickory County. They took great pride in their community, their family, and especially their four sons. Victor and Hellen put in the work to provide for the needs of their boys, and the way they lived life validated that hard work was the Hickory County way.

The Parsons lived the life of sharecroppers for most of their years while raising their sons. When finances were measured, Hickory County may have been one of the poorest counties in Missouri, but if one could measure hard work, commitment, and love, this community would be considered immeasurably rich. Victor and Hellen didn't have much, but what they had mattered.

Early in his life, Victor worked with his father and brothers on their family farm where long hours were non-negotiable. Victor would later be the first in his family to graduate from high school. During his years at Wheatland High School, he was a member of the 1935 state championship basketball team. Listening to Mike describe his dad's basketball experience was like listening to a replay of the movie *Hoosiers* as the Wheatland Mules defied the odds and beat a much larger school from the city in the finals. Nothing echoes pride more than seeing Mike Parson hold the 1935 class ring of his father. Victor always spoke with great pride of his experiences as a Wheatland Mule highlighted by being both a graduate and a state champion.

Victor had one older brother, Gerald; another brother, Lester; and a sister, Velma. Mike and his brothers grew up with a tremendous amount of respect for their father's brother Gerald Parson. Gerald was a decorated World War II veteran who received both a Bronze Star and Purple Heart. Gerald spent his post-military career as a carpenter in Hickory County. Uncle Gerald was quite the craftsman, building many homes and barns in and around Wheatland.

Hellen's childhood had its fair share of challenges. Hellen was three years old when her mother passed away and twelve years old when her father passed away. Left without her parents as a young girl, the people of the area known as Avery Valley sprang into action to help raise her and her identical twin sister, Ellen. When the twins were born, the unique spelling of Hellen with two L's was chosen to match the two L's in Ellen. It was fitting for their mother to spell their names alike because their appearance was the definition of identical. Hellen and Ellen had two older sisters. Zelma was the oldest, and Mabel, who was called "Pete" by family and friends, was the second oldest. Regardless of life's challenges, Hellen proved to be an overcomer.

Hellen attended school through the eighth grade. Despite her limited formal education, Hellen was smart and wise beyond her years. Mike claims he wouldn't be the man he is today without the care, guidance, and values instilled in him through the uncompromising commitment of his mother. Victor and Hellen raised their boys to understand they could not put a price on always helping a neighbor, treating people fairly, and valuing hard work.

One unique gift Mike and his brothers admired about their mother was her handwriting. She was a talented writer who made certain all her letters were perfect. When she wrote, the words flowed across the page like artwork. To this day, Mike says, "Mom's handwriting is the prettiest I've ever seen."

Growing up, Mike did not recall his mother fearing much, but he and his brothers did remember her to be terrified of thunderstorms. This fear of storms stemmed from a tornado she and her sisters experienced that destroyed their home and nearly killed all of them when they were young. Her respect for the power of Mother Nature was evident every time dark clouds neared. "She was scared to death of them," Mike said. He remembered his mother's voice quivering as she would reluctantly share the story from time to time. When the tornado struck, the four girls were home alone. They sought refuge on the floor near the old coal stove in the center of the house when it was completely blown away by the tornado. Pete had hot coals from the stove scorch her back, and she wore the physical scars from that event for the rest of her life. The entire house was displaced, its contents were scattered everywhere, but by the grace of God, the four girls were all that remained.

The girls' encounter with the twister came full circle more than six decades later. When they were little, Hellen and Ellen were each given a wooden dollhouse cradle carved for them by a neighbor. The man wrote their names on the bottom of each cradle. After the house was destroyed, Ellen's cradle was found in the rubble scattered about the yard, but Hellen's was never found. Fast forward approximately sixty-five years when Kent Parson's wife, Mike's sister-in law, was in an antique shop in Warsaw, Missouri, and noticed a cradle that reminded her of the tornado story her mother-in-law had shared. Curious, she decided to pick it up, and sure enough, the name "Hellen" was written on the bottom. Of course, she bought it and saw to it that Hellen got it back.

Kent, the oldest of the Parson brothers, was born in 1938 followed by Lee in 1940. There was a sizable gap between them and the final two Parson boys. James was born in 1953. Growing up, James took on the nickname "Ike." Mike, the final Parson son, was an unexpected blessing to Victor and Hellen. Mike's way of making the impossible possible started when he became the first Parson boy to be born in a hospital. Mike was born on Saturday, September 17, 1955, in Clinton, Missouri, about an hour drive northwest of Wheatland. Mike's brothers were born in their home or at the office of Dr. Briggs, the local doctor in Wheatland.

The Parson boys moved from farm to farm on an annual basis while growing up. When Mike was born, they lived at what the Parson boys referred to as the "Carpenter Place." The Carpenter Place was located about three miles northwest of Wheatland. At this point, Kent and Lee were already seventeen and fifteen years old, respectively. The Carpenter Place would prove to be the final sharecropping destination for the Parson family.

During Mike's early years, the Parson family didn't have the opportunity to enjoy many of the modern residential amenities most enjoy today and many Missourians were already enjoying at the time. Mike and his brothers, however, did not know any other way. They thought everyone in the world were going to the bathroom in an outhouse and taking baths in large tubs outside behind the house. At the Carpenter Place, there was no running water inside. Hellen washed clothes in the same tub the Parson boys used to take a bath. Ike and Mike had to pump water from the well with a hand pump to fill the tub. Ike said, "There was no hurry to get into the freshly pumped water in the tub . . . the sun needed some time to warm that water up." Hellen would sometimes heat a pan of water inside on the stove to pour in the tub, though it made very little change to the temperature of the water. An outhouse was also all they knew. As can be imagined, weather conditions were an important consideration when making the decision to head to the outhouse, but other times, the only factor to consider was the fact that "nature called."

Another feature they thought was the norm was only having one means of transportation for the entire family. Mike and Ike dented a few fenders when they started driving, but the dented fender most impressionable in their minds was provided by their mother in their only vehicle during Ike's early years in school. Mike will never forget it because he was in the vehicle with her, and Ike remembers it because his birthday celebration at school was disrupted because of the accident. Hellen would always make a birthday cake at home for each son and take it to school for all the kids to enjoy. The cake may have still been a little warm when she loaded it and Mike up for the drive to school. The smell of that cake was just too tempting for Mike. As they started eastbound down the gravel road leading from their house, he thought it was only right that someone tested the cake for quality. Mike remembers Hellen turning around in the driver's seat and extending her hand towards him to put a stop to his taste testing session and provide some corrective measures. This, combined with the fact Hellen was traveling a little faster than the old creek gravel road could handle, sent the car off the road into the trees and brush. Hellen had some minor bumps and bruises, and the car had some minor damage, but the cake was totaled. Thankfully, Mike didn't sustain any physical injuries at that moment, but the fear of walking alongside his mother to tell his father, who was working a team of horses in the field nearby, inflicted major mental injuries.

One vehicle for the family was the norm growing up. There was seldom a time their mom or dad would drive them to or from school. When they lived at the Carpenter Place, Ike and Mike were the first on the school bus and the last off. Their dad would always have something for them to do when they got home from school each day. When they didn't feel like riding the bus, Mike and Ike would make the three-mile walk home. That walk often included a stop at the bridge over the creek just east of the house. "Boys will be boys" was a constant theme, and exploration was a must down at the creek. Their adventures often included rock throwing and jumping off the bridge. Physical injury to Mike or Ike usually brought the fun to an end. Regardless, any injury to Mike was always deemed by Mom to be the responsibility of Ike.

When Mike was around ten years old, Victor and Hellen found themselves in a position to purchase a farm they could call their own—a place they'd worked very hard to get. The family relocated to the "Old Home Place," which was previously owned by Victor's parents, in 1965. The Parson Farm was located about three miles north of the Carpenter Place.

When they moved to the Old Home Place, the Parson family finally had an indoor bathroom for the first time. Uncle Gerald and Victor added the bathroom themselves. Along with the bathroom amenities, this was also the first time their home was heated by anything other than a wood stove. Hedge was Victor's wood of choice. He felt hedge burned hotter and longer than all the others. Woodcutting was a family project. Typically, each woodcutting day concluded with a weenie roast for supper that night. The potbelly stove was a staple in the Parson home until their first oil burning stove at the Old Home Place.

Mike and his brothers grew up with a tremendous amount of respect for their parents. Victor and Hellen had very little as a couple and earned every dollar they ever had, which they used to meet the needs of their four boys as best they could. Not knowing any other lifestyle, they didn't want for anything, and this was how the Parson boys grew up. They just assumed this was how it was supposed to be and how most people lived their lives. They owned little of the farm equipment they used. At most of the farms where they lived, there was a cow milking and grain operation.

Victor and Hellen were a great team. Victor oversaw the finances of the family and accounted for every cent passing through the Parson family. He was a stickler for immaculate record keeping. Hellen's focus was on Victor and the four Parson boys. This was a full-time job. Victor had a pretty laid back personality and was a little more "matter of fact." Hellen wore her emotions on her sleeve. She was passionate, and everyone knew it. She was a "firecracker." In a nutshell, Victor made the decisions, and Hellen made the noise. Victor would patiently wait when others were using the community party line phone system, while Hellen would pick up the receiver after a brief moment and say, "You two need to get off here . . . I need to make a phone call." A great team needs variety and mixture of talent, which is just what Victor and Hellen Parson were.

The Parson family focused on using their finances wisely. The boys seldom had an unmet need, but by the same token, they seldom remembered a want being fulfilled. The one thing money could not buy that was instilled in the Parson boys by their parents was a work ethic like none other. The Parson boys didn't know the definition of the word "excuse" because they never witnessed one growing up.

Farming was Victor's primary occupation and source of income. He also did a little carpentry on the side, assisting those in the community with projects like home and barn construction. When Hellen worked outside the home, she worked at the local café in Wheatland and as a cook at the senior center. She also worked in the school kitchen at Wheatland on occasion.

Teams of horses were the norm on the Parson farm while the oldest two Parson brothers lived at home. Kent and Lee considered their father to be one of the best in Hickory County at handling a team and spent many years working in the fields with him. Kent's senior year in high school was the first year they ever had a tractor. Before this, much of the work was done by hand. Mike and Ike remembered many days walking the freshly plowed rows picking up stones (sometimes bigger than a basketball) while following their dad as he plowed with a tractor. These stones can still be found today on the edges of the fields at the Carpenter Place and the Old Home Place.

Technology had improved slightly by the time Mike and Ike were old enough to be valuable hands on the farm, but it still had no resemblance to farming today. Ladders were even a bit scarce back in their day. They had four hand-dug wells used primarily for providing water for the livestock at the Old Home Place. The well walls were lined with stone, and Mike and Ike remember their father periodically sending them to the bottom of the wells to dig them out. Victor would cut down a nearby cedar tree to use as a ladder, and Mike and Ike would scale the branches to get to the bottom. When they reached the bottom, Victor would send a bucket down on a rope. Mike and Ike would fill the bucket by dragging it through the mud. Once it was full, the boys would yell for their father to hoist the bucket back up. This continued until Victor was satisfied with what he saw. When completed, Mike and Ike would climb back up the cedar tree to the surface.

The Parson boys also worked many hours cutting alfalfa, wheat, and corn with a hand sickle or scythe. After dropping the crop, they would bind it into sheaves and arrange in shocks. Since they never owned a thrasher of their own, they would schedule a date with one of the few people that owned one in Hickory County to complete the harvest. The day of thrashing was almost like a holiday event. Since there was only one thrasher, residents throughout the area would gather to assist.

Despite some improvements in technology, there were still pieces of farm machinery few people owned in Hickory County. Mike's dad never owned his own baler. Instead, he would schedule a day with a local farmer who owned one to come to their place a few times a year. Mike remembers a large group of guys coming to the farm to put up hay. A few of the faces changed from time to time, but two particular faces and responsibilities never changed. Mike's dad always loaded the wagon. There was an unwritten rule that no one could do it better. The other face was Johnny Moore. When they lived at the Old Home Place, Johnny, who lived at the neighboring farm to the north, never missed a thrashing or baling day event. In fact, Johnny was the only other person to ever sit in their father's chair at the dinner table. Victor was pretty fond of his spot at the table, but the boys never witnessed their father ask Johnny to move, and they never questioned him about why he allowed Johnny to sit there. To this day, the Parson boys consider it a sign of the tremendous level of respect he had for Johnny.

While the guys were out working in the field, Mike's mother could always be found making a huge spread of food for when the job was complete. Hellen was well known for preparing some of the best food. Mike and Ike still believe their mother's cooking attracted some of the biggest crews in the county. Ike also remains of the opinion that Mike spent most of this time driving the tractor and not throwing bales. Ike regarded Mike as their mom and dad's "chosen one."

Trips to the local grocery store in Wheatland were rare. Hellen would go to the grocery store periodically, but most of what was consumed at the Parson dining room table was raised or grown right there on the family farm. They had cows for milk, chickens for eggs, and butchered their own cows, hogs, and chickens. Despite the fact the Parson boys could harvest deer anytime, Hellen refused to cook deer. Coffee and sugar were the main items reserved for purchase at the grocery store.

Victor would get up at five o'clock every morning to milk cows. He would then return to the house like clockwork to eat the breakfast Hellen had prepared. The meal always included ham or sausage, eggs, biscuits, and gravy. His father would say a blessing before each meal.

In Mike's early years, his dad refused to let him and Ike milk the cows. Victor had a meticulous process of doing things, and Mike thought his dad didn't want him and Ike getting the cows stirred up. When Mike and Ike would help, the cows sometimes got restless, and Dad would spend a considerable amount of time getting them calmed back down. It was thought milking the cows without them was more time efficient than with them. Victor milked the cows twice a day every day. To keep the boys busy, Victor would assign them some other duties on the farm. Mike and Ike recall many hours shucking corn for the hogs. Still today, Mike credits his own work ethic to the standard and benchmark set by his father. Mike considers him the hardest working man he ever knew. He never remembers his dad being sick and certainly never remembers a vacation.

To make a little money during their early years, Mike and Ike would collect eggs from the chicken house and go to Wheatland to sell them from a local business parking lot. As they got a little older, they branched out their business plan and started collecting soda pop bottles which they took to the local grocery store for refund. These were their main sources of income until they were old enough to work at a local business.

Sunday was always observed as a "Day of Rest." The Lord's Day was the Lord's Day at the Parson home. Work was limited to the required chores and nothing more. The Parsons would be found at the Baptist church in Wheatland every Sunday. As with many youngsters, going to church each Sunday was non-negotiable for the Parson brothers. Their Sunday school teacher, Nannie Jenkins, was tasked with bringing the word of God to Mike and Ike each Sunday, though Mike and Ike were not always the best students.

It wasn't all work and no play for the Parson boys. Basketball and baseball were mainstays growing up. Community social time was also important to the citizens of Hickory County. The primary social gathering spot in Wheatland was the local barbershop owned by Faye Smith. Storytelling was the lifeblood for the men and women who gathered there twice a week. The men would gather inside while the women would assemble at the picnic tables in front of the shop. Faye's primary employment was operating a butcher shop halfway between Wheatland and Hermitage, but every Friday and Saturday night Faye would cut hair near the square in Wheatland along 54 Highway. Mike and Ike would trek into Wheatland periodically with their parents for a haircut. With only two options, deciding what kind of haircut to get was not difficult. For one dollar, it was either a crew cut or a flat top. Though the haircuts were a dollar, the stories were free. Mike and Ike remember Faye smoking cigars and cutting their hair with just one arm as he'd lost most of his other arm in a hay baler accident on the farm.

Jackson Equipment in Wheatland was critical to the survival of local farm families, including the Parsons. Ike and Mike aren't exactly sure how their mom and dad were able to make it through difficult times but give Mart Jackson, the owner of Jackson Equipment, a considerable amount of credit. "There is no way our dad could have been able to pay for the items he needed at the time of purchase," Ike noted. "Mart had to float us through difficult times on credit," Mike concluded. Sharecroppers were usually paid at harvest time, and the needs on the farm seldom aligned with the harvest. Seeing friends, neighbors, and customers through difficult times was the way in Wheatland and Hickory County. These lessons served Mike well when he owned and operated a business of his own later in life.

When it came to the purchase of a vehicle, Ike said Victor worked out an agreement with Darby Motors in Wheatland. "Dad would not make monthly payments. He would make payments when he sold cattle," Ike recalled. "Dad kept immaculate records. He knew every dime that went into everything . . . he even kept records of how much he tithed to the church." Mike and Ike still have some of the written records kept by their dad. Victor was a tireless worker, which rubbed off on his sons.

The oldest brother, Kent, and his wife, Shirley, moved to the state of California shortly after graduating from Wheatland High School in 1956. At the time, many people in Wheatland and Hickory County were seeking opportunities to make a good living. Kent could make two to three times more per hour in California, which was hard to pass up. Initially, he went to California to work the summers before his junior and senior years and stayed with Aunt Ellen and her husband. His aunt tried to encourage his dad to join them saying, "You are just killing yourself Vic . . . farming and not making anything." Victor and Hellen never relocated the family to California, but Kent and his wife and many other families from Hickory and Polk Counties did. "Where I lived for 25 years, Santa Paula, was nicknamed 'Little Bolivar' because there were so many people that had moved out there from Bolivar following the depression," Kent said.

Kent and Shirley would make one annual trip back to Wheatland to visit the family. On one occasion, while the Parsons still lived at the Carpenter Place, Kent brought back a couple BB guns he'd bought for his little brothers. Kent thought the BB guns would be more fun than the cap guns he and his brother Lee had growing up. "We got the whole lesson of how to be responsible with the guns or they would take it away from us. Once we got the BB guns, it didn't last an hour. Mike shot mom. She immediately took them away from us. It didn't take us long to lose those," Ike laughed as he shared the short-lived fun when Mike was around six years old.

Lee was quite a prankster. Mike admitted, "I always admired him for that. I'm not sure why. I might have taken after him a little." Lee went to work at Hallmark in Kansas City immediately after graduating from Wheatland High School in 1958. After retiring from Hallmark, Lee opened an antique shop in Weaubleau in Hickory County about ten miles from Wheatland. While he was sheriff, Mike would stop by periodically and visit with his brother. One day, Mike went into the antique shop and noticed a cup on the shelf behind Lee that said "Mike Parson – Polk County Sheriff!" These were cups Mike had given away. Mike noticed a paper tag hanging from the cup with a price on it. It had a dollar on it and it was crossed out. Below that was fifty cents and it was crossed out. Below that was ten cents. Mike proceeded to ask his brother how he got the coffee cup? Mike said Lee answered, "Oh some guy came in here trading that. I gave way too much money for that. I can't get rid of it. I can't even give it away, but I am going to at least get ten cents out of it. That was the worst investment I have ever made. I thought you were popular up there." Lee was really pouring it on Mike. Mike took it like a little brother, but he wasn't done yet.

When Mike came back to town, he approached a guy he knew from Empire Electric in Bolivar who frequented the antique shop. Mike gave the man a couple of dollars and asked a favor of him. Mike said, "I want you to do something for me. I want you to buy that coffee cup. No matter what it costs." The man went to the shop a few days later. He made small talk with Lee as he always did, but right before he left, he got to the point. The man said, "Before I go, I would like to buy your brother's coffee cup off you. Mike has been a good sheriff." The man told Mike that Lee adamantly responded, "I wouldn't sell that cup. That is my little brother's cup. I am not about to sell that cup. It is going to sit right there. I am going to tell everyone that comes in here that I cannot sell that thing." Mike maintains a special place for his late brother Lee and his family.

Growing up, Ike felt his most important job was looking after Mike. When Ike and Mike were able to start working outside the home, they both needed a ride to work at the local service stations in Wheatland. After Ike got his license, he felt he got stuck "babysitting" Mike. In the evening, when Ike would leave the house in his '52 Chevy, he would drop Mike off as quickly as possible at the Dairy Queen in Wheatland. Ike would give Mike a time to meet him back at the Dairy Queen before returning home each night.

After high school, Ike spent a year at Southwest Missouri State University in Springfield before taking a job at the local MFA. He then went into the construction industry working out of the union hall in Springfield. Ike worked on the construction of many bridges in southwest Missouri. He was tempted to take off to Alaska for the construction of the Alaska Pipeline as it took center stage in the 1970s. Ike passed up this opportunity, choosing rather to stay near Hickory and Polk Counties.

Being close in age, Ike and Mike shared many of the same experiences growing up. Since Kent and Lee were so much older, they did not spend much time hanging out with their younger brothers. Regardless, the one thing that is evident when spending time around the Parson brothers is the love and respect they have for one another and especially their parents.

Mike and Ike Parson were dressed for success as they headed to a function at Wheatland High School.

Chapter 2

Know When to Say When
Growing Up—Teenage Years

"Sometimes, silence is the biggest convictor."

One would be hard pressed to find a person more loyal than Mike Parson. He is as dependable as it comes, and his loyalty extends in multiple directions. Mike can always be counted on by his family and he has a tremendous amount of respect for his parents. As the youngest of four, he often found himself being compared to his older siblings. He came up on the short end of a few physical battles as a little brother but eventually learned to hold his own. There was always a bit of sibling rivalry between the brothers, but they had a brothers' bond that was inseparable. Mike has always been tremendously loyal to his friends, which has been reciprocated. Loyalty in itself does not necessarily mean making wise decisions, but it does mean having someone to share in the consequences of poor decision making. Mike and Ike shared some consequences with the Walker brothers.

George and Franklin Walker were Mike and Ike's best friends growing up in Wheatland. The Walker family had moved to Hickory County from the state of Texas to operate a quarry between Wheatland and Hermitage. George and Franklin's father had two artificial legs and walked with the assistance of two canes. He had lost his legs as result of a dump truck accident at the quarry when the truck he was driving on a steep grade lost its brakes. To save himself, he dove from the cab of the truck but was unable to clear himself to avoid being struck. These physical challenges didn't slow him down much, however, and his canes sent a strong message when discipline was needed. George Walker was Mike's age, and Franklin was Ike's age. George and Franklin had many knock-down drag-outs. These were viewed as moments of brotherly love. The Walker and Parson brothers were a force to be reckoned with, and the community learned to be on watch when these guys assembled.

Halloween was a time when Wheatland and Hickory County were on especially high alert for this crew. Ike claimed that "the kids would just take over the town." The fun started with the simple turning over of outhouses. Ike declared that "the outhouse at Aunt Pete's was off limits."

If that outhouse got overturned, Ike or Mike would be called to reset it. Despite the fact they themselves did not overturn Aunt Pete's outhouse, other kids in Wheatland did, and the Parson boys responded each time they were called to rectify the situation.

In fact, Wheatland would hire a temporary night watchman each year in the days leading up to Halloween to help curb the juvenile mischief around town, but the Walker and Parson brothers were always up to a challenge. Water balloons became common as the boys horsed around town, but water balloons were considered "a drop in the bucket" in comparison to the rivers unleashed in one of Mike and George's bigger Halloween pranks.

One Halloween, after spotting the temporary night watchmen and city deputy, Mike and George retrieved a wrench out of the Wheatland city maintenance truck. This wrench had a quick and efficient function . . . to turn the water hydrants in Wheatland on and off . . . and that is exactly what it did on this night. Mike and George turned one water hydrant on after another. It is not certain if the night watchman had a wrench of his own, but it definitely wasn't keeping pace with that of Mike and George. The Good Lord sought justice behind the Christian church when both Mike and George hit an unexpected clothesline. With the city deputy in pursuit, there was no time to be concerned with the injuries they sustained. It's hard to guess how many water balloons it would take to equal the amount of water released that night, but it would have to be enough to fill a water tower as the boys drained it all before the hydrants were closed. This time, Ike and Mike were not summoned to Aunt Pete's house to reset her outhouse, but they did have to hear her adamantly complain about the juveniles that must have drained the water tower as she had no water for some time. The Parson boys did not know what it was like to have running water, but they acted as if they were equally appalled by the actions of the culprits.

Regardless of the time of year, Mike and his brothers did not spend much time in the house. They didn't have a television for most years, and while listening to the radio was an option, Mike remembers it to be reserved for his grandfather and uncle during St. Louis Cardinals baseball season. They would sit on the edge of their chairs leaning up to the large cabinet radio like their lives depended on every pitch.

Basketball was also a common pastime growing up. When the conditions were dry enough, Mike and Ike would spend countless hours on the dirt court behind their house. Playing into the night was common during the warm months. They would hang a lightbulb near the court to play once it became dark. The basketball goal was on an old cedar pole their dad dragged up behind the house. They then nailed a sheet of lumber and a rim to the pole. There was no post hole digger, so they hand dug a hole to put it in; however, this hole was much larger than it needed to be. "The thing never was set. You could actually go down under the goal and move it when people were shooting," Mike chuckled as he told the story. Their friends George and Franklin missed many shots that were right on target thanks to a subtle push of the pole by Mike or Ike.

As Mike got older, he fell in love with driving. It really didn't matter what he drove; he just wanted to be behind the wheel. The first tractor Mike ever drove was a Ford 681. It was a used tractor but new to the Parson family. One day after returning home from town with Ike and their dad, Mike asked if he could take the tractor for a drive down the gravel road that led to their house. Mike was excited to get behind the wheel. As Victor and Ike started on a project near the house, Mike went out of sight over the hill. After about ten minutes, Victor and Ike looked down the road and saw the silhouette of a person walking toward them, quickly realizing it was Mike.

As Mike got closer, Victor and Ike could hear Mike squalling and crying. Mike had a liquid of some kind all over him that at first appeared to be gasoline but was later determined to be battery acid. Mike might have been crying because the battery acid was burning his skin, but Ike still believes he was crying because of the trouble he realized he was in for not returning with the tractor. Now, since Mike was out of sight, the exact details of the incident are still up for debate, but the one thing that is certain is the tractor turned completely upside down and caught on fire.

Ike thought if Mike could make the tractor do donuts, he would try to make that happen, ultimately concluding Mike was probably doing something he shouldn't have been. Mike, however, recalls no horseplay but rather a leisurely tractor ride gone wrong. As he was turning the tractor around to head back to the house, he cut the steering wheel as hard as he could. This caused the steering rod near the wheels to bind up, making it too hard for Mike to straighten up. The front tire of the tractor hit a culvert pipe, tossing Mike to the ground as the tractor turned over. He was fortunate to not be crushed in the process. When Ike first saw the tractor upside down in the ditch, he remembers thinking, "It's a wonder it didn't kill him." The only thing that kept the tractor from crushing him was a small gap between the culvert pipe and the fender of the tractor. This small area happened to be where Mike found himself as the battery acid began to fall.

The tractor soon caught fire, and though Mike escaped before being burned by the fire, he did not escape the burn of the battery acid. Mike required medical attention and didn't return to the scene. The tractor required a total rebuild, and perhaps so did Mike's pride. He was alive but knew he was in trouble. Mike and Ike don't remember how payment was made for the restoration of the tractor, but they are confident their dad did not have the money to pay in full at the time. They both think Victor worked out some type of payment arrangement to make it happen. Small payments until paid in full at the time of the next harvest was likely the plan.

Interestingly enough, Mike's passion for driving soon turned into a passion for racing. Hearing the cars and smelling the burnt fuel and oil at the Humansville racetrack stole his heart growing up. He wanted to experience the power of one of these racing machines. With the help of Ike and some other friends, his wish came true. Mike was quite the driver in his younger days. "I don't remember if Mike was even old enough to have a driver's license when he started driving race cars at Humansville," Ike recalled, remembering how he'd drive Mike back and forth from the racetrack.

Mike's first paying job was at the Apco gas station working for Ronnie Roby along 54 Highway in Wheatland. Mike was not yet fifteen years old, but he was a mover and shaker. After a couple of years at Apco, Mike took his talents across the street to the Skelly gas station on the other side of 54 Highway. The station was owned and operated by Bill Allen. Mike considered both Ronnie and Bill to be "tough as nails." Bill took an interest in Mike. Over the years, Mike took an interest in cars and turning wrenches. Mike was making a little less than $2 an hour working sixty hours a week, but he was a dependable worker and would spend time after hours tinkering with cars and engines. Bill knew Mike and Ike were getting pretty attached to fast cars and racing. He was instrumental in boosting the short-lived Parson racing operation.

Mike and Ike were given an old panel truck by Bill Allen. The panel truck was a retired bread truck. Ike and Mike were able to somehow round up a race car. Getting their start driving race cars at the track in

Humansville, Mike and Ike would load up four or five of their friends in the panel truck and pull their car to the track after throwing a few old tires in the back. The panel truck had an unofficial capacity of approximately ten people. After the race, they would make the twenty-mile trip back to Wheatland. Governor Parson wears evidence of one of these trips. On the way home after a night of racing, Mike decided to slide open one of the doors in the back of the truck and take aim at a sign on the side of the road with a Coke bottle. Bullseye, Mike nailed the sign, shattering the bottle. A piece of the shattered glass came back and pierced his neck. Mike's blood gushed everywhere, and Hellen threw a fit when they arrived at the house to seek first aid. Mike still has a scar on his neck because of his Coke bottle incident.

During high school, Mike played softball in the fall, basketball in the winter, and baseball in the spring for the Wheatland Mules. When Mike was a freshman and sophomore, Ike remembers catching Mike in both softball and baseball the two years they were in high school together. "Mike was a great pitcher in both," Ike bragged. Athletics were an important part of the school experience for all the Parson boys. Studies and homework were not the highest priority on Mike's list during his years in school. Following in his father's footsteps, Mike took basketball very seriously. It just so happened his mother took it even more seriously than Mike. There was no better place to be on game night than the gymnasium at Wheatland High School. It was standing room only when the Mules hit the hardwood. One of the most passionate fans was Hellen Parson. Mike's mother did not miss a game and lived every possession like she was in the game herself.

Mike was an above average player who always gave it everything he had. When asked if he remembered any specific highlights during his high school basketball career, he circled around to the team. But he did relay a story about his mother that is still talked about today. The moment occurred during an intense game against a rival in the Wheatland gymnasium. During this game, from her standard location (front row at center court), Hellen Parson was not certain the game was being objectively officiated. As the game progressed, the game intensified, and so did Hellen. Late in the third quarter after a mad scramble for possession of the ball by both teams, the ball landed in the arms of Hellen in the front row. This is where the details get fuzzy and the legend was born. To get the ball back into play, she threw an overhand fastball into the chest of the unexpecting referee.

Being the youngest of four brothers, Mike found himself wanting to hang out with the older kids in the community. In between his eighth grade and freshman years at Wheatland, some would say Mike "got mixed up with the wrong crowd." Mike was living in the fast lane. The boys his age in the community were envious of the cool kid that was hanging out with the older, even cooler kids. Mike was running hard. He was out late and partying hard with the guys, but he always got up and made it to school on time. He never missed a practice or game, but when the work was done, it was time for play. He loved drinking beer and chasing girls with his buddies.

Mike got his zeal for law enforcement honestly. He did not learn about law enforcement through observation alone but rather by association. Mike first got acquainted with law enforcement one summer night before starting high school. He was out with his friends, drinking beer and running around town. Mike's cousin was in town visiting from California, so she tagged along as well. At one point in the evening, the county sheriff happened to come across the kids. He confiscated the beer they had in their possession and proceeded to take them all home. The sheriff gave the details to the parents but did not ticket the minors. Mike knew his behavior had hurt his parents. He also knew his uncle was not taking the mishap well either, as he heard his belt making contact with his cousin's rear end in the adjacent room shortly after the sheriff departed.

Even still, one time was not enough for Mike to learn his lesson. When he was fifteen years old, he and his buddies hired an eighteen-year-old boy in the community to drive them to Kansas to buy some beer as the age required to purchase alcohol in Kansas was eighteen. The older boy loaded Mike and his friends into his '57 Chevy for the one-hundred-mile or so ride down 54 Highway to the nearest convenience store on the other side of the Kansas state line. Mike and his friends pooled all their money, but it was not enough to purchase a cooler or even ice. In fact, it was not enough to even buy real beer but only lower alcohol content 3.2 beer. Regardless, the alcohol content was irrelevant. The contents of those cans would be golden when secured. The driver was nervous all the way to Kansas, which did not change upon the purchase of the beer. Twenty-four sweet cans of 3.2 beer had been purchased and were ready for consumption by the underage boys.

It sounds like a scene from *Smokey and the Bandit*. Scared they'd be caught with the beer, the boys placed the case between the radiator and grill in the car's engine compartment for the drive back to Hickory County. Too excited to wait, the boys would stop every twenty miles or so to enjoy the now less than cold beverage. Granted, this was happening in the middle of summer. By the time they arrived back in Wheatland, the beers left were now hot to the touch, but they still tasted great. The beer run took so long that by the time they got back, there was not a soul left in town. When Mike got home, he quietly opened the door and maneuvered through the house to his room upstairs, feeling like he and his buddies had pulled off a great one.

Mike and George spent many hours together finding fun. Ironically, most times the "fun" was accompanied by a little trouble. Again, when they were both fifteen years old, they nearly pulled off one for the ages. George had a girlfriend who worked at an area truck stop diner. George came up with the idea they needed to pick up his girlfriend at the diner at closing time. Neither Mike nor George was of driving age, but this wasn't anything two brilliant fifteen-year-old minds couldn't overcome. George's brother Franklin had a '69 Chevy Camaro 428 four-speed. George decided they would ask Franklin if they could borrow his car for the short drive to R & S Truck Stop on 13 Highway to pick up his girlfriend.

Franklin agreed to let Mike and George take his car. Franklin told them his wallet was in the glovebox of the car and they were welcome to use it if they ran into any problems. George drove and Mike rode shotgun as they headed south out of Wheatland. Shortly after they picked up the girl, George asked Mike if he would be willing to drive while he and his girlfriend rode in the back on the way home. Mike was pumped to get behind the wheel of this power machine. Mike said with a big smile, "I got this," as George and his girlfriend moved to the backseat of the two-door Camaro. Mike wasn't concerned about what might have been going on in the backseat as he was fully focused on this 350-horsepower driving machine. It was like a dream come true. He was on top of the world with no worries.

The engine was roaring as he tried his best to pull back the reins of this powerful machine. As they neared Wheatland, there was a stretch of highway that was long and straight. At this point, he failed to tame the horsepower as he stood a little more on the gas, increasing speed as they approached the town. Sixty . . . sixty-five . . . seventy . . . what a rush! It felt so good to be in control. It was close to midnight as they neared the Wheatland city limits. Mike glanced in the rearview mirror and saw a vehicle very close to the back of the Camaro, so close he could not even see the headlights. Mike asked George to knock it off in the backseat and help him identify who was behind them. George quickly identified the car to have "cherries" on top of it. It was not certain if it was county or state, but it was law enforcement. The lights were not on, so George encouraged Mike to turn at the first city street when they rolled into Wheatland.

Mike turned at the first road they came to. The law enforcement vehicle did the same behind them, quickly turning on the red lights. They were being pulled over. As the officer approached the vehicle, Mike, George, and his girlfriend were scrambling to figure out what to do. They remembered Franklin telling them that if they had any problems his wallet was in the glovebox. Red lights constituted a problem, so it was time to get the wallet. Mike got it out of the glovebox as the officer approached the car. The Missouri State Highway Patrolman asked Mike, "Do you know how fast you were going?" Mike said no. The patrolman told Mike he clocked him at over ninety miles per hour. Mike knew he'd opened the engine a little but was not certain exactly how fast he was going.

The patrolman asked Mike for his driver's license, and Mike proceeded to fiddle through Franklin's wallet. Noticing Mike's struggles, the officer said, "You are having a little trouble finding your driver's license." Mike quickly responded, "Yes, my girlfriend has been messing around with the stuff in my wallet lately." After Mike finally found the license, the patrolman asked Mike to join him in his patrol car. The patrolman began asking a few questions as he started to write in his ticket book and said, "I clocked you at 92 miles per hour, but I am going to write your ticket for 80 miles per hour." He added, "It says here that you have black hair." Franklin was seventeen years old and had coal black hair. With his heart pounding, Mike immediately responded, "I dyed my hair." The officer put bleached blonde hair as the color on the ticket.

Ticket in hand, Mike exited the patrol car and walked back to the Camaro. When he got in, relief overcame them all. They took George's girlfriend to her house as they needed to quickly get back home and tell Franklin what had happened. Mike and George told him they got pulled over and used his driver's license. They apologized and said they would pay the fine associated with the ticket. Franklin was irritated but seemed relatively comfortable with the situation and arrangement. George and Mike thought they had pulled off the impossible. Little did they know during the night, Franklin would reconsider his level of comfort with the plan.

While George and Mike were at school the next day, Franklin went to the Hickory County Sheriff's Office to come clean about the situation. Franklin disclosed it all to the sheriff, and the sheriff contacted the highway patrol. After school, Mike went over to George's house as he did most days. As Mike approached the house, he noticed something out of place. There was a highway patrol car parked out front. The patrolman exited the vehicle, approached Mike, and said, "Get in the front seat of my car." As Mike got in the patrol car, the patrolman sat with his hat and sunglasses on, thumping on the steering wheel and dash of the car. Suddenly, the officer took off his sunglasses, threw them against the windshield, and said, "You might have made a fool out of me once, but you will never do it again." There were no words that were going to help Mike at this point. The officer grabbed his ticket book and proceeded to write multiple citations.

It is sometimes hard for young people to learn. One night, Mike and his buddies were running around town. It is not exactly known whose idea it was this time, but the group of young men decided to take four recapped tires from a local gas station that had been left outside. Beer money was a little low, so Mike thought they could sell the tires to replenish their fund. Mike ultimately sold the tires to a buyer in Hermitage. Word of the deal circulated to the school administration and subsequently to law enforcement. This time, Mike had to pay the piper. He had to go get the tires, return the money to the person who bought them, return them to the shop where they were taken, and appear before the judge. Mike vividly recalled the judge saying, "You are not too young to sit in prison." Again, the entire situation crushed his parents.

Mike acknowledged the fact that some things needed to change but running around and drinking with his buddies were not yet going to be eliminated from the plan. The straw that ultimately broke the camel's back occurred at the same time his oldest brother Kent was home from California to preach a revival in the local community. Kent and Mike did not have a close relationship due to their seventeen-year age difference but still had a brotherly bond. On one of the nights Kent was preaching the revival, Mike went out with his buddies and got "shit-faced drunk." So drunk that when he got home, he needed to spend quite a bit of time leaning over the rails of the front porch. The ruckus he made woke everyone. Mike remembers very little being said that night on the front porch or in the house. The defining moment occurred the next morning. Mike partied hard but seldom failed to rise to get things done around the farm.

At the breakfast table each morning, there was a consistent seating arrangement. Victor sat at the head of the table, and Mike sat to his right. That morning, no one at the table acknowledged Mike's presence. When breakfast was finished, Victor headed to the barn. It was common for Dad to review the chore schedule with the boys prior to leaving, but not this day. On this day, the only preaching done at the table came from Mom. As Mike headed out the door, Hellen said in a direct and painful tone, "You hurt us really bad!" By the time Mike got to the barn, Victor already had the tractor out and was driving in his general direction. When Mike got near the tractor, his dad put it in neutral and walked towards the barn without saying a word. The silence said it all. What Mom preached in the kitchen was real. Mike spent the entire day on that tractor discing away pass after pass. Everyone needs a turning moment. Back and forth across the field, that tractor and disc turned many times that day, and on one of those turns, so did Mike.

It is times like this when God sends forth his messengers to pierce one's heart in an effort to reach their soul. Mike had badly hurt those who loved him most. The Parson brothers considered Mike to be the chosen one by his parents; in their eyes, Mike always seemed to be favored. Sometimes, silence is the biggest convictor. Mike had time on the tractor that day to think about the decisions he had been making, the life he had been living, and the people he had been hurting. He came to the realization it was time to put his trust in the Lord. It was in that moment Mike decided to follow Jesus. He had grown up in a home filled with love for the Lord but had got caught up in the things of the world. He had been running, but it was in the wrong direction. One evening during that revival, Mike went forward during the invitation and publicly professed his decision to give his life to his Lord and Savior Jesus Christ.

Once the decision is made to follow Jesus, there is "no turning back." The lyrics to the invitation hymn "I have Decided to Follow Jesus" still resonate in Mike Parson's heart and soul today. "I have decided to follow Jesus . . . No turning back, no turning back . . . Tho' none go with me, I still will follow . . . No turning back, no turning back . . . My cross I'll carry, till I see Jesus . . . No turning back, no turning back . . . The world behind me, the cross before me . . . No turning back, no turning back." This moment was perhaps the most significant of many "no turning back" moments in his life. God knew Mike would someday be governor. Mike didn't know this, but he put his trust in Jesus, and there was "no turning back."

After that moment, God started getting Mike's life in order. Mike graduated from Wheatland High School in 1973. To this day, Mike speaks proudly of graduating in the top ten of his class, though with only about ten students in his graduating class, the verdict is still out on how proud he should be.

When not on construction jobs, Ike Parson spent many hours working for Mike at his service stations in Bolivar.

CHAPTER 2   33

At nineteen years of age, Mike Parson gained an even stronger understanding and love for the United States of America. He grew up and matured while in the army and is grateful for all he learned and the opportunities he received. Mike served in Germany and Hawaii after completing his basic training at Fort Leonard Wood in Missouri. Mike's time and experiences in the United States Army (1975–1981) shaped him into the man he is today.

Chapter 3

Making a Man Out of Him
Military Service (1975–1981)

"I need someone with a pair of balls to step forward."

The theme song for Governor Parson's 2020 campaign was "Made in America" by Toby Keith. From the campaign kickoff in Bolivar in September 2019 to the victory celebration in Springfield in November 2020 to the inauguration in Jefferson City in January 2021, the lyrics of the song speak to a man much like Mike Parson. The lyrics "he's got the red, white, and blue flying high on his farm . . . semper fi tattooed on his left arm" tell of a man passionate about service to his country. When one spends just a few minutes with Mike Parson, they quickly see a man passionate about his God, his family, and his country. This passion for country was a product of both his upbringing and his dedicated service as a member of the United States Army.

After graduating high school in 1973, Mike spent most of his occupational life working at local service stations and detailing cars. He realized he better get used to this lifestyle because if something did not change, it was likely to be his lifelong career. At this time in his life, Mike felt he had two long-term occupational options to consider: move to a city like Springfield and find a job or stay in Wheatland, where his opportunities were limited, and find a way to scrape by. "At the time, I did not have any insurance. I did not have any benefits. I was working for cash every week . . . I had not drawn a bonafide paycheck yet," Mike recalled about his situation at nineteen years old.

Mike knew it was time to get life in order. Part of life's order was marrying his girlfriend when he was nineteen. Next, he began visiting periodically with the local military recruiter. Mike revered his uncle Gerald, a decorated World War II veteran, so in early 1975, he got in his car and drove to the recruitment location in Hickory County for a serious conversation about his options with the U.S. Army. Mike took a liking to the recruiter and the things he was saying. Words like "discipline" and "character" were beginning to resonate with the maturing young Mike. Being an athlete himself, the physical demands of the military did not intimidate him. Mike remembers the recruiter asking him, "What do you want to do?" Mike responded that he grew up on a farm, so he was good with tools and was a good driver, though the highway patrolman from his joyride a few years back might have thought otherwise.

Mike asked the recruiter what options he had. One by one, the recruiter started flipping through a binder giving brief descriptions of the options that might be available to him. The recruiter was not trying to sell Mike on any particular option, but when he finished with the military police page and turned to the next page, Mike remembers saying, "Whoa, whoa . . . let's talk more about that option." In the back of his mind, Mike thought he knew a little bit about law enforcement despite not always being on the correct side in his younger days. It may not have met the exact definition of "paying it forward," but Mike had his own encounters with law enforcement. He thought, "Maybe I can change it around for somebody else. Maybe it's a good way to make up for all my misdeeds."

Mike asked the recruiter to tell him more about the military police. As the recruiter provided details about the roles and responsibilities, Mike asked one more question, "What if you have a juvenile record?" The recruiter's response to this critical question still echoes through Mike's mind. "The Army does not care about what you did as a kid . . . the Army will make a man out of you." Mike entered the recruiter's office that day thinking his options might be limited based on his less-than-ideal life choices growing up. He had experiences with law enforcement few others had. Some of these experiences were wanted, and some were unwanted. When Mike learned that juvenile records would not be a factor, he knew the door of opportunity was open.

Mike did not dwell on the decision to enlist in the army long. Soon after making the decision, Mike went home to tell his parents. He remembers his dad not saying much and being very practical in his response. "If that is what you want to do, it is your decision to make," he said, but Mike thinks his dad expected him to take over the family farm at some point. He remembers his mom being scared at first and reluctant to get behind the decision.

After enlisting, Mike spent a considerable amount of time thinking about how this new opportunity might collide with some of the dreams he had growing up. Mike felt if he could get stationed at Fort Sill in Lawton, Oklahoma, or Fort Hood in Killeen, Texas, he would be close enough to Wheatland that he would still be able to run around with his friends when on leave. In the back of his mind, Mike also envisioned a bonus benefit of being stationed in or near Texas. He always had the dream of someday going to the famous Gilley's honky tonk in Pasadena. If he was sent to Fort Sill or Fort Hood, this dream could soon be a reality.

Regardless of where he was stationed, it was first things first—basic training. Victor and Hellen drove Mike and his wife to Fort Leonard Wood in Missouri. Mike remembers being mentally and physically prepared for basic training. He knew going in that it would be an intense and a challenging experience, but his uncle and cousin had both survived, so he knew he could. His relatives in the military also offered him a piece of advice. They repeatedly reminded him, "Whatever you do . . . do not volunteer for anything during basic training."

Mike also learned that with his last name starting with a "P," he seemed to be drawing less assigned duties during basic training than those at the beginning or the end of the alphabet. When duties were assigned, he determined they started at the beginning or the end of the alphabet on most occasions. With "P" being closer to the middle, he felt like he heard the name "Parson" shouted a few less times than the others.

On one occasion, Mike let his ego win out over the advice given by his family members. "One time, we were in formation. Suddenly, they were asking for volunteers. They wanted to know if anyone had his driver's license. They needed someone to drive," Mike recalled of the moments prior to his lapse in judgment. Mike began to process what he had just heard. Of the one hundred-plus soldiers in formation, he considered himself to likely be the best driver of all. He thought they probably needed someone to drive the trucks during training exercises. He had driven race cars and various pieces of farm equipment growing up, and he remembered telling himself, "Ain't nobody can do it any better than I can . . . I'm the guy."

Mike also reminded himself, "Whatever you do . . . do not volunteer." He remembers the drill sergeant continuing to vocally prod for volunteers. The drill sergeant declared, "I need someone with a pair of balls to step forward. Someone with a driver's license. Someone who really knows how to drive." The line of soldiers remained motionless until the words "someone who really knows how to drive" reached Mike's ears. He thought not volunteering at this point was a personal attack on his skills as a driver, so he stepped forward from the formation. Soon after, another soldier did the same, and the drill sergeant immediately yelled affirmation to the two volunteers. "Now these are real soldiers," he said.

The drill sergeant dismissed the other soldiers and approached Mike and the other private to give them their driving orders. They were going to get an opportunity to showcase their skills. Mike remembers walking alongside the drill sergeant as he announced, "Boys . . . here are your drivers" as they entered the officers' barracks. Mike and the fellow soldier were assigned to drive (operate) a floor buffer all night. Waxing, polishing, and buffing was their mission. "This thing was shining like a diamond in a goat's butt before they got us out of there," Mike remembered of their quality work.

At the end of basic training, Mike recalled being in the best shape of his life. He knew some of the soldiers would be sent overseas, but he never dreamed he might be headed to a foreign country. He thought the odds were in his favor to be assigned to one of the lower forty-eight states, preferably in or near Texas and Gilley's. When the orders for Advanced Individual Training (AIT) were assigned, his dream of trips to Gilley's and weekend hangouts with his friends in Hickory County was squashed. Mike was sent to Fort McClellan in Anniston, Alabama, to learn the skills needed to be a military policeman. Fort McClellan was best known for two different military establishments, one of which was the Military Police Corp. The other was the Chemical Corp. The base closed in 1995.

"I was a better student during that time than I ever was. The reality of it all was that I started liking it a little bit. Working crime scenes, solving crimes, what to look for, interview techniques . . . I just started liking the training," Mike proudly recalled of his experience at Fort McClellan. "Although growing up I might have been doing a few things I should not have been doing, I still respected officers. Wearing that uniform was a big deal," Mike said of his adolescence. Firearms training was also a major component of the experience. Competition was always a part of life for Mike Parson and still is. The posted results from firearms training became his motivator like the scoreboard once did at Wheatland High School. Competing to win was always the goal. Not everyone can win, but competing to win was mandatory.

Private Parson remembers competing alongside some of the greatest individuals the United States had to offer. He remembered state by state the physical talents many of the individuals brought to the company, but the greatest competition during this period was against himself. Being a farm boy paid dividends at the shooting range. When asked if he set the standard in anything, a humble Mike Parson answered, "Some of the things I am most proud of . . . fired expert level in the M-16 rifle . . . in the M-60 machine gun . . . in the 45 caliber handgun . . . and in hand grenades." The M-16 rifle target was about three hundred yards away. He had to aim above the target to account for gravity and, to top that off, he had to hit the target ninety-seven out of one hundred shots.

At the end of training at Fort McClellan, Mike vividly remembers the sergeant first class informing the newly graduated privates of their assignments and where they would be stationed. The sergeant first class started with privates with last names starting with "A." Things were looking good for a stateside assignment as approximately four out of every five he heard were in the states. When he got to Mike, however, he shouted, "Private Parson . . . 21st Replacement Division . . . Frankfurt, Germany!" Mike's first thought was how far is Frankfurt from Gilley's, and his second thought was how far is Frankfurt from his buddies in Wheatland? "I remember going back into the barracks . . . in the main entryway was a world map . . . it was definitely a long way away from Wheatland," Mike recalled.

Private Parson remembered the stay in Frankfurt being a short one. Mike received his orders, had them stamped, loaded into a truck with about twenty other soldiers, and took off for the Miesau Army Depot within hours of arrival. Miesau was approximately eighty-eight miles from Frankfurt. When asked about his first impressions, Private Parson recalled, "The first thing you realize is you cannot read any of the signs. You are an outsider. You don't even have the currency." It was quickly apparent to Mike that he was not in Wheatland anymore.

"When you are in the military police, they give you white gloves, white hat, black patent leather, and your boots are spit-shined," Mike recalled about his anticipated expectations. "When we go into the entry gate, the MPs are in full combat gear. Helmets, fatigues with the patch of the MP on it . . . this was not garrison duty. No fancy patrol cars, one jeep with a light on it . . . this is no white hat assignment," he recollected of his first impression. The Miesau Army Depot was a relatively small post, but within the boundaries of the post was an installation that required security clearance by all personnel. Private Parson and his MP colleagues' primary responsibility was to secure the front gate and the entire perimeter of the installation. The installation had a perimeter of about two miles and eight elevated towers. Being a so-called "tower rat" was not the most high-profile job of an MP, but with Mike's upbringing, he and high profile had never crossed paths. He and hard work were acquainted well, however, so that is what he did.

"Your job was to look out the window of the tower for three or four hours. Then you would take three hours off, then go back for another three or four hours. Seeing a rabbit or a deer every once in a while would break up the monotony," Private Parson recalled of his duty. It was a mentally draining task. Going to the tower day after day took its toll on the MPs. "It just worked in your mind. A lot of guys couldn't handle it," Mike said. Since this was such a mentally taxing assignment, MPs would often be given greater input into their next duty employment.

While in Germany, Mike was selected to participate in French Commando School competing with fellow American soldiers against French and German soldiers. Overcoming barriers was a key component of commando school. The mental and physical challenges would indeed separate the men from the boys. Mike was among an elite group of soldiers selected to represent his country. Again, competing to win was all Mike ever knew. If one was going to play cards with Mike, he expected to win. Mike could even make a competition in a hay field.

While in French Commando School, there was no shortage of competition. Survive and advance were his and his fellow soldiers' daily goals. Each obstacle presented its own set of challenges to overcome. Representing one's country in this competition was a grueling honor. If a soldier did not pass one part of an obstacle, they put their uniforms in their bag and were sent back to their post. Mike proudly remembers being among six or seven American soldiers left of approximately fifteen that had started.

Of the many obstacles faced during the competition, which was about two weeks in duration, one in particular resembled the hard working, find a way, "no turning back" attitude Mike has exemplified his entire life. Mike always understood the military would teach him and his fellow soldiers that they could always do a little more if they had to. They have just a little more in them. The obstacle he remembers testing him the most began even before it started. As Mike stared at a rock cliff just over fifty-feet high, he first had to decide if he could overcome his fear of heights. His feet firmly on the ground was a comfortable position, but staying on the ground was not an option. He was told he was going to the top, along with his full gear—backpack, M-16 rifle, combat boots, helmet, belts with ammunition.

As he started up the cliff, he was very intentional with every hand and foot placement. The cliff had no natural hand or footholds. Mike moved to the left and right to find a secure hold while gravity seemed to tug harder and harder at his backpack with each passing inch. About halfway up, Mike glanced to the bottom of the rocky bluff and, without hesitation, fixed his eyes upon the top. It was at that moment, Mike realized there was "no turning back."

Governor Parson has never been a person to back down to a challenge, especially when the stakes are high. When he walked through the doors of the governor's office to take the oath of office on June 1, 2018, he knew he was put in that place at that moment for a reason. Missouri was at a crossroads. God had placed him in this position to right the ship and bring stability to the state. This was not about a man and a position. It was about a man poised to be on a mission to rescue Missouri. The moment he said, "I will" and took Missouri and its highest political office by the reins, there was "no turning back."

Like that day and the day he accepted Jesus as his Lord and Savior, he recognized there was "no turning back" on that cliff in Germany. It would be harder to try to work back down the cliff than continue up, so up he continued. He was like a leech gripping his fingers with all his might and strategically placing the soles of his boots on every step. He knew one slip would be his only slip as momentum toward the ground would likely take him all the way to the bottom. The weight of his gear was light in comparison to the responsibility he had to his team of fellow soldiers.

At the top of the cliff, the ledge jutted out. Mike took a moment to glance down, confirming up was still the only option. The overhang near the top blocked his view of what was ahead. The sky was all his eyes could see. In that moment, it came down to faith, courage, and grit. This was bigger than himself. "At the top I was grabbing for anything . . . grass, sticks, whatever. When I got up there, I was shaking like never before. I have never been more exhausted in my life," Mike recalled of his final moments before completing the obstacle. Although he felt prepared for the challenge, it was ultimately his commitment to the plan that led to success.

Mike selected the Augsburg Army Installation for his next duty assignment. Augsburg was approximately fifty miles from Munich. Mike considered this part of Germany a much prettier part of the country. At Augsburg, Mike finally received that "white hat." He had a patrol car and did regular police work—quite a change from the duty assignment in Miesau. In Augsburg, Mike started to get involved in the Military Police Investigation (MPI) piece of military law enforcement. Within weeks, he set his sights on becoming a detective, wasting little time learning the route and plotting a strategy to get there. Determining who the key people were along that path became his focus.

Mike continued to hit the books while at Augsburg and set out to obtain an associate's degree through the University of Maryland. He did not know much about the requirements to get this degree, but he quickly learned it would require sixty hours of coursework. Mike was in a very different place in his life as a student and did not see the requirement as one he could not fulfill. "I will just start taking courses in everything I like," Mike recalled of his initial strategy. He soon learned there were certain required categories of courses to obtain an associate's degree. Not every course he needed to take was going to land in the Mike Parson academic wheelhouse, such as English language arts. Over the years, these courses had proven problematic. Regardless, he committed to the general education courses and electives required.

As his interest in learning grew, so did his strategies in managing the classroom environment. While taking an elective in philosophy, Mike decided to take the opposite stance of that taken by his professor and argue a point on every occasion. "He probably thought I was a dumb, old hick, country boy," Mike remembers. Opinion versus fact became the primary theme during that course. Mike is not sure he learned much, but he still passed. It was one more requirement he could mark off the list. Despite crossing off several courses along the way, Mike continued to avoid English language arts.

Sports continued to be a big part of his life, and the assignment at Augsburg allowed Mike more opportunities to participate in sports during his down time. "I would go snow skiing in the morning and play tennis in the afternoon," Mike remembered of his leisure time. The geographic location of Augsburg in relation to the Swiss Alps offered about every climate daily.

"Do I stay in or do I get out?" Mike remembers of the decision that presented itself near the end of his duty in Augsburg. By this time, he had earned the rank of sergeant and the pay was improving, creating a sense of stability. By not taking much time away from his service duties, he had accumulated more than sixty days of leave and was headed home to Wheatland to think over his decision. On his way home, Mike had to pass through Fort Polk in Vernon Parish near Leesville, Louisiana, for a few days. At the end of his leave, he would be required to report back to Fort Polk with his final decision for the future. He figured some time with family and friends back home would help him decide his next course of action. "It was like the whole world had changed," Mike remembers of returning home. After more than three years away, things as he once knew them were no longer the same. Many of his friends had gotten married. Some of them had relocated out of the area.

Looking back now, Mike laughs at one of the things that garnered so much of his attention upon return. Of all the Parson boys, Mike had been the one who was all country. Wearing cowboy hats and boots was his norm. Few people lived the country lifestyle like Mike did. Of all his brothers, he considered his brother Ike to be the least country of them all. Living on a farm didn't necessarily mean one was a farmer. "He was not a farm boy to say the least," Mike recalled. Mike returned to Wheatland shortly after the release of the movie *Urban Cowboy* starring John Travolta as Bud Davis and Debra Winger as Sissy. Mike had always envisioned himself at Gilley's growing up, but little did he know that a movie set in the same place would change the world and people he once remembered.

"I come back from Germany and people are wearing cowboy hats and boots, driving pickup trucks with hat racks. I thought what in the world is going on here," Mike recalled. "Here comes Ike driving a pickup truck, hat rack hanging off the ceiling, wearing a cowboy hat, wearing boots . . . this is bullshit. I have never seen him look like that in his life," he remembered upon first seeing his brother. This really got his attention. Mike remembers not only his attire changing but also additional evidence of Ike's "Bud Davis" transformation. When he went to the family farm, Ike and his friends had a wooden barrel wired to a couple of trees, the barn, and an electrical pole that supported the wires providing power to the house. The wires would make an ear-piercing buzzing sound as each rider mounted the barrel for an attempted eight-second ride. On the day Mike happened to be there, the buzzing sound was accompanied by another thunderous sound as the electrical wires were pulled from the house due to the power pole violently moving as the barrel shifted.

"It was nothing like I had expected when I came back home," Mike said. It did not take all sixty days for Mike to decide on his next course of action. Within three weeks of being back home, he decided to reenlist in the army. When he went to Fort Polk to declare his intent to reenlist, Mike was hopeful to get an assignment in the states. It just so happened there were two locations available but not in the lower forty-eight states. Alaska and Hawaii were the only two locations available at the time for MPs, especially with potential opportunities in investigations.

Sergeant Parson accepted a duty assignment at Schofield Barracks Army Base in the Twenty-fifth Infantry Division at the foot of the Waianae mountain range on the island of Oahu in Hawaii. Serving in the MPI Division, Mike wasted little time trying to figure out a pathway to be elevated to the Criminal Investigation Division (CID). The major roadblock between MPI and CID was the requirement of an associate's degree. Although Mike had been diligently working on it, two three-hour credits of English still stood between him and the degree. However, Mike learned that from time to time, the CID would select members from MPI to move to CID. Mike regarded the CID as the top law enforcement agency, and he wanted to be a part of it. When he inquired, he was reminded of the associate's degree requirement. Mike focused on learning "the powers to be" in possibly making the elevation to the CID and quickly learned the colonel was a significant player in the process. If the colonel was a significant player, Mike needed to form a relationship with him.

Being able to "game the system" can be critically important in making it in this world. This was early evidence that Mike understood it. There is perhaps no deeper thinker in relationship building than Mike Parson. "I got to know who the Colonel was, see what he liked. He liked to play racquetball," Mike said of his relationship building maneuvers. Sergeant Parson made it a point to frequent the racquetball area of the facility when the colonel would be playing. This is one of those moments when preparation meets opportunity. One day, the colonel's racquetball opponent did not show up. Mike acknowledged the colonel and expressed his desire to learn how to play racquetball. The colonel immediately responded, "Today is a good day to learn." Mike had little experience at the game, but he competed. When they were done, the colonel asked if Mike would be interested in playing again in the future. Of course, Mike took him up on the offer.

A positive mindset and skilled listening were key during every chance to dialogue with the colonel. On one occasion, Mike remembers the colonel bringing up some concerns about his car—another preparation meets opportunity moment. Mike quickly offered a solution in his wheelhouse. Mike said, "Colonel, I used to turn wretches a little bit. I can come take a look at it." Mike went to see his car and, over the days ahead, made some minor repairs and did some detail work.

The relationship door had been opened. Within a few weeks, Sergeant Parson had created the opportunity to discuss his desire to be in the CID. The colonel ultimately responded with the phrase Mike wanted to hear. "We could probably get you on there," he said. Mike reminded the colonel he was working on his associate's degree. The colonel agreed he would need to get the degree completed but went ahead and recommended Mike move to the CID.

Mike's law enforcement roles turned to major cases during his time in Hawaii. An army installation is like a society within a society. A post has everything needed to survive independently. Law enforcement personnel were respected on the bases, but they were also "law enforcement." Every person on the base has a role and is an important part of the whole. Being a soldier is not easy. Training can be very taxing, so when soldiers have down time, they often want to have fun. Sometimes the fun crosses the boundaries of the law. Soldiers are human. Dealing with societal situations as they arose is just what Mike and his colleagues did. Being in military law enforcement had similarities to public law enforcement. Being an MP made the biggest difference on the intramural courts and fields. "You got infantry, artillery. We were seen as the pretty boys on the block. Everyone wanted to beat the MPs," Mike recalled of the competitive nature of all, but the bottom line was "we were all soldiers."

Mike's experience in Hawaii was a positive one, but near the end of this tour of duty, he again contemplated his future. It was indeed a tough decision. This time, he looked a little further to the future—five years, ten years, etc. A lifelong career in the military was a possibility. "There were two things I knew – law enforcement and turning wrenches," Mike said. When jokingly asked if he thought he was going to go home and be governor someday, Mike quickly responded, "Not in a million years." He felt a few less than ideal decisions he made as an adolescent guided him towards law enforcement. "I knew what it was like on the other side of the fence, dealing with people, interviews and interrogations. I kind of knew why they did what they did. I was able to build rapport with a lot of people," Mike said of the decision-making process. He knew he had the potential to succeed at either law enforcement or a service station, so he decided to head back home.

When Mike landed on the tarmac in Springfield, Missouri, after serving two tours, he knew he never wanted to leave Missouri again. Missouri was home. He loved the state, and he loved the people. Mike went to work for Sheriff Verl Kennedy in the Hickory County Sheriff's Office. He also detailed cars in the evening to make a little extra money. Due to those adolescent decisions, Mike believes Sheriff Kennedy knew Mike before Mike knew him. He was honored to go to work for a sheriff who had seen the best in him when it may have not been deserved. Mike still believes he would not be where he is today without the support and encouragement of Sheriff Verl Kennedy.

Mike has never wavered in his passion for the United States of America. There is no greater country in the world, and Mike is proud to be an American. He feels blessed to have had the opportunity to serve the red, white, and blue. Toby Keith's "Made in America" continues, "He won't buy nothin' that he can't fix with WD-40 and a Craftsman wrench. He ain't prejudice, he's just Made in America."

Although Mike is extremely proud of his military career, at this point in his life, it was time to see what else he could make of himself in America.

Governor and First Lady Parson visited the Schofield Barracks Army Base in Hawaii in the summer of 2023.

Governor and First Lady Parson were joined on Faurot Field by members of the U.S. military for Mizzou Football's Military Appreciation Day.

Governor and First Lady Parson joined family and friends to welcome home 110 veterans who participated in the Fifty-ninth Central Missouri Honor Flight.

Mike and Ike Parson discussed the potential solution to getting the service station tow truck back on the road.

CHAPTER 4

Playing to His Strengths
Law Enforcement and Turning Wrenches (1982–1992)

"He was not only a loyal customer, but also a loyal friend."

After serving in Germany and Hawaii in the United States Army for nearly six years, Mike returned to Missouri in November 1980. He loved Missouri and was excited to get back to the area in which he grew up. He felt this would be where he would spend the rest of his life. When he returned home, Mike and his first wife bought a small house in Hermitage in Hickory County. Mike then played to his strengths—law enforcement and turning wrenches—and began working as a deputy for the Hickory County Sheriff's Department.

Despite not being the most devoted student in high school, when Mike got into the military, he really took a liking to the learning and training that accompanied each experience. When he got out of the army, he felt extremely confident in every facet of law enforcement. If anything, he may have even been a little overqualified for a position in a county sheriff's office. When Mike was preparing to leave the army and return home, he reached out to Sheriff Verl Kennedy of Hickory County. The relationship between Sheriff Kennedy and Mike Parson had originally started on opposite sides of the legal system, but what's important is not how one starts but rather how one finishes. Mike remains grateful to Sheriff Kennedy for seeing potential in him in his youth that he did not see in himself. Part of who Mike is today was shaped by those experiences. Mike chooses to see the best in people because someone saw the best in him.

Hard work and long hours were just part of the job as a deputy. It was not a glamorous law enforcement position, but Deputy Parson loved serving the people of the county he grew up in. The Hickory County Sheriff's Office was located on the third floor of the Hickory County Courthouse in Hermitage. The Hickory County Jail was located on the courthouse lawn northwest of the courthouse. The jail was a standalone building sitting on a corner of the square. They did not even have a jailor at the time, so Mike was sometimes assigned to go check on the inmates. The inmates were on their own. On hot nights, the inmates would sleep on the concrete floor to stay as cool as possible, and on cold nights, they would get out of the metal cells and sleep atop them to stay as warm as possible. Names of many inmates remain present on the stone walls of the jail as they would often carve their names into the stone. The jail was constructed in 1870 and remained in use until 1982.

Mike used his training and experiences as a military policeman in the army as one of the lead investigators for the Hickory County Sheriff's Department. While in Hickory County, Mike worked in conjunction with multiple law enforcement agencies across the state and the nation. Through investigations over the years, Mike got to work closely with Sheriff Charlie Simmons in Polk County. Sheriff Simmons and Mike had a great working relationship and got to know each other well over time. Sheriff Simmons ultimately asked Mike to leave the department in Hickory County and come to work for him in Polk County. Mike saw this as a step up in the profession. It was an opportunity to move to a larger department and make a little more money. Mike worked in Hickory County for about a year before moving to Bolivar to take the deputy position in Polk County. Soon after moving to Bolivar in early 1982, Mike and his first wife divorced. The divorce was not a result of irreconcilable differences but rather similarities. They both desired to just go their separate ways. Having no children, this annulment could be done with little collateral damage. The separation was peaceful and in the best interest of both.

The move to the Polk County Sheriff's Department did provide some additional financial resources, but life's challenges required more of Mike. During this period, money was tight. Mike described his finances as so low he "did not even have a pot to pee in." To make ends meet, he diversified into his other strengths while continuing to work as a Polk County deputy. He also began detailing cars on the side to earn extra money.

Mike rented an apartment in Bolivar and commonly frequented a small local service station. When Mike stopped by the station, he and the owner would always talk business. Mike would tell him about his time working at stations and on cars while growing up in Wheatland. In late 1982, the owner encouraged Mike to take over his service station and begin operating it himself. Mike ultimately decided to take him up on the offer and began leasing the station. Mike's first service station had just one island with two pumps and a two-bay garage, but everyone must start somewhere. Regardless of the size, Mike was full speed ahead on his new venture.

Mike was never afraid to put in the work. He loved serving people, and gas stations back in those days were mostly full service. Taking care of the needs of patrons was mandatory to maintain and grow a customer base.

It was all about creating relationships. Mike's days were full and he was all in! There was not enough time in the day to dedicate himself at the level he expected of himself, however, so he had to refocus his priorities. Mike loved the service station business and law enforcement, but something had to give. Sheriff Simmons did not want to totally lose his top investigator, so he decided to allow flexibility in Mike's hours at the sheriff's office. Mike took him up on the offer. He could not wait to make his mark with his station in the local community and began fixing up his newly acquired station. He decided to paint his station inside and out, so he borrowed a paint sprayer from a local friend and went to work.

He was so proud of the way his new full-service gas station was looking. Mike got even more excited when Dan Bishop, the owner of the neighboring car dealership, came to talk to Mike and ask him how he thought his paint job had gone. Beaming with pride, Mike spoke of the improvements he had made to the station, especially the paint job. Dan asked Mike to walk over to his dealership, which Mike assumed was to get a better view of his quality work. It was at this point Mike learned he had literally made his mark when Dan proceeded to show him some paint of his own.

The paint color he showed Mike was eerily similar to that on the outside of his station. The paint from the sprayer Mike used had been blown by the wind, landing on the fence and numerous new cars for sale in the dealership lot. At this point, Mike's experience in detailing cars came in handy as he spent the next few evenings on cars for which he would receive no compensation. He was very regretful of the situation and wanted to make it right, so that is what he did over the next few days.

When Mike owned and operated his first gas station, he was living day to day. He often did not have enough money to have cash in the register. But soon, Mike began to make a name for himself. His station, like most service stations at the time, had an air hose bell system to alert him when a patron was pulling up to the pumps. When Mike heard the ring, he answered the bell shifting all focus to the customer. "Whatever you are doing, you drop. If you are changing oil, if you are fixing a tire, you stop. You have to get out there to the customer's car. That is the priority," Mike said. Washing the windshield and checking the oil while filling the vehicle with gas were mandatory, but more important was treating everyone with respect. In the early years, Mike had a part-time employee to keep the station open when he had to be gone, but otherwise, it was a one man show.

If someone pulled into the station with a low tire and asked if he had time to fix it, the answer was always yes. Regardless of how busy he was, he always made the time. If he did not, they would take their business down the road. Mike quickly learned when he engaged the heart, magic happened. Over the years, Mike continued to expand his customer base and started making a little money. The paths of Mike and Teresa eventually crossed because of this. The trips to the bank with cash to deposit brought the two together. After they were married, Teresa started providing some assistance with the records. Mike was putting in fourteen-hour days, but when the office manager operating the cash register needed to leave, Teresa would stop by after she got off work at the bank.

Mike eventually got to where he had maxed out the capabilities of that first station. It was time to go big. Moving in the direction of a larger service station came down to whether Mike had the manpower and money to do it. If he could come up with the workers and finances, there was no question in his mind he could produce a winner. He had built a good customer base at the small station and knew no one was going to outwork him. The only competition in town that ever concerned him was owned and operated by Joe Lemon, the longtime mayor of Bolivar. Joe ran a great business. The "who's who" of the local businesses all had an account at Joe's station. "He just had a heck of a business," Mike remembered.

One day, Ronnie Jump, the owner of the largest station in town, stopped by Mike's station. This was the moment Mike got called up to the majors. Ronnie had observed Mike's success from a distance and was looking to get out of the business. Ronnie offered to sell his business to Mike. Ronnie told Mike to think about it. Mike told Ronnie his only concerns were about workforce and finances. Ronnie was not certain he could help with the workforce but offered to carry a portion of the loan for Mike to begin leasing the station from him. Donald Roberts, a longtime resident of Bolivar and owner of the local sale barn, became acquainted with Mike and his business. He had also watched Mike's success. Mike looked to Don on several occasions for advice early in his service station days, and the two became good friends over the years. When Ronnie Jump wanted to sell his service station, Mike turned to Don. "If you work hard at it, you can make it," Mike remembers Don telling him. Don told Mike he could make money at it if he was willing to work from sunup to sundown. Mike ultimately began leasing the station in early 1985. The new service station had five islands with a total of ten pumps and a five-bay garage. This was the Taj Mahal of service stations in comparison to his first.

While Mike played to his strengths and the service station business started to prosper, the Mike and Teresa Parson family started to come together. When Mike and Teresa were united in marriage, Teresa had a young daughter, Stephanie, and a young son, Kelly. The details of how the Parson family became the Parson family will be detailed later, but Teresa, Stephanie, and Kelly were critical team members in making the service station business a winner.

Shortly after Mike and Teresa were married, they made the decision to purchase the station from Ronnie. Finances were still very tight, so they had to be creative in getting it done. Teresa's parents put forty acres of one of their farms up as collateral on the original loan to purchase the station. The demands of the new station and new family did not allow Mike to give the deputy position the attention it and the citizens of Polk County deserved so he temporarily stepped away from law enforcement.

Mike and Teresa then worked hard to transition the station into a family business. Stephanie and Kelly spent a considerable amount of time there. During the school year, the bus would drop them at the station each day. When Stephanie worked the cash register, she would turn an old milk crate over to reach the counter. This is how she first learned to count money. Being young, her attention to the register and customers didn't last long, but she would spend about an hour each day attending to this duty. Mike would work until 6:00 PM each night before taking Stephanie and Kelly home shortly after closing time.

Kelly put in his time at the service station as well. Mike remembers his signature "grease rag" hanging from his back pocket as he pumped gas for customers. Kelly recalled the celebrity status he reached in his first-grade classroom when his teacher announced to the class that Kelly Parson had pumped her gas the day before.

Mike prepared a room in the back of the station for Stephanie and Kelly. The room was like a mini playroom for kids, equipped with a couch, chairs, table, and a television. After completing their daily routine in the front of the station, they would go to the back room to play, nap, or watch TV. As they got older, completing homework became part of the daily routine in the back room.

Growing up in the service station business, Stephanie and Kelly always knew when the end of the month was near. Their mom took care of the financial records, and at the end of each month, she would have to put in a few additional uninterrupted hours to process payroll, taxes, and billing statements. Mike vividly remembers the financial challenges of the service station business. He remembers his dad thinking he was crazy when told how much money he and Teresa had borrowed to get this second station. Looking back, it was an interesting business model—borrowing money with interest from the bank while at the same time allowing customers to run credit without interest on gas purchased at the station. Mike remembers credit to customers exceeding $20,000 some months, but he learned early on to keep his eye on the goal. True progress often requires a large investment of money, and it always requires an investment of time and hard work. One may never get the time back, but a well-designed plan can still create a significant return on investment. It is often hard to quantify the return of working hard and doing right for others, but Mike knows no other way. This is the Mike Parson business model.

Teresa was a Bolivar and Polk County native. Mike, on the other hand, was a Wheatland and Hickory County native. Over the years, Mike earned his acceptance in Bolivar and Polk County. Always treating people right made this a seamless transition, and as his business ventures grew, so did his relationships within the community. Getting involved with community organizations through his stations helped him establish relationships he values to this day. Mike always trusted the process and knew strong relationships yielded positive results. Unbeknown to anyone at the time, this man washing windshields and pumping gas would one day be the fifty-seventh governor of Missouri.

Mike diversified his operation when he bought a wrecker to tow customers to his station. He remembers most towing companies charged $40 to $50 to tow a vehicle. He knew once people had an opportunity to experience the first-class service of his station, they would return. He set his initial towing fee at $12.50. This was not popular with the competition, but business started pouring in. The two towing companies in town once approached Mike about increasing his price to be more comparable so no one had an advantage over the others. Mike said he was happy where he was and was not interested in increasing. He just wanted to serve people. He even remembers agonizing a few months later over raising the price to $17.50.

Don Roberts ultimately became a loyal customer at Mike's station. As the owner of the sale barn, Don would send multiple vehicles to the station each afternoon to be filled with gas to be ready for the next day. Mike determined this was good for his business, but it did create some challenges. Don was notorious for loafing around the service station visiting with customers daily. In Mike's mind, a blocked gas pump was a liability to the operation. Instead of demanding Don move his vehicles, Mike would move them around back after filling with gas. Don agreed he was there almost every day but for good reason. "I would stop at the full service pump each day and get out and walk to the two funeral homes near the station to see who had recently passed," Don said when asked.

Mike remembers one little known measure of success when it came to a good gas station—the number of "loafers" around. He never had a loafer working for him, but the loafers he referred to were the local patrons that frequented the station to hang out and "shoot the bull." If one had loafers around, they were likely running a pretty good business. Don Roberts, Garland Roberts, Max Roweton, and the Cheek brothers were like clockwork every afternoon at Mike's station. The Cheek brothers brought their own chairs with their names on the back and told everyone to stay out of them. Don said Mike barely had a water fountain for them in his service station. "Those boys drank more free coffee than you could ever imagine," Mike respectively disputed. They were also willing to give advice to anyone who would listen.

Any time a new business is opened, there are always unexpected challenges. When these moments happened, God always put someone in Mike's path. One evening at closing time, Don pulled up in his truck and Mike got in. Don gave Mike an envelope with something in it. Mike put his hands in the envelope and pulled out $5,000 in cash. Don told Mike to use the money and he could pay it back in the future. Don wanted to give Mike an opportunity to make it. He was not only a loyal customer but also a loyal friend.

Mike was always skilled at being ornery and pulling jokes on others, but there are times loyal friends turn the tide. Don seldom did much driving. His wife, Dolores, often drove him, and when he was with Mike, Mike would do the driving. Mike made many trips to the Humansville sale barn and Don often rode along. Mike remembers one occasion soon after he and Teresa were married that his father-in-law, Bob, rode along with them. Mike considers Don to be "the king of one-liners" and was always serious when he would say them. Mike and Teresa had been married less than a year, so he wanted to be as respectful as possible to his father-in-law. About halfway to Humansville, Mike asked Bob if he could come out to his house the next day and borrow his rake. Don, in a completely composed manner, responded, "Well, hell no he doesn't care if you borrow his rake. You have been making love to his daughter. Why would he care if you borrow his rake?" Mike remembers nearly dying when Don delivered this line. "My father-in-law was sitting right there. I had to be white as a sheet," Mike recalled. He first remembered what felt like forever silence before Bob started chuckling and Don joined in. Mike was speechless; they couldn't get to Humansville fast enough. "What in the world are you doing, Don Roberts?" Mike remembers asking as they exited the vehicle.

Mike and Teresa Parson and Don and Dolores Roberts became great friends over the years. They would go out to eat together a few times a month and take some short excursions to sightsee around the country at least once a year. Tunica, Mississippi, and Las Vegas, Nevada, were common destinations. To save money, they would often take the "red eye" flight out of Kansas City. It was routine for Mike and Don to get fifty or one hundred one-dollar bills and play "liar's poker" with the serial numbers on the dollar bills the entire flight to not only entertain themselves but other passengers on the plane.

Pulling jokes on one another were just a part of the routine for Mike and Don. Mike laughs thinking back to a time he thought he saved the life of himself and all the other passengers on a commercial flight from Las Vegas to Kansas City. When Don got up to use the restroom in the back of the plane, Mike waited a few minutes and went back to the restroom door. Mike proceeded to wedge his foot into the bottom of the door. When Don was finished, he pushed the door to exit but it would not open. He backed away and shoved the door a little harder. This time the door opened slightly at the top but did not open. On the next attempt the door opened several inches at the top but did not budge from the bottom. The commotion began to get the attention of the stewardesses and the concern of Mike. His concern was not with the trouble he may be in with the stewardesses but the safety of the plane if he were to remove his foot from the bottom of the door on the next attempt. Big Don may just go through the side of the plane when he comes full throttle. Mike thought, "If I let go of this door, we are all going to die." At that moment, Don realized who was the problem and yelled out, "Get away from the door you son-of-a-bitch." Boys will be boys. The good news: all lives were spared.

While Mike built quite a business at his service station, he never lost his love for law enforcement. He would assist Sheriff Simmons as time allowed. Not only did Mike have loyal customers, but he eventually filled his business with loyal employees. When he won the race for Polk County sheriff, he wanted to make sure he took care of the people who had taken care of him. He had to sell the station but decided to build a garage on the property adjacent to it. As sheriff, he would not be able to do much himself, but the four-bay garage would keep his loyal mechanics in business. They did not actually need him. They just needed a place. His desire to take care of them ultimately turned Mike's Service Station into Mike's Garage.

The Parson family had a lot of irons in the fire. Sheriff Parson! Farmer Parson! Mechanic Parson! Something had to give. Mike would soon sell the garage operation.

The Hickory County Jail sets on the northwest corner of the courthouse square in the heart of Hermitage. The standalone jail was constructed in 1870–1871, costing $4,500 to build, and was in use when Mike served as a deputy sheriff in the county. The jail was used for 110 years before closing in 1982.

This sign, in its prime, welcomed loyal patrons to Mike's Service Station and later Mike's Garage in Bolivar.

Mike and Teresa became husband and wife at "High Noon" on October 13, 1985, at the Little White Chapel in Las Vegas.

Chapter 5

Coming Together
Marriage, Family, and Fatherhood

"He could tell most thought he had outkicked his coverage being with Teresa."

When the focus is put on Mike, Teresa, and the Parson family, it is important to backtrack to where it all started. The early years of his first service station were not easy. Mike found himself working long hours. He understood the key to a successful service station business was winning over the community and creating a people first, family-friendly operation. This started with offering a product or service at a fair price and, to make a lasting impact, providing dedicated service and building strong relationships with his customer base. Mike knew this was going to take some hard work, but he was never afraid of a little hard work.

If Mike was going to own a business, he was going to make it the best it could be. Without a full staff, Mike would often open and close the station himself. His first and most valuable early employee was Renee Meadows, who served as the station's office manager. She took care of all the office needs, operated the register, and kept the financial books. Each day, either Renee or Mike would take the cash to Citizens State Bank in Bolivar for deposit. Renee was never afraid to assert her thoughts to her boss related to business or life. She was often heard encouraging Mike to "settle down and find a good woman."

In early 1985, Mike began to notice a good-looking lady each day when he would make the deposit at the bank. Renee happened to know her because they were cousins. Initially, Mike did not know she and Renee were related, but he quickly learned that when he asked Renee about her. Renee told Mike her name was Teresa. Mike began to inquire more and more about Teresa, and Renee and Teresa began having conversations related to Mike. Mike and Teresa were both in their late twenties. Other than small talk over the counter at the bank, Teresa didn't know a lot about Mike, but she knew him to be a successful, conservative businessman in the community who worked hard for the money he had. She also knew him to drive what people in town regarded as the "coolest car." Being a farm girl herself, she knew Mike was a farm boy at heart who owned his own business and knew what he wanted.

Teresa was the daughter of Robert (Bob) and Darlene Seiner. The Seiners owned acreage in various parts of Polk County. Dairy farming was a big part of life on the Seiner farm. The dairy operation was Bob's focus, but he also did quite a bit of construction on the side building many homes in and around Bolivar. Darlene ultimately followed her daughter Teresa into banking over the years.

Like Mike, Teresa had just been through a divorce of her own. She had two children—a five-year-old daughter, Stephanie, and a three-year-old son, Kelly. Following the divorce, Teresa and her children moved in with her parents in Bolivar. After about a year, and after her grandmother transitioned into a nursing home, she and the children moved into her house. When Teresa divorced, her first husband repeatedly told her "no one will want you with two kids." He must have underestimated a man like Mike Parson.

One day, Mike asked Renee if she thought Teresa would go out on a date with him. Renee responded that she and Teresa had discussed the possibility, and Teresa said he'd have to ask her himself. In July 1985, Mike worked up the nerve to ask her out. Teresa said yes and, as they say, the rest is history!

Mike and Teresa's first date was on July 25, 1985. Mike picked Teresa up in his "cool" ride for a trip to Springfield for dinner at Western Sizzlin'. Mike's heart was pounding as they started south down 13 Highway towards Springfield. Shortly after leaving Bolivar, Mike learned this might indeed be the shortest date of all time. About five miles out of the city limits, Teresa said, "You know my brother." Mike immediately asked her who her brother was. Teresa replied, "Rocky." Mike was instantly taken back. The Rocky he knew was one of his closest friends who he'd spent a considerable amount of time with after moving to Bolivar, but Mike had never heard him refer to a sister. Teresa was Rocky's only sister, and during all he and Mike's running around, he never mentioned her. Mike and Rocky were in the fast lane—there was not much idle time on the docket. Even though he'd never seen her before, Mike thought for certain Rocky would have told Teresa about the hard running, hard living Mike Parson.

Despite his initial panic, this moment turned out to be the first time Teresa caused Mike's heart to skip a beat. Mike had survived his first cardiac moment, and the date continued. Mike and Teresa enjoyed dinner before stopping by a bar inside the Holiday Inn in Springfield.

After some boot scooting on the dance floor, the night ended. Mike and Teresa headed back to Bolivar. After a short but sweet goodnight kiss, Mike headed home, knowing immediately this might be the start of something special.

For a guy with limited financial resources to keep the station going, Mike somehow found enough money to send Teresa flowers periodically at the bank. He was now setting the stage to ask Teresa out on a second date. He also began making more deposit trips to the bank. Before the first date, Mike took about one of every five deposits. Now, he was taking one out of every three.

It is often said one doesn't get a second chance to make a first impression. In the days following the first date, Teresa invited Mike over to the house to meet her children. The ultimate thing a man can do to impress a woman is love her children, and perhaps even more impressive to her is when her children love to be around him. Let's just say Mike nailed the first impression with the kids. Stephanie and Kelly instantly gravitated towards him, and his relationship with them brought Teresa around very quickly.

In fact, there were only two dates that ever happened without the kids. The second date occurred just days after the first at the popular Ozark Empire Fair in Springfield. Few were aware of their first date, so this second date was the first time their relationship was put on public display. They saw many people they knew at the fair that night. Mike felt like he could read people's minds that night as he looked them in the eyes. He could tell most thought he had outkicked his coverage being with Teresa and thought they were thinking he was not worthy of a lady like her. Mike looked forward to the challenge of doing what few expected him to be able to do. Most may have thought Teresa was out of Mike's league, but he committed himself to winning her over.

Mike soon realized Teresa was almost too good to be true. He could not let her get away; he needed to get on the stick and tie the knot on this relationship, so he went on a search for the perfect ring. Now, Mike was a farmer who ran a gas station. Jewelry was not exactly his area of expertise, but he committed to the process and put his heart and soul into finding just the right ring all on his own. One evening about two months after their first date, Mike got down on one knee in the living room at Teresa's house and asked her to be his wife. She joyfully accepted the opportunity to be Mrs. Parson and unite not only herself but Stephanie and Kelly to the family team.

Wedding planning soon started. Since Mike and Teresa had both been divorced, neither wanted a large wedding. Mike asked Teresa if his brother Kent, who was a Baptist pastor, could officiate the wedding ceremony, and Teresa agreed. This sounded relatively simple, but Kent lived in the state of California. Mike and Teresa have never backed down to a challenge, and this was among the first challenges they would overcome together. If Kent was going to officiate the wedding, either he was going to have to come back to Missouri or they were going to have to go to him in California. The solution ended up being somewhere in the middle. Work was critically important to both Mike and Teresa, and neither felt like they could be away from work for long, so they decided to meet Kent in Las Vegas.

With fall approaching, Columbus Day in October was the perfect opportunity to make it all happen. Columbus Day was a banking holiday, so Teresa would have an extra day off. Mike had established a solid staff with a few more employees, and he had Renee to help oversee things.

On Friday after work, they began the twenty-four-hour drive to Las Vegas. That weekend, Mike and Teresa joined Kent, Mike's Aunt Ellen and her husband Everett, and Mike's cousin Wendy and his wife Linda in Las Vegas. Mike and Teresa were united in marriage at "High Noon" on Sunday, October 13, 1985, at the Little White Chapel in Las Vegas. The chapel had its own pastor to officiate the wedding, so Kent took on a different role for the day serving as Mike's best man. Ellen served as Teresa's maid of honor. The wedding went off without a hitch, though there was little time to celebrate as Mike and Teresa were adamant on getting back to Bolivar as soon as possible. They were grateful for those family members that attended, but getting back to work and the kids was paramount. They arrived in Bolivar early Wednesday morning, both returning to work after what might be the most eventful four-day weekend in history.

Mike moved out of the apartment he was renting and joined Teresa, Stephanie, and Kelly in their house. After saying "I do" in Las Vegas, Mike not only took on the role of husband to Teresa but also the role of stepfather to Stephanie and Kelly. Teresa knew both Stephanie and Kelly loved Mike immediately. While courting Teresa, Mike would play with the kids on every occasion possible. They loved that. They needed that.

Mike and Teresa then and today view the unification of this family as a natural fit. Just like the speedometers on those cars Mike liked to drive that could go from zero to one hundred in a short period of time, his level of responsibility as a father did the same. After marrying Teresa, he immediately transformed from a bachelor to a husband and father of two. He took this responsibility seriously then and still does today. He loved every moment of his time with them during their early years. He loved teaching them, and Teresa loved watching the joy Stephanie and Kelly found in Mike. Mike was a natural, but Teresa remains quick to remind him with a grin that through all his love for the children, he never had to change a diaper.

Mike's love for Stephanie and Kelly was not a short-lived experiment to win the heart of his bride. When Mike said, "I do," there was "no turning back." He was all in and wouldn't have it any other way. He was going to be the best father he could be, and part of this meant sharing experiences with them. Experiences for the Parson family included hard work and life on the farm. Teaching was a passion of Mike's, but sometimes teaching was less about talking and more about doing.

In 1987, Mike and Teresa saved enough money to purchase forty acres with an old farmhouse about eight miles outside of Bolivar from Johnny Johnson. Both Mike and Teresa loved being back on the farm and spending time with Stephanie and Kelly. Mike loved watching the kids learn new things with each passing day, and it wasn't long before Kelly became Mike's right-hand man. Teresa remembers Mike making them grow up a little faster than she planned. One day, Mike and Kelly were out in the hay field, and after a few hours of raking hay, it was time to return to the house. A good farmer must always be thinking about the most efficient way to get things done.

Mike first looked at the challenge—he had a truck and a tractor in the field that needed to get back to the barn. Mike then looked at his resources. He had himself and Kelly, who was around seven years old at the time. This was another one of those moments when a challenge and an opportunity came together. There were no mobile phones back then to see if Teresa thought it was a good idea, so he made an executive decision. He would put the truck in the lowest gear and have Kelly drive it back to the house and he would drive the tractor. A young man never forgets his first driving experience. Kelly responded in a time of need. He could not steer and work the pedals at the same time. Mike put the extended cab pickup in low gear and off to the house Kelly went. Teresa remembers the scene vividly as her and Stephanie stood in front of the house. As they looked toward the setting sun, they could see a truck topping the hill coming slowly toward the house. It was too bright to see the driver, but as the truck got closer, they soon saw the tractor with Mike driving close behind. Who was driving the truck? The driver had his hands at ten and two just like a professional, though few professionals had such poise. Teresa then spotted the eyes of Kelly peeking through the steering wheel just over the dash. Mike may not have gotten Teresa's blessing, but when there is a will, there is a way!

Stephanie and Kelly loved spending time with Mike on the farm. He loved to teach them things, but some things, he learned, were just better taught by Mom. Mike had extensive training in the military on investigations, interviews, and interrogations, but his experience in each was put to the test when the topic of reproduction was broached by the kids while out watching the horses. As they watched, Kelly asked the question of all questions. "How do horses have babies?" Mike immediately thought, "Oh my!" This was his first birds and bees' moment as a father. He was going to have to pull this answer out of his ass to overcome this challenge. Suddenly, Stephanie emphatically answered, "I know!" Mike was amazed and relieved by the sudden show of knowledge, but he was only off the hook temporarily. Mike was taking it in as Stephanie continued to explain, "See there, when they touch noses . . . right there." Mike quickly gave his approval on this reproductive theory, saying, "See . . . she's right." He went on to add, "If you have any other questions, you need to check with your mom!"

Teaching and learning were a huge part of the fatherly way for Mike Parson. Although he ultimately reached the highest political office in Missouri, he learned early on his own limits in the teaching process. Love for family has always been a focus of Mike and Teresa, and if one wants to put their love for family to the test, a good old family vacation across the country will certainly do it.

Mike and Teresa felt it was finally time to take a family vacation when Stephanie was eleven and Kelly was nine. When visiting with Mike and Teresa about their first family vacation experience, it was almost as if some of the scenes in the *National Lampoon's Vacation* movie were based on the real-life experiences of the Parson family vacation. Mike and Teresa owned a minivan when they decided to make the trip to Walt Disney World in Orlando. Why fly when they could drive? It was time for some quality family time! A vacation of this length consists of defined stages, and everyone generally starts in a good place in anticipation of the fun-filled adventures ahead. Their vacation plan included a Saturday departure from Bolivar and a Sunday return after a week of sightseeing and fun for the whole family. This was a big-time trip for a family that had not ventured very far from the farm over the years.

Every great vacation requires extensive planning, and the Parson plan focused on wise use of fiscal resources to maximize the benefits for all. They planned places to stay, places to eat, and places to see. This included a multiple-night stay in a Holiday Inn in Orlando, which provided free breakfast each morning for the entire family at the Denny's restaurant adjacent to the hotel. This seemed to be a wise use of fiscal resources. After all, who can go wrong with a good Denny's breakfast? But when stacking the good Denny's breakfast on a limited menu day after day, it gets a little old. Stephanie and Kelly laugh thinking back to pounding down the same Denny's breakfast day after day. "We ate at Denny's everyday because it was free," Stephanie laughs thinking back to the first ever Parson family vacation. Stephanie and Kelly started doing everything possible to break the streak as the days became repetitive.

Mike and Teresa both admit the first few days were fine, but the kids had their fill of Denny's. By day three, they were recommending an alternate option, even if only for one day, to break the streak. Each time the kids asked for an alternative, Mike and Teresa emphasized the value of the free breakfast. An alternate option was not an option.

Like most farm families, the Parsons are early risers. Why change anything when on vacation? When it was time for the day of fun at Disney World, after taking advantage of the free Denny's breakfast, of course, they were amongst the first to arrive at the park. The plan was to optimize their experience by spending the entire day there. People had told Mike and Teresa that traffic in the big city and area around the park could be a little challenging, but the Parsons from Bolivar, Missouri, defied the odds. Getting to the park early, parking was simple when they found a spot in a nearly empty parking lot. Unexpectedly, it was a "no sweat" experience into Disney World. They entered the park just as it opened. It was a day of fun for the entire family, although everyone was beginning to wear down as the day ended.

Just prior to the park closing for the day, Mike and Teresa decided it was time to leave for the hotel. Mike thought it would be a quick exit and they'd be able to walk straight to the car, but this was not the case. For every action, there was an opposite reaction. When they exited the park, there were thousands of cars now in the lot. Walking straight to their car was indeed an option if they knew where their car was. Excited to be at the park, Mike took no notice of the section signs in the parking lot when they'd arrived, so they decided to ride the parking lot tram while trying to find their vehicle. Stephanie and Kelly had laughed all day on the rides in the park, but the forty-five-plus minute ride on the tram repeatedly circling the lot was not quite as entertaining. They never told the kids they could not find the car but repeated "almost there." The kids began squalling as the tram ride continued. This ride was like the bonus free breakfast as there was no charge for every lap. Finally, their car was spotted, and the day was over.

As they were preparing to leave Orlando for the trip back home, Mike inquired with the hotel staff about places to stop on the way to break up the trip. Mike was told spring break was going on, and hotels and motels along the way would likely be hard to find. Mike and Teresa had heard about college life during spring break but remained confident they would be able to find a place to stay in Panama City. They had not called ahead for reservations. As they neared Panama City, they saw sign after sign saying, "No Vacancy!" The whole Parson crew was beginning to wear down with each passing sign. Mike ultimately decided the first hotel or motel they saw with a vacancy would be their destination.

Finally, they saw a motel without the "No Vacancy" sign lit in the front. Mike quickly pulled into the parking lot. The kids scurried around in the car and prepared to exit as Mike left for the front desk. Suddenly, a sound rang out on the second-story balcony. Two college kids on spring break must have gotten into a small drunken disagreement. Mike recalls it to be one of the most intense fights between two individuals he may have ever seen. "It was fist city," Mike recalled. The fight was accompanied by some less than ideal language at the loudest volume. There appeared to be no sign of surrender in either spring breaker.

Mike proceeded to initiate a less than ideal situation of his own, not with the spring breakers but with his children. Despite the pleas from Stephanie and Kelly, "Dad please!" Mike ordered them back in the car. Even with the little bit of night that remained, this would not be their final destination. Back on the road they went, and soon they found a place just down the road. Mike went into the motel, right along the coast of the Gulf of Mexico, only to be shocked by the price of a room at $100 a night. Although this was way over the family budget, this was not a time for negotiation. Teresa and the kids loaded up enough belongings to get through the night and headed for their room.

When they woke the next day, the kids were excited to see the proximity they were from the water. A beautiful beach lay between the motel and the water. Scattered all over the beach were hundreds and hundreds of chairs, each tilted forward lying on the sand. Getting up on Parson time, there was not another soul on the beach when they arrived. The kids quickly ran for the water and Mike and Teresa set up four of the beach chairs preparing for some "family fun in the sun." The kids returned from the water to Mike and Teresa in a short time. What a great moment! This $100 a night price may not have been so bad after all. The Parson family from Polk County was living an upscale lifestyle, even if only temporary. Within thirty minutes of arrival, a man from the motel approached the high living Parson family, proceeding to inform Mike, "You know we rent those chairs." Mike was astounded by the comment. He could never recall anyone in Polk or Hickory Counties ever charging for the use of lawn chairs. Mike answered, "I am not going to pay you to sit in these chairs." The man was not amused by the comment. Mike told Teresa and the kids to "move their rear ends to the sand" and turned the chairs back over. Even under less than ideal circumstances, the Parson family enjoyed the day before departing for home.

Like a well-run 400-meter dash (or 400-yard dash in Mike's day), the final stretch is always the toughest. This first family vacation was no different. As they neared the Missouri state line, the kids had all they could take of this trip. Stephanie and Kelly had put in a long week and had about all of each other they could handle. The two found more and more to disagree about and elevated their volume with each passing mile. Mike was wearing down as well. The arguing in the back of the van was starting to take its toll on him. While Teresa was attempting to negotiate peace, she remembers Mike demanding, "If you kids do not stop, I am going to pull this rig over and you are going to wish you had!" Within a few miles of the Missouri border, Mike's patience reached its end. He suddenly slammed on the brakes and pulled the van to the side of the road. "He pulled over and stopped on the side of the road so fast that we knew we were in trouble," Stephanie remembered. Kelly remains uncertain they left the driving lane, but he is pretty certain he left some black marks on the highway. If Dad or Mom was going to lose his or her temper, Stephanie was putting her money on Mom. She doesn't remember her dad losing his temper that often. On this occasion, Stephanie concluded, "He was done!" He got out of the van, slammed the door, and walked to the passenger side. As he walked in front of the van, he took his belt off for all to see.

This not only got Stephanie and Kelly's attention, but also Teresa's. Mike had never spanked the kids and she'd never seen him quite this angry

CHAPTER 5   67

before, but she knew he was definitely a little upset. Stephanie's and Kelly's eyes filled with tears as Mike headed around the van. When Mike got to the passenger side, he grabbed the side door and slid it open. Stephanie found a small amount of enjoyment in the fact he had thrown the door open so hard it recoiled back into him. Kelly remembers his dad holding the belt high and smacking it onto the floor mat under their feet. As the belt hit the mat, Mike yelled, "Do I need to use this belt or not? If I hear one more peep out of you, you are going to find out what this belt is all about!" Since he never spanked Stephanie and Kelly, he did not on this occasion but felt it was important that a clear message be sent. Stephanie and Kelly remember it being clearly received. Once they crossed into Missouri, Mike does not remember hearing a sound from Stephanie or Kelly. "It was total silence from the state line to Bolivar," Teresa stated. As a matter of fact, Mike does not remember hearing Teresa say a thing, either. Despite a few eventful moments, the first ever Parson family vacation is still regarded as a success today.

 Being great is a process, and to be a great husband and a great father, a man must experience the highs and lows that come along the way. Often, more is learned from missteps than triumphs. There are experiences that fill one with pride, and there are experiences that one finds no pride but never seems to forget. Mike had a couple of "I thought I blew it moments" as a husband and a father, but he was a quick learner. The greatest people make mistakes, but they don't make them twice.

 There are some things never forgotten, and then there are some things only forgotten once. Mike and Teresa were still mere newlyweds in April of their first year of marriage. Mike was about to drift to sleep one April night when Teresa broke the silence in the room around 10:00 PM with the comment, "You could have at least said happy birthday!" No man wants to hear those comments coming from their wife. Mike had forgotten it was Teresa's birthday. There is no way to work out of a jam like this. Not even the verbal judo techniques he learned during law enforcement training were going to help him in this moment of desperation. There was only one option, and it was to take what he had coming.

 Mike survived the night. With his psyche fractured, he got up and went to work at the station. That morning, Teresa's dad stopped by the station as he did almost every day. He was notorious for never filling his gas tank but rather putting $10 worth of gas in the tank on each trip to the pump. On this day, Mike's father-in-law skipped the pump and came directly into the station. When he entered, Mike went up to him and asked,

"Why didn't you tell me it was Teresa's birthday yesterday?" Surprised, her dad responded, "You mean it was her birthday yesterday!" He had forgotten it was her birthday as well.

Fathers-in-law sometimes pull off father-in-law magic, and sons-in-law just have to accept it. Near closing time that day, Teresa's dad returned to the station after Teresa had arrived from the bank. With no mention of anyone forgetting anything, he handed Teresa an envelope and in earshot of Mike said, "Here you go sis . . . here is your birthday money. Sorry I did not see you yesterday." Mike wanted to throw up. His father-in-law had made an escape greater than any made by the famous Harry Houdini. He glanced at Mike with a grin, and Mike did what a son-in-law is supposed to do at that moment. Shut his mouth and go back to work, and that is exactly what he did.

It is not easy to recover from a wife's birthday "I blew it moment." Making that mistake twice is never an option, and it is safe to say he has not made this mistake again. Now, Mike's "I blew it moment" as a father was self-imposed and not even realized by the Parson kids for years.

When Kelly started kindergarten and Stephanie was in second grade, the bus would drop them off each day after school at the family-owned gas station. The station would open at 7:00 AM and close at 6:00 PM. To accommodate the kids, Mike turned the backroom in the station into a very nice hang out. The room was equipped with all the necessities and more. Stephanie and Kelly were pretty self-sufficient in the back of the station. If they wanted to watch TV, they had a television. If they wanted to take a nap, they had a couch. If they wanted to do some homework, they had a table and chairs.

When Teresa got off work at the bank each afternoon, she would come to the station and operate the register until closing time to allow Renee to go home. Shortly after 6:00 PM each night, Mike or Teresa would load the kids up for the eight-mile trip home. Teresa would take them home some days and Mike on others. On one particular night, Mike was working to complete a couple of jobs in the shop. He was not ready to leave when Teresa closed the station, and neither were the kids. Teresa told Mike and the kids she was going to head home and start dinner.

Mike finished up the jobs and headed home. As he walked into the kitchen, Teresa asked, "Where are the kids?" Mike did not answer and headed straight out the door. He didn't verbalize what he was thinking, but the only thing going through his mind at that moment was "Oh crap!" Soon after he got out the door, Teresa heard the truck start and drive away.

Mike recalls it to be one of the longest fifteen-minute drives in his life. After completing the jobs in the shop, Mike had turned off all the lights and locked everything up. The one important thing he had forgotten to do was get Stephanie and Kelly out of the back room. During the trip back to get them, he had a bunch of think time. One haunting image kept coming to mind as he drove. All he could picture was Stephanie and Kelly with their faces pressed against the glass and crying uncontrollably. From his years in law enforcement, he knew officers would be going from business to business checking to see if their doors were locked. He could only imagine the sight the officer would see as he walked up to find the kids locked in the gas station. The former sheriff's deputy has blown it as a dad!

When Mike arrived at the station, it was dark and quiet. His heart was pounding as he unlocked the door and headed into the station. He noticed light under the door to the backroom, and when he turned the knob and opened the door, Kelly sprang up and asked excitedly, "Is it time to go?" Stephanie and Kelly did not even know they were the only people manning the station for the past forty-five minutes. What a relief it was to Mike! It was not for another five or so years that Stephanie and Kelly learned they had been left at the station.

The governor is a survivor. When he gets knocked down, he gets up again. Looking back now, Mike, Teresa, Stephanie, and Kelly laugh at these moments. There was little laughing the days they occurred, but it is a perfect example the Parsons are just like most others across the country. The bottom line is love conquers all.

Growing up, Stephanie and Kelly often stayed overnight with Grandpa Victor and Grandma Hellen. In true grandma fashion, Grandma Hellen thought Stephanie and Kelly could do no wrong. Hellen really loved Mike, but Stephanie was confident she and Kelly outranked their dad in Grandma's eyes. Victor and Hellen were Gramps and Grandma to Stephanie and Kelly. When they would go to the farm, Stephanie and Kelly loved to ride horses. They would help garden and take care of the chickens. They said there was no mistaking Grandma's fear of storms. Gramps and Grandma would make the trip to Bolivar every Friday to get groceries for the week and go to Grandma's favorite McDonald's for lunch. About the time Stephanie and Kelly were graduating from high school, Gramps and Grandma moved from the Parson Farm to a house in Wheatland.

Grandma Hellen is known as the "best cook ever" to Stephanie and Kelly. Every meal she prepared was a feast. After meals, the family would go outside and circle up lawn chairs in the front yard. With no air conditioning in the house, this was mandatory in the summer. Playing cards, including Hearts and Pitch, was common in the cooler months. Gramps was much quieter than Grandma, who was the feistier of the two. He did not say a lot, but when he did, everyone listened. Gramps was always the first one to go to church, and missing church was not an option.

Although he was not their biological father, there is no mistaking the fact Mike Parson fulfilled that role and responsibility for Stephanie and Kelly. Their biological father passed away when Stephanie and Kelly were starting elementary school. Stephanie loves her mom, but she considers herself a "daddy's girl." She sees her dad as the voice of reason. He is calm and patient in almost every situation. She can count on one hand the number of times he has been truly mad at her. There is nothing Stephanie and Kelly like more now than seeing their dad interact with their own children.

Kelly loved to farm alongside his dad growing up. Before becoming governor, Kelly and Mike shared a lot more time on the farm. Tending to the cattle is a mainstay on the Parson Farm. Cutting, raking, baling, and gathering hay are also a major part of the operation. The governor and Kelly bale about three thousand bales a year. Being a third-generation cattle farmer, Mike was proud to pass on his love and passion for farming to his son Kelly. While governor, Mike has had to downscale his cattle operation.

When Mike and Teresa were married, their first home was one Teresa and the kids were living in Bolivar. Their journey from then until now resembles a story a realtor and a moving company would be proud to tell. It also seems to speak to Mike Parson's "horse trader" strategy. Teresa even says looking back now, it looks like they moved a lot, but she asserted that "we didn't move nearly as many times as we had vehicles." Mike was always looking for an opportunity to turn a home or a vehicle to make a dollar. Teresa learned to never be surprised when Mike presented her a new used car. Buy a car for $850 one week, detail it, then sell it for $900 the next week. One cannot argue the numbers. The same man today serves as the governor of Missouri with the same philosophy. If the state is going to spend a dollar, let's make sure it will generate two dollars but on a much larger scale.

Life moves quickly, and life for the Parson family was no exception to the rule. God's will ultimately elevated Mike Parson to the highest political office in the State of Missouri. That journey had included six years in the United States Army, six years owning and operating service stations, twelve years as Polk County sheriff, six years as a state representative, six years as a state senator, a year and a half as lieutenant governor, and will conclude politically with six and a half years as governor. For much of his life, he had also been a proud Missouri farmer. Along the way, Stephanie and Kelly grew up, got married, and had children of their own. In 2023, one of those children extended the family an additional generation, making Governor and First Lady Parson great-grandparents for the first time.

Stephanie serves as an assistant principal at the public school district in Springfield and resides with her husband, Jonathan, in Sparta, Missouri. They have two sons and three daughters (David, Alicia, Michaela, Benjamin, and Isabella). In August 2023, they became grandparents when Alicia and her husband (Tyler) had a son (Urijah), and Michaela and her husband (Gabriel) will make them grandparents again during the year ahead. Kelly serves as a branch president at a bank in Bolivar where he resides with his wife, Tara. They own some acreage a couple of miles north of Mike and Teresa's farm. They have one daughter (Sophie). Only God has known what would be in store for the Parson family. It can be relatively certain that none of the original four (Mike, Teresa, Stephanie, and Kelly) said the word "governor" while eating all those somewhat free Denny's breakfasts in Florida many years ago, but that is where life landed for Mike and the Parson family.

Being the governor of Missouri has its benefits, but only a few Missourians have the firsthand experience of the toll it can take on many aspects of normal life. From afar, watching the governor and his team maneuver about the state appears to be a pretty favorable gig. Governor and First Lady Parson will admit they get to do some cool things, but there is so much more people do not see. Governor Parson is the governor twenty-four/seven. Seeing the governor in person at a public event or on television at a press conference or other function does not begin to do justice to the grueling schedule or the continuous stressors that accompany the position.

Life as it was known immediately changes when taking on the position of governor. Life is not altered just for the governor but also for all those that have direct or indirect contact with the governor. Family is the first thing that is greatly impacted. When looking at the family, the first person to be considered is the first lady. From the moment Lieutenant Governor Parson called Teresa while shopping at Battlefield Mall on Tuesday, May 29, 2018, her life would never be the same. The political process can be taxing on a spouse. Teresa had been alongside Mike every step of the way during his political career, but this was not the same. There is no greater teammate in life than a person's spouse. When celebrating one, the other is also celebrated. When one is criticized, so is the other. When one is attacked, so is the other. There may be a special characteristic required to be married to Mike Parson, but tenfold of that characteristic might be needed and then some to be married to Governor Mike Parson.

The wife of the governor is not immune to the public judgements of the governor. With the rise of social media, everyone is now an expert, and many people fail to observe respect and decency when making a public comment. Social media is what it says it is. Many people make comments on social media based on the perceived audience and not the direct person involved—in this case, the governor. Though some of the interactions are positive, often they are intended to be hurtful. The governor, however, has some thick skin. It is often said that "blood is thicker than water." Family members are not exempt from the public scrutiny that arises as part of the position of governor, but the great news for Missourians is the fact Mike Parson and his family love one another and know the governor is making decisions he feels are positive for the state. Some people and families may find motivation in the number of likes they get through social media, but the Parson family and the Parson administration do not rest their faith in one another based on positive or negative feelings expressed by others through social media. Sometimes, there is not much "first" about being the first lady, but Teresa Parson is honored to be the wife of the fifty-seventh governor of Missouri.

Early on, Stephanie remembers the hurt social media would cause her. "When people go on the offensive against your father, it hurts," she said. When people are downright cruel to someone one loves, it can take its toll, but both Stephanie and Kelly learned how to manage social media and negative opinions in general. When told she might have a little of Grandma Hellen in her, she laughed and indicated she just might. Stephanie concluded that Grandma Hellen would struggle with social media if she was still alive. "Grandma Hellen took it personally when the Cardinals would lose. I couldn't even imagine her when someone would be talking about her son," Stephanie noted.

When it came to Hellen, Kelly said, "If Grandma could see her son as the Governor of Missouri, she would be so proud and have a smile from ear to ear." He seconded the fact she would not handle the negative opinions well. Kelly remembers people stopping by the bank he works at during the pandemic. People sometimes think the governor's children are a pipeline to the governor. Stephanie had the same happen to her as an educator. There is no escape from politics when their dad is the governor, especially during that polarizing period.

The grandchildren think it is pretty darn cool their grandfather is the Missouri governor. Getting to spend the night at Gramps and Grandma's house that also happens to be the Governor's Mansion is special. The grandchildren do not take the benefits for granted. Kelly feels Gramps would rather spend all day with kids than adults saying, "He is just fantastic with all the grandchildren." All the grandchildren are very proud of Gramps, but when Gramps is the governor, it comes with some downfalls. There are times when the governor's children and grandchildren wish he could be around more. Governor and First Lady Parson try to attend as many events of their grandchildren as possible, but this is not easy. When one of the grandchildren seeks advice from him, they often reach out to their grandfather by phone. During these phone conversations, the governor wishes he could see them to provide a hug, encouragement, and guidance in person.

The first grandson has a great understanding of the position his grandfather is in and has feathers like a duck when it comes to hearing public criticism about him. The granddaughters, however, took a slightly different position during their early years. The governor considers them to be as fiery as anyone when talking critical of Gramps. Governor Parson laughs at the temperament of his granddaughters saying, "You have someone saying something about their Gramps . . . they took it personally. They just don't think people should get away with saying what they say sometimes. It's just not right." Governor Parson loves knowing his grandchildren come to his aid when the public is turning up the heat. Social media is king in the life of young people. One doesn't have to look far to find haters of everyone and everything. "There have been times when I have had to sit down with my entire family and remind all of them to be mindful not to respond to the foolish rhetoric on social media . . . reminding them that it only escalates things," the governor disclosed.

The bottom line is being governor takes them away from many of the little things most husbands, fathers, and grandfathers take for granted. Being under the watchful eyes of the Governor's Security Detail (GSD) has its positives, but it also carries a few negatives. Having a personal family conversation, even with the first lady, can be a challenge. The GSD not only has the privilege of having a front row seat to the emotional rollercoaster that is a typical day in state government, but they can also find themselves front and center for emotional Parson family discussions. Sometimes while traveling from event to event, family topics are too critical to delay. Governor and First Lady Parson have a great working relationship with the GSD. The GSD must focus on protecting them while also maneuvering through the emotions of both the professional and personal lives of the governor. "That is not easy. We have a great deal of respect for the members of the GSD. They understand the emotions of this position . . . they know their job," the governor spoke of the GSD. Despite their role, all the participants are human. No one is exempt from the high pressure roles they all hold. Kelly said he was a little apprehensive about the GSD at first, remembering his initial thoughts that family life would be very different stating, "Our family gatherings are never going to be the same. We are going to have strangers in the house with us. It is going to ruin the vibe of our family." He now admits his original thoughts couldn't be further from the truth, concluding they are now more like family. The GSD is often part of the family meal during the holidays but departs to allow for Parson family time after dinner.

When Mike decided to run for sheriff of Polk County, Stephanie's feelings on the possibility of him being sheriff was one unexpected hurdle he had to overcome. She was just getting ready to start high school when she overheard her mom and dad talking about the decision to run for sheriff. Teresa remembers Stephanie entering the room with tears in her eyes declaring her dad becoming sheriff was going to ruin her life. "I thought I would never be able to get a date. If my dad's the Sheriff, there is going to be no boy that wants to date me," Stephanie recalled when she first heard her dad was considering running. Stephanie walked a pretty tight line growing up, but her friends did not consider it that big of a deal since she never found herself in trouble. Kelly, on the other hand, thought it was the coolest thing he had ever heard. He declared, "My dad gets to carry a gun."

"My dad is by far the hardest working man I know. Since the gas station days, through the sheriff days, through representative and senator, and now as Governor, he runs circles around me, and I consider myself to be a pretty hard worker," Stephanie spoke of her father.

One of the most memorable moments for the Parson children related to the political journey occurring after Mike won his first statewide election for lieutenant governor. The win was followed by some physical challenges that put life in perspective for all. "Right after, he had heart surgery. He is getting ready to walk down the steps of the Capitol.

Everyone around here is not thinking the same thing I am thinking . . . oh my goodness . . . I hope my dad makes it down the stairs and he is safe. As he was walking down the stairs, it actually hit me. My dad is the Lieutenant Governor. That feeling was something that I had not ever experienced before. I was so concerned about taking care of my dad . . . then it just hit me," Stephanie recalled of the day her father took the oath as lieutenant governor. Teresa slowly and deliberately walked Mike down the capitol stairs that January day, and Stephanie and Kelly joined them for the swearing in ceremony. They were prepared to assist their dad as a human crutch if they needed to. At that moment, they were both so proud of their dad, and if it would have been the Lord's will, they would have proudly served as a crutch.

Little did they know at the time, but their dad had another role to play for the Great State of Missouri.

Governor and First Lady Parson are often photographed on the beautiful grounds of the Missouri Governor's Mansion.

Photographed are Governor and First Lady Parson's daughter Stephanie and her husband Jonathan House.

Photographed are Governor and First Lady Parson's son Kelly and his wife Tara Parson.

Mike Parson served as Polk County sheriff from 1993 to 2004. During Mike's tenure as sheriff, his goal was to build a professional law enforcement agency for the citizens of Polk County.

CHAPTER 6

Creating a Winning Culture
Life as the Sheriff of Polk County (1993–2004)

"When I first became sheriff, it was like the floodgates opened."

Charlie Simmons served as Polk County sheriff for sixteen years prior to Mike. Despite a limited amount of law enforcement training and experience, Sheriff Simmons brought stability to the position during his tenure as the county's top law enforcement officer. Mike enjoyed his years serving as a deputy for Sheriff Simmons. During Mike's time working for Sheriff Verl Kennedy in Hickory County, he worked in conjunction with Sheriff Simmons on multiple investigations. Soon after, Sheriff Simmons invited Mike to join his department in Polk County.

Mike served as an investigator for the Polk County Sheriff's Department for five years before stepping aside to concentrate on family and the service station business. Mike loved law enforcement and serving the citizens of Polk County, but at this moment, family was his highest priority. Mike had thought about being a sheriff someday, but that day would not happen under the watch of the respected Sheriff Simmons.

In 1992, business was good for the Parson family, and Mike had no intention of running for sheriff. He and Teresa purchased their first farm and were operating a thriving service station in Bolivar. One day, Sheriff Simmons stopped by the station. The sheriff was never a man of many words, and on this occasion, he had even fewer. This caught Mike by surprise as Sheriff Simmons paced around the garage. Finally, he got to the reason he was there stating, "I think you need to run for sheriff." Mike was surprised by this statement. Why would he run against the trusted sheriff of over sixteen years? He continued to tell Mike he did not plan to run for another term. He knew Mike had more experience and training for the position than anyone in the county and he was also a trusted businessman and citizen of Polk County. These characteristics did not guarantee victory, but they were a great place to start. The ball was now in Mike and Teresa's court to make the decision.

Mike thought the experience he had gained as a member of the military police could bring a professional level of law enforcement to Polk County. Most county sheriffs were just county citizens with a desire to serve. Few had little, if any, law enforcement training. Mike's level of training even exceeded that of most county sheriffs in the state.

Mike and Teresa ultimately decided to pursue the position. The only thing tougher than deciding to put a name on a local ballot is watching the results roll in on election day. When telling this story, Mike had his name on the ballot on numerous occasions, but he regarded that election as one of the most humbling and gratifying moments of his life. Mike considered a county-level election to be a true test of the democratic process. "When you put your name on the ballot in front of those that know you best, you are reassured that those you serve have confidence in you to best serve them," Mike said of the local experience.

Mike defeated his two opponents in his first ever election for any public office in the Republican primary election on August 4, 1992, by a 42.14 percent to 35.22 percent to 22.64 percent margin. Mike was able to rest easy in the general election on November 3, 1992, because he was unopposed. Polk County is a Republican stronghold. Historically, few Democrats have run for public office in Polk County. The political culture and climate of Polk County reflects its conservative foundation rooted in the Bible Belt. Mike is very proud of all his elections, but his first race for sheriff is very special to him.

When he was first elected to the position, Mike went back to work in the sheriff's office as a deputy. The incoming sheriff is often unable to get started until their term officially begins, but this was not the case for Sheriff Parson. Mike had many years of experience with the department, and he and Sheriff Simmons wanted to create a seamless transition. Sheriff Parson would have a staff that included nine deputies and five dispatchers. Nine deputies were six more than the department had when he stepped away in 1985. Kay Williams was the only Polk County deputy that remained from the original department Mike worked.

On January 1, 1993, Mike Parson was sworn in as Polk County sheriff. "When I first became sheriff, it was like the floodgates opened," he remarked about his first year. Law enforcement business picked up shortly after Sheriff Parson took the reins. Multiple homicides and drug offenses led the way, but it was a recovered stolen helicopter that was the first newsworthy investigation during his tenure. In January 1993, the Polk County Sheriff's Department recovered a helicopter from Midland, Texas, and took into custody the individual who allegedly stole it. Few, if any, sheriffs have recovered a stolen 1976 Hughes 269C Helicopter in their career, but Sheriff Parson put that on his resume during his first month on the job.

Mike is very proud of many things during his tenure as Polk County sheriff, but three things rise to the top when reflecting on those years. The first was actually one of his biggest goals when he assumed the position. Sheriff Parson wanted to make the Polk County Sheriff's Department a professional law enforcement agency. He thought he could use his time in the military police to catapult the agency to one of the best in the state. The U.S. Army had afforded him the expertise through both training and experience to make it happen. The second thing was a product of the culture he had created in the department. For years, the department struggled to maintain full and consistent staffing. He wanted to create a department in which everyone wanted to work and serve. Last, Mike created a winning culture. His commitment to this can be seen in the continued success of the department and its legacy of leadership. With his first hire in 1992, Sheriff Parson hired his future successor Steve Bruce to the department as a deputy. Sheriff Bruce's future successor, Kay Williams, was a deputy in the department working for Sheriff Simmons, Sheriff Parson, and Sheriff Bruce. Sheriff Danny Morrison would then follow Sheriff Williams in the position. Danny was another deputy Sheriff Parson hired.

Another of Sheriff Parson's proud accomplishments was the agency's success rate in closing criminal cases, including multiple homicides. The goal in law enforcement is to serve the people. When crimes are committed, the goal is to get them solved. Under Sheriff Parson's leadership, crimes were solved in an environment where people enjoyed working professionally to serve the people in the community they loved.

Mike always attempted to have a good relationship with the inmates of his county jail. Obviously, the inmates were not there because they sang too loud in the local church choir but because they had broken the law. He always wanted fair treatment for all and understood it was not his job to ultimately determine the guilt of an inmate. He knew most, if not all, would be back in the community soon. Relationships are important to Mike. He understands a good relationship with a person can lead to many positive outcomes in the future. He knew when presented with a tough decision in the future, these inmates might make a different decision. If their paths were to unfortunately cross again, they knew why he and his officers would do what they had to do. He also knew those who frequently made poor decisions related to the law were very familiar with others who did the same. In his experience as a military policeman and sheriff's department investigator, information important to investigations comes readily from a person with whom you have a positive relationship—even if that positive relationship initially resulted from a negative situation.

Mike prided himself in having a great relationship with the media. He understands everyone has a role and responsibility in society. He understands the media has the essential function of informing the public, and it is critical to have a respectful relationship with all media outlets. Dave Berry was among the first members of the media Mike worked alongside. Sheriff Parson brought a high level of professionalism to the Polk County Sheriff's Office, but he brought a little humor as well.

Dave Berry was the editor of the *Bolivar Herald Free-Press*. The newspaper covered Bolivar and the surrounding area and was circulated weekly. Dave would meet with Sheriff Parson each week for an update. Mike still considers Dave to be a good friend today, but both remember with a laugh when a disgusted Dave Berry had to launch his interview notepad across Mike's patrol car. Sheriff Parson and Dave were meeting in a local café one morning going over the weekly events. Sheriff Parson needed to run to Buffalo for some business, but before leaving, he told Dave he was working on something big and asked if he had time to ride along with him.

Dave agreed and grabbed his notepad. Sheriff Parson told his deputy with them to position Dave right behind him in the patrol car, and the three men started east on 32 Highway toward Buffalo. Dave got his notebook out and prepared to write notes. Sheriff Parson started by saying, "Let me give you the background of what happened here." Dave excitedly begins to write down all the details. As they pass by the sale barn at the edge of town, Sheriff Parson points toward the barn and begins to explain, "There were some boys unloading some hogs over there." Dave jots some words down and asks, "Now, how many hogs were there?" The sheriff answered, "There were three of them . . . kind of fat hogs." He continued, "While the guy was unloading them, another ole boy backed in beside his truck and he loaded the pigs up right in his truck as he was pulling out. When the guy noticed, he yelled 'Hey, those are my pigs!' The guy who loaded them up paid no attention to the guy and drove away."

The guy who had his pigs stolen immediately called the sheriff's office. "Our boys got in a pursuit with them," Sheriff Parson added as Dave wrote everything down. "About 3 or 4 miles down 13 Highway, the guy took down a gravel road." Dave continued to request more details, asking, "What kind of truck was it?" The sheriff added, "It was an older model Ford truck, 2-ton truck, not in very good shape, with a set of stock racks on it." As Dave continued to write, Sheriff Parson continued, "The gravel road was a dead-end road. When the guy got to the end of the road, he got out and on foot with what looked like a 357." Dave continued to feverishly write and asked if the gun was chrome plated.

The sheriff continued with the details, "The deputies were right there and almost had him. Then suddenly, the guy takes the 357 and shoots all those hogs dead in the back of that truck and takes off on foot." Dave is writing as fast as he can. Sheriff Parson continued, "The Deputies chased after him and finally got him on the ground and took the gun away from him." Dave is writing it all down and periodically asks some follow-up questions. Sheriff Parson purposely put Dave behind him in the patrol car as he knew he would have a tough time keeping a straight face as he told the story. Dave asked, "Mike, why did he shoot those hogs?" Sheriff Parson empathically answered, "So they wouldn't squeal!" Dave then jerked a few pages from his notepad and launched them and the notepad across the car. That was going to be a great news article—if it was real.

Mike's time was filled with a little bit of everything. While serving as sheriff for twelve years, there were many highs and lows that came with the territory. Sheriff Parson considered it his role as sheriff to not only serve all those in the county that elected him but also look after all his employees as if they were family members. Leading and teaching were significant parts of his calling as sheriff, and that is what he did.

The paths of Brad and Rachel Mabee and Mike and Teresa Parson crossed when a young man full of piss and vinegar applied for a position at the Polk County Sheriff's Office. Mike remembers sitting at the table with Brad and his parents before hiring him, discussing the risks and rewards of being a law enforcement officer. Brad's enthusiasm to learn and serve reminded Mike of his younger self. Mike emphasized to Brad and his parents he would look after Brad and do his best to guide him to be the best man, husband, father, and law enforcement officer he could be. Brad and Rachel had no children when they arrived in Polk County, but he knew fatherhood would happen at God's will. Just over two years later, Mike would gather again with Brad's parents at that same table to discuss the ultimate sacrifice their son had made in service to citizens of Polk County.

Sheriff Parson hired Brad to serve as a dispatcher in the Polk County Sheriff's Office. It was Brad's first position in law enforcement, and being a dispatcher was only the beginning. Brad was taking law enforcement classes at Drury College in Springfield when he and Rachel moved to

Bolivar shortly after he accepted the position. When they made the move to Bolivar, Rachel was working at a bank in Springfield and would make the thirty-plus minute commute daily. Mike noticed the strain this arrangement was putting on the young couple and proposed a possible solution. Mike let Brad know Teresa worked at Polk County Bank and Rachel might want to apply for a position there. Rachel reached out to the Polk County Bank and was ultimately hired. "At that time, I worked with Teresa and Brad worked with Mike," Rachel recalled about her first interactions with the Parson family. Rachel was only nineteen years old at the time.

Brad quickly started advancing up the law enforcement ranks. He moved from dispatcher to jailor, and once he graduated from the Law Enforcement Academy, he went on the road as a deputy. Daily, Brad did everything he could to learn as much as possible and really valued his time working alongside Sheriff Parson. "He really thought a lot of Mike. He liked the way Mike ran the Sheriff's Office. It was very much about professionalism, following the rules, very family oriented," Rachel recalled of Brad's feelings for the sheriff. Rachel recognizes the law enforcement world and the world in general is much different now than it was then, but she and Brad loved the value Sheriff Parson put on family. "He encouraged spouses to ride along with the officers to spend time with them," Rachel said. Sheriff Parson understood the stress being on the road put on the family of a law enforcement officer. "Sheriff Parson was a huge proponent of that. He wanted to make sure his officers took care of their home life," Rachel recalled. Sheriff Parson felt a happy home made for a happy officer (and spouse). Rachel recalled riding along with her husband many times. "When he would have to do some prisoner extraditions, I would ride along with him. We would get to spend the afternoon together, with an inmate in the back of the car, but it was still time together," Rachel chuckled.

Brad aspired to someday be a sheriff himself. He hoped to be promoted to a detective before moving back to Dade County where he grew up and would someday run for county sheriff. Brad was proud to be a Polk County deputy and strived to serve the community to the best of his ability. He did this by being a great learner, a great teammate, and a great ambassador for law enforcement. He knew Rome was not built in a day. Much like Sheriff Parson, he understood that hard work and commitment to others were the keys to success.

Deputy Mabee drew the night shift on October 19, 1997. This Sunday started like most fall evenings in Polk County. Not much mischief was occurring as Deputy Mabee patrolled the county completing standard security checks. At 10:40 PM, Deputy Mabee called into dispatch after completing a security check near Halfway. Shortly after, a passing motorist called the sheriff's office to report an accident involving a sheriff's vehicle on Route P about five miles north of Halfway. After receiving the phone call, the dispatcher called out on the two-way radio to Deputy Mabee with no response. The dispatcher attempted the same a few more times, again receiving no response. The accident reported by the caller involved Deputy Mabee.

Teresa distinctly remembers that night. Soon after she and Mike had gone to bed, the phone rang. When Mike got the call, Teresa remembers him immediately leaving the house. "I knew it was bad because of the way he was acting," Teresa remembered. Based on one side of the conversation, Teresa had put together that one of the deputies had been in an accident and dispatch could no longer contact him. She was not sure Mike knew it was an automobile accident at that point, but based on his reaction, she could tell he knew it was serious. Teresa said being the spouse of a law enforcement officer herself, she did not go back to sleep after he left. Less than an hour later, Teresa remembers getting a call, this time from Mike.

Mike told Teresa to get dressed and Tony Bowers, who was the chief deputy, was coming to pick her up. This is when she learned Brad had been in a serious accident and was being airlifted to Cox Hospital in Springfield. Teresa remembers Mike anxiously saying, "I need you to go with me to get Rachel. We need to get her up there as quickly as possible." Deputy Bowers picked her up and she met Mike at the sheriff's office after he returned from the scene of the accident. They went to the Mabee residence where Rachel was sound asleep. "I can remember that ride to Springfield because it was the fastest trip I had ever made in my life. Lights . . . sirens . . . 100 miles per hour plus. We tried to get her there as quickly as possible," Teresa spoke of the rush to get Rachel to Brad.

Sadly, Brad passed away shortly after arriving at Cox Hospital. He was twenty-six years of age. "She is a strong lady, let me tell you," Teresa recalled of Rachel after their arrival in Springfield. Teresa remembers the rest of the early morning hours being a blur, but while talking to Rachel about her recollection of that night some twenty-five years later, she pointed towards a door of what is now the jail building saying, "I can remember walking through that door." After visiting briefly with the doctors, Rachel had a few private moments with Brad. When they left the hospital, Mike drove the three of them back to Bolivar. There are no words to describe the emotion felt by Rachel, Mike, and Teresa on that trip. They arrived back at the sheriff's office around 3:00 AM. By this time, all the deputies had gathered at the sheriff's department. It was an emotional scene for all.

"We don't know why he lost control. We may never know," Sheriff Parson told the *Bolivar Herald-Free Press*. According to the Missouri State Highway Patrol, the car was traveling south and ran off the right side of the road. It then started sliding, crossed both lanes of the roadway, ran off the left side of the road, and hit a hedge tree. Sheriff Parson said the car hit the tree sideways on the driver's side and wrapped around the tree, which was about three feet in diameter. He added the light bar had been turned on and was flashing. Mike thinks he had likely just started a pursuit of a vehicle based on the speed and direction he was originally traveling when he reported into dispatch at 10:40 PM.

"He was a sponge for learning. He's the kind of officer you like to have working for you and with you," Polk County Sergeant Kay Williams told the *Herald-Free Press* about his late colleague. Sergeant Williams had worked in law enforcement for twenty-two years with the last seventeen years in Polk County. He had never worked in a department where someone had been killed in the line of duty. In the same article, Kay referenced the kind of officer Brad was. He said he "was always asking questions and always wanted to know more about law enforcement."

The death of one of his young deputies took its toll on Sheriff Parson. "It affected him very deeply. He took it very personally. I wouldn't equate it to losing a son, but at the same time, it was pretty darn close," Rachel recalled of Sheriff Parson following the death of her husband. She said Mike and Teresa almost accepted her care as their personal responsibility. "They made sure I was taken care of. I am not talking financially. I am talking about the little things," she recalled. "He mowed my yard. He changed the element in my water heater. I don't know how to explain it other than I was just looked after. They made sure that I was okay," Rachel emphasized.

Rachel feels Sheriff Parson felt it was his responsibility to take care of those under his watch. This also meant Teresa shared in the responsibility. "It was like their calling to step in and help out until they were no longer needed in that capacity," Rachel said. Evidenced by the relationship Rachel and the Parsons still have today, the phrase "no longer" actually has no end. "It was a really bad thing. It was tough and hard, but so much good came from that. Our friendship is one of those things. I hold those two

(Mike and Teresa) very near and dear. They are like second parents to me. Their thoughts and opinions matter very much to me," Rachel declared from the heart.

The following is an excerpt on Deputy Mabee posted on the Officer Down Memorial Page – Remembering All Fallen Law Enforcement's Heroes:

BRAD A. MABEE

Deputy Brad Mabee was killed in an accident after striking a tree half-mile south of Goodson on Polk County P.

It is thought that he may have been attempting to catch up with a speeder or swerved to avoid hitting a deer. His emergency lights were on.

Deputy Mabee had served with the Polk County Sheriff's Office for two years. He was survived by his expectant wife.

Those last three words may have been a surprise. God's blessing proved to be a surprise to all but God. Rachel returned to work at the bank after a couple of weeks. The loss of a spouse is a traumatic experience, and physical illness is often one of the responses after such an event. When Rachel returned to work, it was accompanied with stomach sickness. People continued to attribute the vomiting to stress from the loss of Brad, but Teresa started to think it might be more. "She was still having times when she was nauseated," Teresa recalled of Rachel a few weeks after she returned to the bank. Rachel thought it was stress related, but one of Teresa's colleagues at the bank began to have similar concerns like Teresa. "Do you think she might be pregnant?" Teresa's co-worker asked her. Together and respectfully, they encouraged Rachel to go get a pregnancy test. Shirley, Teresa's co-worker, accompanied Rachel to the doctor. "Come to find out, she was three weeks pregnant at the time of the accident," Teresa recalled. Blessings from God are often not explainable here on earth—only God knows. Rachel (and Brad) were blessed with a daughter, Miranda. "When Miranda was born, they treated her like a grandchild," Rachel recalled about Mike and Teresa.

After Brad passed away and Miranda was born, some thought Rachel might move back to Barry County where her parents lived. Like many who have faced tragedy, Rachel thought this might be her one opportunity to do something else, but leaving Bolivar and Polk County never crossed her mind. She did leave the bank and went back to school. Soon after, she met her now husband, Randy Lightfoot. Rachel loved her new career path, but circumstances did not allow her to dedicate herself at the level she expected. Rachel was at a career crossroads. Randy encouraged her to reach out to Sheriff Parson. She did and ultimately went to work for the Polk County Sheriff's Office. During her time there, Rachel remembers getting to see Mike "the boss" just as her late husband had.

Mike and Teresa continue to hold Rachel, Randy, Miranda, and the entire Lightfoot family dear to them. The tragic events that occurred in October 1997 were heart-wrenching for all involved, but it is often those moments when one shows the outside who they are on the inside. The Parson family was committed to the Mabee family and equally committed to the Lightfoots. In turn, the Lightfoot family today remains committed to the Parson family.

When Sheriff Parson decided to not run for a fourth term as Polk County sheriff in 2004 and instead run for the Missouri House of Representatives, Rachel told the sheriff she would help him in any way needed and took a position on the Parson campaign team. She remembers walking the communities and going door to door during the early campaigns. She ultimately became campaign treasurer and worked on all his campaign teams. Regardless of the position she held, she was willing to work at the grassroots level of all campaigns. Working hard was the only way she knew how to do things, but she learned early on that outworking Mike Parson was an impossible task. Raising money became her focus when Mike was in the House and Senate, and hosting golf tournaments at the Silo Ridge Golf Course in Bolivar became her specialty. When Governor Parson started running for statewide positions, she characterized them as "another kind of beast," so her roles on the campaign team transformed over the years. "He outworked everybody. It is literally what he did," Rachel said about Mike on the campaign trail. "If there was a town, he went. If there was an event, he went," she recalled.

These words speak to who Mike Parson is and has always been. His commitment to work hard and serve has paid dividends to Missouri. The words "Parson Works for Missouri" are real.

ABOVE: Mike Parson and his brother Kent have spent many years as public servants.

RIGHT: A bronze plaque dedicated by Rachel Mabee (Lightfoot) is displayed in the Polk County Sheriff's Office in honor of her late husband Brad, who as deputy sheriff gave his life in the line of duty under Sheriff Parson.

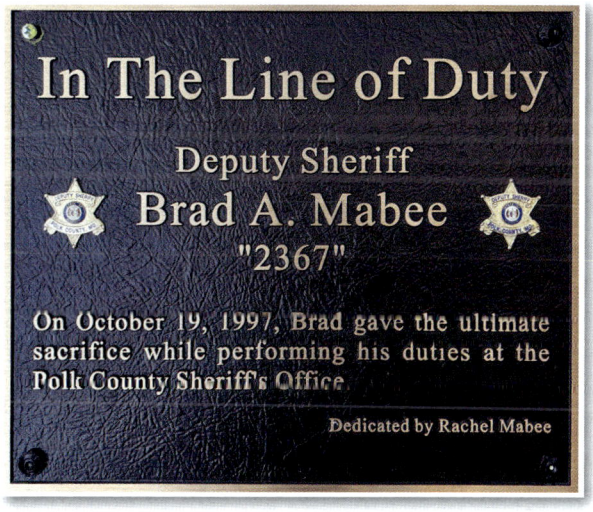

CHAPTER 6   89

Representative Ron Richard, Kent Parson, Representative Mike Parson, and Representative Steve Tilley posed on the House chamber floor. (Photo credit: Tim Bommel.)

Speaker of the House Rod Jetton recognized Representative Mike Parson as Freshman Legislator of the Year for his outstanding work in rural highway improvement during session in 2005. (Photo credit: Tim Bommel.)

Chapter 7

The Bus Has Only One Driver
Life as a Missouri State Representative (2005–2010)

"He was playing chess when others were playing checkers."

Near the end of his twelfth year as the Polk County sheriff in 2004, Mike and Teresa determined his third term would be his last. Sheriff Parson was proud of the work completed during his years serving the community. He was proud he had brought a professional level of law enforcement to the people of Polk County. He was proud all major cases in the county, including multiple homicides, had been solved. He was most proud of the fact he had created a solid foundation for the future of law enforcement in Polk County. The future without Mike as sheriff was critically important to him. Like a great football coach, Mike was ready to turn the reins over to the next play caller. When some speak of the greatness of Nick Saban and Andy Reid, they view their coaching to be even greater than all their championships. It is not necessarily about what was done at a point in time, but rather about the influences one had on creating other leaders along the way. Mike's influence is still evident in the law enforcement leadership in Polk County today. On a personal note, Sheriff Parson said that after twelve years, "You just know too much about everyone" and felt it was "the right time to get out of the sheriff business."

Mike and Teresa were not sure what the next step was going to be, but they were certain it was time to end that chapter. They spent a considerable amount of time thinking about what that next chapter would be, though they never considered a career move in the direction of politics. Mike thought he might open a lawncare business, detailing shop, or sell used cars. All those ideas were slashed from the list moments after he hit a slice into the trees with his driver on the second tee at Bolivar's Silo Ridge Golf and Country Club in 2004. The foursome Mike was playing with that day included longtime Missouri State Representative Ronnie Miller. Term limits were approved by Missouri voters the previous year, and Representative Miller was one of the first legislators affected. During Mike's backswing, Representative Miller said to Mike, "You ought to run for that." Mike responded by slicing the ball into the trees on the right. Governor Parson has now made the big slice a consistent part of his golf game, but that slice was a monumental moment.

First Lady Parson remembers her and Mike's first conversation about the possibility of running for the Missouri House of Representatives. She knew Mike had played golf with Ronnie Miller that day, and when Mike returned home, they had a few minutes of small talk before Mike hit the punch line. Teresa remembers Mike saying, "Ronnie thinks I should run for his position." Teresa's immediate response was "Oh," before a moment of hesitation followed with "in Jefferson City!" Mike went on to confirm that Ronnie had encouraged him to do so. "Are you going to? You have got to do something," Teresa remembers saying. She remembers some hesitation in Mike's initial response to her question. She remembers Mike looking at her and saying, "I don't think I can do that . . . I don't really know anything about that."

Now when working with the JAG (Jobs for America's Graduates) students, both Mike and Teresa use that initial conversation as an example of stepping out of their comfort zone. Teresa remembers exactly what she told Mike. "You don't know you can't do it until you try," she said. They discussed his steadfast interest in politics. He had never run for a state office, but he had grown up in a family with parents who were always in tune with politics. A decision was not made at that particular moment, but the seed was sown. Teresa remembers there was no rush to a decision, but as a family unit, they decided in the months ahead to file for the District 133 Missouri House of Representatives seat in the Republican primary taking place on Tuesday, August 3, 2004. This decision, one that could have been a "no" just as easily as it became a "yes," would prove to be yet another consequential moment in the journey of Mike Parson, fifty-seventh governor of Missouri.

In August 2004, Mike Parson won the Republican primary election against three other candidates vying for the nomination, garnering 44.1 percent of the votes. In November 2004, he went on to win the general election against a Democrat and a Libertarian, securing 74.7 percent of the votes cast. What was unique to Mike Parson's time in the Missouri House of Representatives was he ran unopposed in both the primary and general elections in 2006 and 2008. Aaron Willard, Governor Parson's chief of staff, identified this trend coming out of a four-way primary to be extremely rare. "When you come out of a multi-candidate race where there are a lot of different people that think they can do this job, there is usually some bitterness," Aaron said of election history. Running unopposed after winning an election against multiple candidates is not the norm. Aaron added that Governor Parson not only did it in the House but also the Senate. Aaron concluded, "You see that from members that really work their districts hard . . . people that are well liked." He stressed there are multiple factors and characteristics evident when this happens. "That really speaks to the type of legislator he was, the kind of person he is. People in the community thought 'This guy is doing a good job. There is no need to challenge him. I would rather be on his team and get behind him and support him than try to challenge him,'" Aaron highlighted.

When Mike Parson entered the state house, the landscape of politics in Missouri was changing. On November 3, 1992, Missouri voters approved by a 75 percent margin an amendment to the state's constitution limiting the years a legislator can serve in the general assembly. Prior to this, Missouri had no legislative term limits. The amendment limited terms to a maximum of eight years in the Missouri House of Representatives and eight years in the Missouri Senate. The period of so-called "lifetime politicians" and those in long-standing leadership positions started to become a thing of the past around the year 2000. If people were thinking about making politics a career, they now had to be strategic. Corresponding with this period was the first time the Republicans gained control of the legislature in over fifty years. This occurred after a special election in the Senate in 2001 but was retained after the general election in 2002. Following the 2002 election, Catherine Hanaway was the first female to serve as speaker of the House in 2003. Rod Jetton, who served as speaker pro-tem under Hanaway, advanced to the position of speaker of the House in 2005 when Hanaway decided to run for a statewide office.

Aaron Willard recalls the 2004 Missouri General Assembly having a very strong freshman class. There were many legislators in the House with countywide elected experience. Among the group were prosecutors and mayors as well as sheriffs like Mike Parson. With the onset of term limits, legislators started doing the math, and Representative Rod Jetton proved to be a benefactor. Term limits combined with Catherine Hanaway's decision to pursue a statewide office allowed Rod Jetton to quickly advance to speaker of the House. This was not common, but things were changing as a result of the new limitations. Being a former United States Marine, Speaker Jetton was prepared for the challenges. Aaron remembers Speaker Jetton immediately taking the helm with a "command and control" approach. "We are going to be a team. We are going to have a strategy," Aaron said as he summarized the speaker's approach. This method resonated with the members of the strong freshman class, especially with newly elected representative and veteran of the United States Army Mike Parson.

Although there was a lot of jockeying for positions in leadership at that time, Mike remained behind the scenes early on. He watched where the chips were going to fall and concentrated on being the best legislator he could be. This was the beginning of a strategy that would prove to be a signature feature of the "Parson approach" throughout his political career. As a result, Mike was not seen as a threat by other members who were seeking leadership roles. In fact, many of the other members of the House wanted to work alongside him and confide in him as they advanced their own agendas. Aaron said Mike was a person most legislators saw as "a good guy . . . not trying to be someone else. He just really wants to get things done." In doing this, members naturally gravitated towards Mike, making him a leader whether he sought it or not.

During this period, Republicans reintroduced a framework around the House Rules, including how floor activity would be governed, how committees would be governed, and how overall day-to-day activity would be conducted. This was not a new framework but one that had been partially implemented during most of the multiple decades of Democrat control of the legislature. During the first session of Republican control, the legislature operated under the old set of rules. After that session, Republican leadership decided they could do things better—just because things have been done a certain way didn't mean they always needed to be done that way.

Despite Republican control, there were a small number of Republicans who were not supportive of the rule changes. Those Republican legislators with a seat on the political bus quickly learned their political position and influence in the capitol could be significantly altered if they purposely made too much noise. Some of the opposed legislators not only lost their leadership roles on committees but even lost their physical offices in the capitol. The concepts of team and strategy were real, and legislators quickly learned that adhering to the code of the team was not negotiable. If one did not respect the team, they may be going it alone.

When Republican State Representative Mike Parson started his political career in Jefferson City, it was the first time the Republicans had control of both chambers (House and Senate) and the governor's office in recent history. Newly elected Republican Governor Matt Blunt, who had replaced the outgoing Democrat Governor Bob Holden, swore in Mike Parson and the other members of the legislature on January 5, 2005. Like most, if not all, of the other freshmen legislators, Mike spent much of his time learning the ropes and getting his footing during his first year in office.

With Mike's extensive experience in agriculture and law enforcement, most people would naturally expect Mike to want to be assigned to committees focused on these topics. This was not the direction Mike wanted, however. He wanted to broaden his knowledge and expertise. Instead of being assigned to committees such as Agriculture, Corrections and Public Institutions, or Crime Prevention and Public Safety, Mike was assigned to the committees of Senior Citizen Advocacy and Transportation. Mike served as a valuable member of both committees. He and his other freshmen Republicans absorbed as much knowledge as possible during their first year about what would be required to make the biggest positive difference in the political process.

Mike quickly learned every member of the general assembly had a role and seat on the political bus, but only a few had the ability to drive and determine the direction. Mike did not want to just be in one of the seats; he wanted to be as close to the driver's seat as he could. He knew the speaker of the House had a firm grip on the steering wheel, but he also realized early on there were other positions of leadership important to the speaker and ultimately determined the road map to get there. Mike realized going it alone was not an option if he wanted to make the biggest positive impact in the political process, so he charted a course for himself and his freshmen colleagues to position themselves to be in the driver's seat in subsequent years.

Mike established a strong relationship with many freshman members of the House. Kenny Jones was one of those members. Kenny and Mike shared similar career paths and ultimately became great friends. They both spent time in law enforcement before joining the Missouri State House of Representatives in 2005. Kenny was elected Moniteau County sheriff in 1984 after nine years as a trooper for the Missouri State Highway Patrol. Mike was elected Polk County sheriff in 1992 and assumed the position in 1993. Kenny and Mike first became acquainted through the Missouri Sheriffs' Association. Kenny remembers Mike's colleagues in southwest Missouri talking about him in high regard.

Originally from Greenfield, Kenny remembers stopping by the Polk County Sheriff's Office in Bolivar to visit with Mike on his way to visit family. "We often drift to people that are like minded," Kenny recalled of his relationship with Mike. Kenny regarded Mike as "an active sheriff who was always trying to make his county better and consequently was well-respected . . . a good honest reputation."

Mike went to Texas after the space shuttle *Columbia* burned and crashed upon reentry and to Louisiana after Hurricane Katrina. Kenny remembers Mike always putting others before himself and service before benefit. "He was not only thinking of his county . . . he was always thinking further than that. He was thinking about his state and his country. He had the bigger picture. Mike made the most of his life experiences," he said. Kenny insists this is still the Mike Parson he knows to this day.

With Moniteau County being the western neighbor of Cole County, home to Jefferson City and the Missouri capitol, Kenny found himself representing the sheriffs' association on numerous occasions regarding political issues important to law enforcement. Mike also traveled to Jefferson City to testify on legislation related to law enforcement during his tenure as Polk County sheriff. During that time, Mike testified on two landmark pieces of legislation. The first was related to property searches known as the Open Fields Doctrine. The second related directly to a high profile case he worked as Polk County sheriff, which ultimately improved laws associated with the abandonment of a corpse. Concealed Carry Weapons (CCW) was another piece of legislation they both took a personal interest in while sheriffs. To this day, Kenny and Mike still debate which one of them signed the first gun permit when CCW passed. The debate may never be fully resolved, but the power of the legislature on important issues was very apparent to them both.

Kenny feels Mike's time in the service prepared him as much for leadership as anything. He then had his own business that proved to be very successful. In his interactions with Mike, he found him to be a thinker who was always looking for ways to do things better. He found him to be one of the hardest workers he knew. Kenny considered Mike to be a master at relationship building. Mike knew no strangers and had the innate ability to talk to anyone. Getting to know people is easy for Mike. A person's worldly status has no bearing on Mike getting to know people. Everyone is on an equal playing field with him. He understands he can learn from everyone. Mike is indeed a special and unique relationship builder.

Both Kenny and Mike had friends who preceded them in their political districts who encouraged them to seek election. Both regarded their time as sheriff as fulfilling; for similar reasons, they knew it was time to make a change. Like Mike, Kenny felt it was time to get out of the sheriff business when he started arresting the children of the parents he had once arrested. While on the campaign trails, neither Kenny nor Mike remembers having significant conversations about their futures other than in passing.

During his freshman year as a state representative, Mike was instrumental in organizing groups of fellow first-year Republican representatives in an effort to make a lasting impact and set a trajectory toward future leadership. The name of one such group is still up for debate. Mike continues to refer to this group as the "Apple Dumpling Gang" while others recall them to be the "Apple Pie Caucus." The group of eight or so freshmen representatives would meet about once a week at the local Country Kitchen in Jefferson City. During their visits, most would eat a piece of apple pie with some ice cream. The Apple Dumpling Gang also shared interests outside of politics. The average age of the members was about forty-five in 2005. These representatives were from rural Missouri and had favorable relationships with members of both sides of the aisle in the House. The Apple Dumpling Gang ultimately became a powerful force within the Republican caucus.

Kenny Jones could be considered a "charter member" of the Apple Dumpling Gang along with Mike. Other members included Ward Franz, Darrell Pollock, David Sater, Rodney Schad, and Don Wells. "We were not there just to talk about how good the pie was. If you were not trusted, you would not have been there," Kenny recalled. The group spent time discussing how all the committees worked. They talked, but more importantly, they listened. The knowledge of the group was more important than the knowledge of any single member. Kenny remembers most of the freshmen Republican representatives were put on the right side of the aisle with the Democrats when session opened. Being in such daily proximity with the Democrats helped the group learn to understand them and their different backgrounds. "We figured out why they vote like they vote. It made us all better because of that," he said.

With their extensive experience in law enforcement, Representative Parson and Representative Jones were called upon on numerous occasions on important legislation related to public safety. "If he thought something was good, he would definitely promote it. He would not just sit back and see what happened," Kenny recalled of Mike. One important piece of legislation was the use of force to defend oneself, often referred to as the Castle Doctrine. Both Mike and Kenny sponsored or co-sponsored bills related to the Castle Doctrine, and their testimony from a law enforcement perspective was critical to its passage in 2007. After the Castle Doctrine passed, Kenny remembers some of the Democrats apologizing that they could not vote in support of the legislation. They felt the language was sound, but they could not support the passage. He and his Republican colleagues sympathized with their position, and thanks to the relationship they had created from the onset, they could all respectfully "agree to disagree." Still today, Governor Parson considers this piece of legislation to be an important landmark in history for individuals to provide personal protections for themselves and their property.

Kenny remembers Mike having very good rapport with Speaker of the House Rod Jetton. Mike was focused on leadership and influence, but this focus was not for personal gain. Mike wanted to see all people around him have self-worth and be successful. Mike was a loyal Republican, but he treated all people with dignity and respect. "When you are in the majority, you can just roll over them or you can work with them," Kenny spoke of the importance of having relationships with all legislators regardless of party. Mike was always a leader and got along with everybody who wanted to get along.

Representative Steven (Steve) Tilley entered the Missouri State House of Representatives the same year as Mike. Both took the oath as members of the Ninety-third General Assembly of the State of Missouri. Steve and Mike would become good friends over the years. Although Steve did not necessarily consider himself a member of the Apple Dumpling Gang, he did recall joining the group, which he referred to as the Apple Pie Caucus, on occasion. Representative Tilley, being thirty-three years old, felt this group of men were a little old to be hanging out with but knew there was something special about them. Steve considers it God's gift that he and Mike were placed on the same floor and complex of offices in the capitol.

Steve would be quick to point out that few, if any, would envision the relationship that developed between the two. Looking back now, not even Steve saw it coming. "Mike and I were not likely friends. I was 33 years old, and he was a retired sheriff with some gray hair. Because of our age and interests, you would not pick us to be close friends," he recalled.

Steve remembers Mike seeing potential in him he did not see in himself. The result was a natural bond still existing today. "We had no reason to be hanging out together," Mike laughs thinking back.

Steve Tilley learned early on that Mike Parson was "playing chess when others were playing checkers." He quickly noticed that Representative Parson saw things others did not see, and if others did see them, he saw them first. Representative Parson quickly came to the realization that the years of continuous leadership were over—term limits were going to change the landscape of political leadership. In four short years, this group of freshmen representatives would be the senior group, and Mike considered it critical to plan ahead. Steve learned Representative Parson was not just glad to be there but fully intended to make a positive difference. He learned from Mike there were 163 members in the House and all were important, but there were four or five who were truly in the drivers' seats.

Steve vividly remembers Representative Parson calling him into his office just over a month into their first session. In that meeting, Mike told him, "I think you need to be Speaker of the House someday." Representative Parson's kind words gave Steve a rush. He considered himself a young, aggressive, ambitious politician when he entered the House and was humbled when Representative Parson reiterated, "I want you to be the leader."

The second group of first-year Republican representatives Mike assembled was a different group than the Apple Dumpling Gang but did include a few members. A "preparation meets opportunity" moment does not happen without preparation. Mike did his homework. In the early part of the session, Mike did his best to determine the members in the freshman class who were born leaders, who were difference makers, and who were confident in being there a while. Kenny Jones and Steve Tilley recall Mike convening a group of eight or nine freshmen representatives in the weeks that followed, including themselves. Mike organized the unnamed group to support the future of the party, the representatives, and their ability to be a part of the leadership and influence moving forward. Kenny recalls Mike directing the meeting with laser focus. Some of the representatives were still in their honeymoon period and just happy to be there, but not Mike Parson. He was driven by a bigger purpose for them all. Mike encouraged the group to be forward thinkers, and that is exactly what they became. "The biggest goal of the group was to make Missouri better," Kenny remembers.

Steve remembers Representative Parson leading the meeting, saying, "We are freshmen . . . we need to lay the groundwork so that everyone in this room can be successful and achieve their goals." At that point, they went around the room identifying their goals and intentions for the future. Some identified House officer positions such as speaker and floor leader, while others identified House committees they would like to serve as chairman. Mike realized the group working together as one would be more beneficial to the team. If three different representatives thought they someday wanted to be speaker of the House, it was important to know sooner than later. Kenny remembers identifying the position of chairman of the Accounts Committee as his goal.

When discussing the legislative process, there are a lot of people on the political bus, but as Kenny stated, "There is one driver." However, the driver still has other people with roles and responsibilities that need to be respected. Kenny felt Mike learned before most what those positions were. During the meeting of freshman representatives, Kenny remembers Mike stating he would like to be Rules chairman. Kenny immediately thought the leader with laser focus had lost his focus, but he later learned the wit of the silver fox. At first glance, the Rules chairman does not seem to be influential, but the driver cannot turn where the Rules chairman does not direct. "He is the turn signal," Kenny emphasized. With a smile and laugh, he remembered no one in the meeting saying, "Mike Parson, you will be the Governor of Missouri someday!"

Kenny became chair of the Administration and Accounts Committee, which has sole and complete control of all financial obligations and business affairs of the House. The committee is responsible for the operation funds of the representatives' offices and governs the expenditure of funds allotted to the members. The committee assigns all offices, chamber seats, and parking spaces. Kenny put his focus on spending money where he felt it should be spent. He focused on taking care of everyone in a fair and just manner.

From the same meeting that resulted in Kenny one day becoming chair of Administration and Accounts, Steve Tilley remembered leaving feeling like the group had entered into an unwritten pact to help everyone in the room achieve their goals. He also recalls Representative Parson identifying "Chairman of the Rules Committee" to be his personal goal, which caught himself and many of the others in the group off guard. Steve considers this to be yet another example of Mike playing chess while the rest were playing checkers. "Mike knew how powerful rules were going to be before the rest of us," he reiterated. Mike knew when it came to policy, the Rules Committee chairman would be as influential as the speaker and floor leader. Representative Parson remembers visiting in the back of the House chamber with whom he considered the "young guns"—the representatives he felt would be the ones to run for statewide office someday. Mike felt like he spent much of his energy in the early years supporting the career aspirations of his younger colleagues. Mike told Steve he would likely be governor someday, not knowing the script would be totally flipped. Both laugh today remembering Mike Parson, the political architect, designing the plans and putting them in motion. Mike saw a statewide candidate and winner in Steve Tilley. He viewed him as a mover and a shaker with the potential to someday be governor, but the Heavenly Architect had a different set of plans.

Steve Tilley was a successful businessman. He was an optometrist by trade and owned some pharmacies as well. Most optometrists probably do not know much about farming, and farmers do not know much about optometry. This was the situation for Mike and Steve, but regardless, they both found value in the other. Steve was obviously not a legislator for the money. Rather, he was giving up a lot to work in Jefferson City. While in the House, Steve spent a considerable amount of time helping other legislators get their priorities accomplished. He supported those who supported him. Mike and Steve worked on a number of pieces of legislation together. They were alike yet very different.

While in the House, Mike regarded Steve as the best of salesmen. "What he was selling, he could convince you to buy. He just had that ability," he said of Steve. Mike also felt there were times Steve was too fast even for himself. This is when Mike felt he was most valuable to him.

Representative Parson flew in the face of the norm when he supported Steve, who was from Perryville in southeast Missouri. It was customary for legislators to have coalitions with others in their general geographic location, and Mike got behind Steve for the position of majority floor leader. He ultimately won the position and began serving in that capacity in January 2008, which was a big step toward the ultimate goal of becoming speaker of the House in the future.

While Steve Tilley eyed the speaker's gavel, Mike kept his focus. He wanted to have influence that extended the entire spectrum of legislative issues. As Rules chairman, he could have an impact on every piece of legislation. The Rules Committee did not specialize in anything but dabbled in everything. Everything had to funnel through the committee, which was brought back into existence with the changes recommended when the Republicans assumed the majority. Shannon Cooper from Clinton served as the first Rules chairman when it was reinstituted followed by Mike. Shannon was a talented and well-respected member of the House. Before he left, Mike did what he could to learn as much as possible from him. Being from Clinton, this made it geographically possible. Mike considers Shannon a mentor still today.

Before any piece of legislation could go to the floor, it had to pass through the Rules Committee. Mike recognized early on that this committee had an awesome responsibility with the ability to have a powerful influence. After a piece of legislation got to the floor, it became the responsibility of the floor leader, but it had to make it through the Rules Committee first. The committee served as the check and balance of the legislative process. Mike and his committee would be called on to negotiate through disagreement. As chairman, he spent most of his time building bridges to advance pieces of legislation. Relationships and conflict resolution became his specialties.

Steve remained patient in his pursuit of becoming speaker of the House. He enjoyed his position as floor leader, and when former Joplin mayor Ron Richard expressed his desire to be speaker of the House, Steve agreed to continue in the position of majority floor leader. Representative Richard was characterized as an elder statesman in comparison to Steve, who was a highflier. Along with this came general personality differences. Representative Parson had a good relationship with both Ron and Steve and was able to serve as a liaison between the two. Rules chairman combined with strong relationships with both the speaker and floor leader ultimately made Mike one of the most powerful leaders in the legislature without even being in an official leadership position.

Steve considered Mike to be like a father figure. "He was the wiser one of us two," he recalls. He remains of the opinion the two were put together for a reason bigger than themselves, realizing Mike served as his "third-party validator" as he progressed through the ranks of the House. "When people would say, 'Steve is too young for that position. He has not been here long enough,' Mike was able to calm them down," he recalls. "I would have never been Speaker of the House without Mike Parson."

Mike is a master at "gaming the system." When it came to parking in the early years, Representative Parson identified an opportunity and moved on it. As chairman of the Accounts Committee, one of Kenny Jones' responsibilities was to assign parking places. Only those in leadership positions like the governor, lieutenant governor, speaker, floor leaders, a select group of senators, and of course the Accounts chairman, got to park in the Capitol Police gated basement garage of the capitol. There was no better place to park than the climate-controlled environment of the basement garage. Steve Tilley remembers the garage to be a coveted area to park. Early during his tenure in the House, he remembers the cold, the rain, and the snow and still to this day is convinced he was parking in the furthest outdoor spot assigned.

Having a freshman legislator parking in the basement was not common; Kenny Jones was an exception to the rule. Being the Accounts chairman comes with its perks. Mike remembers Kenny always tinkering with old cars, and Kenny took pride in his mechanic ability and often drove the old cars he was fixing to the capitol. Mike laughs thinking back to the attention Kenny drew when he was parking in the basement garage after replacing an engine in one of the trucks he was working on. "It must have had one cylinder out of it. It would smoke like a dickens when he would go into the garage. It looked like he was fogging for mosquitoes," Mike remembered. A friend who responds to a friend in need is a friend indeed (maybe), so Mike offered Kenny some advice. "Jones . . . park that piece of shit outside," Mike said. Kenny replied, "I am going to have to . . . they are starting to complain about that." This is when the always-thinking Mike Parson created a preparation meets opportunity moment. "Why don't you let me park my car in here. We usually don't go anywhere during the day. I will leave my keys in it . . . if you need to go anywhere just take it," Mike offered as a solution. Kenny agreed to take him up on the deal. Soon after, Mike started parking his car in the garage, and Kenny started parking whatever he was driving out in the elements.

"What I love about Mike . . . he is intellectually smart. He sees things that others don't see. His personality gives him a way about him . . . an oh shucks thing. It is very sincere, not an act," Steve Tilley adds about his early perceptions of Representative Parson. "I remember walking to and from my parking spot to the Capitol and seeing Mike drive into the basement for like a year and a half." He remembers one day asking Mike, "'How in the world are you parking in the basement?' He just laughed and shrugged his shoulders."

Mike remembers a second and more significant encounter in the basement garage about two weeks after he started parking there. He remembers getting out of his car at about the same moment "Tilley and the Young Guns," as he referred to them, were coming into the garage.

Among them was the "Big Gun" Rod Jetton, who was speaker of the House. As Mike exited his car, Speaker Jetton yelled, "Parson! Why are you . . ." then a moment of hesitation followed with "I don't even want to know about this." Mike remembers Steve behind Rod laughing, shaking his head, and silently mouthing, "I can't believe you." "He just has a way of getting things done," Steve emphasized. Throughout the years that followed, the bond between Steve Tilley and Mike Parson continued to grow. As in any great relationship, Steve remembers it was not all take and no give. A true friendship involves give and take.

With term limits fully implemented, Mike and his colleagues in the House had to contemplate and decide in a timely manner the political trajectory they intended for themselves. With the support of his constituents, Representative Parson proved through the years he could make winning reelection a foregone conclusion. Nonetheless, his tenure as representative would end not due to the lack of favor by the citizens but rather by term limits at some point.

During Mike Parson's third term, State Senator Delbert Scott from Lowry City, a fellow Republican, reached his eight-year limit in the Missouri General Assembly. Senator Scott had been elected to the Senate in November 2001. He was later reelected to a second term as Republican senator of Missouri District 28 in November 2005. Mike had two options—run for one more two-year term as state representative or seize the opportunity to run for a four-year term as state senator in his home district. If he chose to run for representative, in a race he would have likely won, he would be term-limited at the conclusion of the term and not have the opportunity to run for Senate. Since the timing of the House of Representatives and the Senate seats were not perfectly aligned, he had to decide quickly.

Mike decided to forgo a fourth and final term in the House of Representatives to pursue the Senate seat. Steve Tilley remembers Representative Parson asking, "I want to run for Senate. Will you help me?" Steve responded he would be behind him all the way. He remembers about a month or two into the Senate race coming across what appeared to him to be a downtrodden Representative Parson. He remembers asking Mike what was on his mind, to which he responded he was reconsidering his run for the Senate. Steve then asked, "Why?" Mike responded, "Because I don't have a college education. I don't know how that will look." Steve remembers picking up a dejected friend and dusting him off, saying, "Don't let your willingness to serve be impacted by what you think is a shortcoming . . . because it is not." He considered Mike Parson to be one of the smartest guys he knew despite the fact he lacked a few widely judged words on his resume. Steve's display of confidence in him would prove to be just the push Mike needed.

When Mike, Teresa, and the Parson family ultimately made the decision to pursue the seat, they never turned back. It was another moment in Mike Parson's life where preparation meets opportunity. Mike worked hard to be an effective and well-respected state representative, and his constituents rewarded him by electing Mike Parson as a Missouri state senator.

Representative Kenny Jones, Representative Mike Parson, and Kent Parson posed on the floor of the House. Kenny and Mike shared many memories from their time in political office and always had a lot of laughs when they were together.

Mike Parson was never afraid to put in the work as he prepared to participate in a parade during his Senate race to meet and visit with the citizens he hoped to serve.

CHAPTER 8

Blessed by an Unexpected Turn of Events
Life as a Missouri State Senator (2011–2016)

"He had two options – respond with bitterness or respond with kindness."

Hitting the campaign trail was nothing new for Mike and the Parson family. Once the decision was made to run for Senate, the work began. Mike was challenged in the Republican primary by Larry Wilson and Ed Emery. Both Representative Wilson and Representative Emery were at a similar crossroads as Mike when making the decision to run for Senate. Mike had represented Cedar County and a portion of Polk County. Representative Wilson represented St. Clair and Hickory Counties, and Representative Emery represented Barton and Dade Counties and portions of Jasper and Polk Counties. Although they were neighbors and had spent six years together as Republican colleagues in the state capitol, only one of them would represent the party in the November general election—a known risk when running for the state senate. However, Mike was focused on the reward. On August 3, 2010, Mike took 47.4 percent of the votes to take him into the general election. After winning the primary, it became clear there would be little contest in the general election. Mike defeated his opponent, taking 83.7 percent of the votes.

Mike Parson now was a member of the Missouri Senate representing District 28. District boundaries changed slightly during his tenure in the Senate, but while in the seat, he represented all or portions of Barton, Benton, Cedar, Dallas, Henry, Hickory, Laclede, Pettis, Polk, and St. Clair Counties from 2011 to 2017. He had a new title, Senator Parson, and was very active and involved in and outside the Senate chamber, quickly becoming well-respected among his new constituents.

Given the timing and full implementation of term limits, many of the Missouri Senate winners in the general election were former members of the Missouri House of Representatives. This was a huge class of senators who had served together in the House, which was a very unique situation. Approximately one-third of the Senate body had worked together as a unit in the House. Until then, senators often worked independently of one another; each member was like an island. The mindset of the Senate was changed in one election cycle.

When the Republican caucus met in 2010 after the election, the newly elected group of senators, including Mike Parson, quickly realized there were "more of us than them." They concluded they needed a seat at the leadership table. Before Mike was even sworn in as senator, he was chosen to be the majority whip during the caucus meeting. The duties of political leadership positions vary, but regardless of the specific responsibilities, he had a seat at the table where decisions were made. His ability to foster positive relationships across the capitol during his time in the House was the preparation that met this opportunity.

Representative Steve Tilley did not run for Senate but did demonstrate his loyalty to many of the members on his House team by endorsing them in their Senate bids. Steve still had two years left in the House and continuing to work with those he worked with in the House in the Senate seemed like the right thing to do. Having allies in the Senate chamber would assist in advancing critical legislation. He supported many of the eventual winners, but he also supported a few that came up short when the election results came in. One such individual was Representative Kenny Jones, a longtime friend and ally of Mike Parson, who ran in the Republican primary against eventual winner Mike Kehoe. Unlike Kenny, Mike Kehoe didn't come from the House, yet the political careers of Mike Parson and Mike Kehoe would cross many times over the years, each with varying degrees of consequences.

Steve Tilley outwardly supported Parson and others, including Kenny Jones, and sometimes, the concept of association can have consequences. A level of bitterness is natural when the legislators one will be working with want someone else to be in one's seat. Even in the same political party, when a person fails to support someone, they remember. Despite wearing the same jersey, there are sometimes teams within the team. Some legislators thought the influence of Steve Tilley was overreaching and unhealthy to the political process; he should not have this influence across both chambers. As a result, an unnamed coalition of legislators evolved to see to it Team Tilley was derailed.

When Mike was a senator, two particular leadership elections had the fingerprints of a group of senators fixated on silencing the influence of Steve Tilley. The first was the president pro tem position for the Ninety-sixth General Assembly in January 2011. There is typically a sequence that occurs when senators are advancing up the leadership ladder. For president pro tem, the previous majority floor leader is typically next in line for the position. The majority floor leader in the Ninety-fifth General Assembly was relatively confident he would be the next president pro tem. This particular year, on the day the Republican caucus met in November 2010, a new, unexpected senator was nominated for the position. The nomination for the position was a surprise to many, but not to those who supported the shadow candidate. The advancement of a senator from Appropriation chairman to president pro tem was not typical.

Senator Mike Parson was the casualty in the next leadership election at the Republican caucus meeting in November 2012. God had a different plan. In the Ninety-sixth General Assembly, Senator Parson served as majority whip. Being majority whip as a freshman senator was not the norm, but he was not your typical freshman legislator. His strong legislative relationships made it possible. The natural leadership progression for Senator Parson was majority floor leader in the Ninety-seventh General Assembly. He set his sights on the position, which could very likely lead to the president pro tem position in the Ninety-eighth General Assembly.

Senator Parson made his intentions to pursue majority floor leader known to his colleagues in the Senate, many of whom were supportive of the idea and pledged their support. Some of the senators who pledged their support directly to Parson must have done it with their fingers crossed, though, because unbeknownst to him, conversations of many of the same people behind closed doors must have been different. Senator Parson was confident he had the support he needed and there was a good chance he would run unopposed. When it was time for the official vote, evidence of the private conversations and a subversive campaign became evident. Ron Richard (Joplin) was surprisingly nominated for the position of majority floor leader. The person who was most surprised was Senator Parson. Mike subsequently lost the election of his peers in the Senate by one vote to Ron Richard.

Mike was taken aback by what occurred on the Senate floor that day. When an event like this happens in the life of most legislators (or most people in general), their mind usually records three people groups: the people who helped, the people who left, and the people who put you there. The difference between Mike Parson and most people is the fact he is not most people. Mike is human, so it hurt him. He believes when a moment of adversity occurs, it is 5 percent what happens and 95 percent how one deals with it.

Fast forward to today, it is conceivable to say Mike Parson would not have been the fifty-seventh governor of the Great State of Missouri if he would have won majority floor leader then. It is more likely he would have been elected to president pro tem in two years and, instead of leaving after year six in the Senate to run for lieutenant governor, Mike feels he would have ended his political career after eight full years in the Senate. Like fishing, the fish that drops off the hook and gets away sometimes becomes the biggest. The story certainly gets bigger and bigger over the years for Mike Parson. The election for majority floor leader was the only election Mike ever lost in his lifetime, and it was one of his peers, not of the people. Mike lives the percentages few can. The one that got away was indeed a big one. When hearing the word "loss," most people assume the political trajectory will most likely regress, not advance. In Mike's case, the loss of the position of the Senate floor leader ultimately catapulted his trajectory in the state.

Now, Mike still had to mentally rustle through the carnage, which he had more than a few minutes to do on his drive back home to Bolivar that night. It was as if he was at a crossroads. He had two options—respond with bitterness or respond with kindness. Mike Parson chose the latter, and there was "no turning back." It was a defining moment. Working with some of the same senators who had lied to him—a few right to his face—would not be an easy task.

However, Mike ultimately committed himself to moving forward. He dedicated himself to be the best senator for all Missourians he could be. It was only natural many of the senators were anxious to observe Mike's response. One never knows how a man is going to respond to an unexpected haymaker. His positive response was almost eerie to many of the senators who had deceived him. Mike was able to continue forging great relationships in the Senate, including with the coalition that essentially did him wrong. As a result, he became a powerful leader in the caucus with a magnanimous attitude who senators gravitated toward. Instead of being a roadblock, Mike served as a catalyst for critical legislation even though his positive attitude was almost too good to be true.

On August 5, 2014, Missouri voters narrowly approved a constitutional amendment referred to as Missouri Right-to-Farm. With a name like Right-to-Farm, a person would expect it to be favorable for farmers and agriculture in Missouri. However, just as a headline does not always speak to the content of an article, this title was a wolf dressed like a sheep. Farmers and ranchers having the right to engage in their livelihoods and produce food for others sounds great on the outside, but like many pieces of legislation, there are layers of impacts resulting from these basic words.

Supporters of the amendment argued all farmers and ranchers need protections due to out-of-state interests in restricting certain practices. Opponents countered it would provide protections to large corporate and multinational agribusiness and make it harder for family farmers and ranchers to protect themselves from business interests. As a farmer himself, Mike was an obvious choice by his colleagues to spearhead the effort to unwind and best explain the detrimental impacts of the amendment to Missouri farmers and ranchers. The voters had approved the amendment, and now the legislature was going to adjust the language. Mike boldly walked the line, accepting the responsibility and challenges it presented.

During Mike's time in the Senate under Senator Richard's leadership, the body began to operate using the team approach many of them operated under while working together in the House. A team approach was critical to success. Although Mike did not carry a leadership title during his later years in the Senate, he was undoubtedly a leader. He was a true example that one did not need an official title to be a leader. His colleagues knew he got things done. His ability to build relationships with people on both sides of the aisle was critical. When his colleagues in leadership ran into obstacles, Mike was often called upon to thread the needle. He is a Republican. He supports a conservative agenda. He fundamentally rejects liberal agendas, but he fundamentally respects people, and there is always extremism on both ends of the pendulum.

Right-to-Work was another controversial piece of legislation Republican senators turned to Mike to take the lead. The Republicans wanted to fast-track the bill while the Democrats were convinced it was just a poor piece of legislation. Mike focused on moving conservative items forward by respectfully listening to legislators who were liberal without sacrificing his conservative ideals. Instead of digging his heels in and getting nothing accomplished, Mike listened and created open dialogue. A few minor concessions in a piece of legislation to ultimately pass a conservative proposal was how he operated. Mike led the process with a thoughtful approach and provided adequate time for debate. The bill moved through and ultimately passed with conservative impressions. When a bill passes, the Republicans or Democrats sometimes want to publicly parade the moment in the face of the other party like a trophy. Mike likes to win, but he views one's reaction in victory to be even more defining than one's reaction in defeat.

Mike continued to be a senator who got things done. For this reason, many important pieces of legislation were directed his way. "If he sets his mind to something, it is going to happen. He was so respected by everyone. Most senators knew who Mike was from his years in the House, and if they didn't, they quickly learned who he was. He worked so hard to get things done. He ran circles around everybody," Marylyn Luetkemeyer, his executive assistant, stated of Senator Parson. During his time in the Senate, he was asked to sponsor a piece of legislation to address the maintenance of many state-owned buildings and facilities. This would require the need for bonds and subsequent payments by the state. Spending money on maintenance did not have the same appeal to legislators as a ribbon cutting at a new facility. As a result, Missouri had accumulated a significant deferred maintenance backlog. Mike loved the thrills of a ribbon cutting just like every other legislator, but he understood the critical responsibility of taking care of what the state already had. Mike learned early in Wheatland that if he was going to invest in something, he must do routine maintenance to keep it around for its intended lifespan. The Parson family never had the means to buy new very often, so finding ways to maintain what they had, and even repurpose when needed, was a way of life.

Mike dislikes debt just like any other Missourian or American, but utilizing debt to preserve the initial asset was not wasteful spending in Mike's eyes. Rather, it was a wise investment. Many bonding bills had been attempted and failed in the past due to the baggage attached in the political process. The bills ultimately killed themselves with their own weight. When Tom Dempsey was president pro tem, he approached Mike about leading a bonding bill. Mike knew the dismal history of bond bill legislation, so he shared his thoughts on a practical bonding bill that might have an opportunity to pass. Mike remembers telling him, "The biggest thing facing state government is deferred maintenance. We have built new shiny stuff with people's names on it. We have not taken care of what we got. If you want to do that, things that really move the needle, I will do that . . . only if you see to it that it does not turn into a Christmas tree with everyone attaching their wants, not needs, to it." Mike Parson was and never has been a fan of others in the general assembly attaching senseless amendments to an omnibus piece of legislation.

Tom Dempsey gave Mike full authority to move forward and do what he needed to do, so Mike sponsored the bond bill with a price tag around $600 million. It was not a very sexy bill. Bond sales would be used to refurbish buildings on university campuses and make repairs to state parks. Mike immediately identified the obstacles he would need to overcome to pass the bill. Senator Rob Schaaf was one senator he instantly knew would oppose any bond legislation. He knew Senator Schaaf was not going to support the bill, but Mike wanted to do what he could to make sure he did not kill it. Relationships are the backbone of the Parson way, and Mike did not hesitate in meeting with Senator Schaaf about the bill. Mike knew the senator would see opportunities in his bill that others would not see. Mike told him early in the meeting that he did not expect him to support the bill, but asked him, "How can I make this better?"

Senator Schaaf went to work. He provided multiple ideas to make the bill better and more efficient. Mike attributes Senator Schaaf with overall savings in the bond bill of approximately $12 million. The university portion of the proposed bill included such things as the renovation of bathrooms and replacement of carpet. The senator pointed out that many items like this would not last twenty years. Why would you bond items like this out to twenty years when they will likely need to be replaced again in five to ten years? Senator Schaaf recommended shorting the term on certain bonds would be more appropriate and save money. Mike went on to make these changes. Senator Schaaf reminded Mike he did not actually support the bill, to which Mike responded he did not request his support, he just wanted to get it through. Mike knew Senator Schaaf could have killed that bill, but he didn't. He voted against the bill, but he did not filibuster. It was all about relationships!

Although Mike was ready for another session in 2015, it had a different feel to it than other years. Nasty campaigns were in progress. People were doing and saying despicable things to get votes. It was just different.

Following the suicide of Missouri State Auditor Tom Schweich on February 26, 2015, Senator Mike Parson gave a moving speech on the Senate floor on March 2. The speech ultimately garnered national attention, though that was never Mike's intention. He has always been a man who just follows his heart. In his legislative column on March 5, 2015, Mike published the following for his constituents of Senate District 28 and all Missourians:

This week was unprecedented in the General Assembly as we paused to honor Missouri State Auditor Tom Schweich, who unexpectedly passed away last Thursday, February 26, from an apparent self-inflicted gunshot wound in his hometown of Clayton, Missouri. Busloads of lawmakers and staff traveled from Jefferson City to Auditor Schweich's funeral. His eulogy was given by his close friend and mentor, former U.S. Sen. John Danforth, who condemned the negativity that permeates the landscape of politics today in Missouri.

I wholeheartedly agree with Danforth's statements, and I made a speech on the Senate floor asking lawmakers and campaign organizers to take a closer look at how negative propaganda affects us all. How do we gain the trust of Missourians and their belief in all of us? We could start today by making a commitment to the people of this state and ourselves that we are not going to use propaganda. We are not going to destroy people's lives at all cost just to win elections. Instead, we can start talking about who we are and articulating the differences between ourselves and our opponents by being honest with the facts. I will personally commit that I will no longer stand by and let people destroy other people's lives using false accusations and demeaning statements in the name of money and winning elections. Nor will I support candidates that use such tactics. Tom's tireless dedication and service to our country and our state is the memory I will hold on to.

The column concluded with the words "Nothing is Politically Right Which is Morally Wrong" centered at the bottom. There may be no phrase that better speaks to the leader Mike Parson strived to be then and strives to be now for all Missourians each and every day. Better yet, it speaks to the man Mike Parson strives to be for all those he has an opportunity to influence daily.

Mike was moved by the events that may have contributed to governor candidate Tom Schweich taking his own life, and on Thursday, April 30, 2015, at the Bolivar High School Gymnasium, he announced he was entering the 2016 governor race. The next day, on Friday, May 1, at the North Jefferson City Recreation Area, he made the announcement official in the Capital City. Senator Parson announced his candidacy promising to clean up dirty politics and "bridge the gap" he believed existed between the state's urban and rural populations. "I've been questioned several times about why I'm running and, without a doubt, some of the tragic events that happened in this state over the last couple of months has probably given me more of the ambition," Senator Parson expressed to those in attendance at the announcement. He continued:

> I think Missouri politics, for one, needs to take a serious look at the way we do business. And we need to start putting out a positive message to the people of Missouri. Number one, if you want to talk about your opponent, and the differences of why (and how) you view issues, then I think that's what a campaign is all about. You build a reputation of who you are for that many years, and the people who know you know you the best. When people try to destroy that – try to destroy your honor and your integrity, just to win an election – that's wrong. And I think Missourians are fed up with winning at all costs.

During the announcement, one of the reporters in attendance asked "the elephant in the room" question, "What if another campaign runs negative attack ads against you during the race?" Senator Parson emphatically responded, "If people run negative ads about you, they're going to run negative ads about you." He then turned to what Missourians could expect from his campaign. "We're going to talk about the positive side of who I am. That's going to be my entire campaign message." He ended the announcement with, "Without a doubt, my family's the backbone of who I am. The people who know me the best– that I've lived with, grew up with–and that humble beginning, I want to say, (this) is who Mike Parson is."

Mike met with his political advisory team approximately one month after making the announcement he was running for governor. Steve Tilley vividly remembers that meeting and recalled the room being filled with a bunch of "yes" people. He felt many of those present would benefit either in position or financially if Mike were to win the race for Missouri governor. During the meeting, Mike posed the question to those in the room if he should continue in his pursuit of the bid for the Republican nomination for Missouri governor. Steve remembers the yeses coming out repeatedly as each person in attendance answered. Then the question got to him. Steve remembers first providing some basic friendly, supportive comments saying, "Listen, I am on the train with you. I am going where you are going." He then turned to his short and honest answer. Mike remembers Steve saying, "Senator, you cannot win." Mike

CHAPTER 8   115

was at a crossroads with his political future. He could complete the final two years of his second term in the Missouri Senate, or he could set a new course and run for the office of lieutenant governor.

On Sunday, July 25, 2015, Senator Mike Parson announced via Twitter that he was dropping out of the Missouri governor's race to pursue the position of Missouri lieutenant governor. He stated this position "will give a better path to win real reform for Missouri and promote positive politics." The switch came just three months after announcing his candidacy for governor. The race for governor had become a crowded one, especially on the Republican ticket. Five Republicans were in the race at the time with one more expected to join. The five candidates included Lieutenant Governor Peter Kinder, former Missouri house speaker Catherine Hanaway, Springfield State Senator Bob Dixon, St. Louis businessman John Brunner, and former state representative Randy Asbury. Former Navy SEAL Eric Greitens was expected to declare his candidacy in the near future. The only Democrat that had announced candidacy was Attorney General Chris Koster.

When Mike made the decision to run for lieutenant governor, he consulted with Aaron Willard, who would later serve as his chief of staff during his time as governor. Mike had consulted with various political campaign consultants about the recommended strategy to win the election, but he reached out to Aaron because over time he had observed him to have a sharp political mind. His strategy was not the same as that of most consultants. Aaron did not speak by gut feeling but rather by the numbers. He presented a model to Mike founded in data. Rural Missourians were a critical base to winning an election. The numbers showed voters in rural counties played a significant role in winning a primary election, so Mike put the strategy to the test and went to work.

Many Missourians are likely unaware of the role of lieutenant governor or that the political position even exists. Mike Parson admits the job lacks a high profile, but its potential significance is unmistakable. What does the lieutenant governor do? First, the lieutenant governor fills in when the governor is out of the state or incapacitated. If the governor dies, quits, or is ousted, the lieutenant governor typically closes out the term. This had last happened in 2000 when Democrat Roger Wilson finished Governor Mel Carnahan's term after he was tragically killed in an airplane crash in southeast Missouri while traveling to a campaign event for the United States Senate. Secondly, the lieutenant governor serves as the state senate's president and on boards and commissions involving seniors, veterans, tourism, and economic development. Unbeknownst to him at the time, in the case of Mike Parson, the words "potential significance" quickly became "real significance."

During the campaign for lieutenant governor, Mike vowed to fight for veterans, seniors, the tourism industry, and blue-collar workers across Missouri. When it came to environmental regulations and agriculture, he committed to pushing back against federal government overreach. He vowed to not sit idle in the face of the issues confronting Missourians and, as a result, Missourians didn't sit idly at home when asked to elect Mike Parson as their next lieutenant governor.

Senator Mike Parson spoke from the heart on the Senate floor in March 2015. (Photo credit: Harrison Sweazea.)

Senator Mike Parson took the helm of Missouri Senate District 28.

Growing Up: Early Years and Beyond

LEFT: Rarely did Mike and Ike Parson get dressed up, unless it was for occasions like Easter or Christmas. These boys were headed to church for Easter.

BELOW: Mike Parson turned two years old.

Ike Parson looked after his brother Mike through the years, even at a young age. Although the boys fought and bickered, they have a very special friendship.

Ike Parson found great pride in entertaining and watching after his little brother Mike.

GROWING UP: EARLY YEARS AND BEYOND 119

ABOVE: "Cops and robbers" was one of Mike and Ike Parson's favorite games to play. They would run around outside and pretend to shoot anything in sight. This was where Sheriff Parson got his start.

LEFT: Ike Parson drew his knife at the Carpenter Place. Mike thought his older brother was pretty cool.

LEFT: Hellen Parson always prepared a birthday cake for the boys' birthdays. Ike was celebrating his fifth birthday.

BELOW: Hellen Parson always made an effort to make Mike and his brothers' birthdays special.

Mike and Ike Parson were dressed up for Easter Sunday.

Mike and Ike Parson showed off their Easter goodies.

With Mike Parson's birthday on September 17, he often celebrated outside on the farm.

122　Growing Up: Early Years and Beyond

Lee and Kent Parson were several years older than Ike and Mike. Their parents, Victor and Hellen, loved when they could all get together.

From a young age, Mike and Ike Parson have enjoyed cars and car races. They proudly waved their Indianapolis Speedway flags.

In his younger days, Mike enjoyed fishing as a hobby. Mike posed with his catch of the day.

At a young age, Mike and Ike Parson worked on the farm with their dad, Victor. Victor taught the boys what hard work was and how to farm. It was very common for the boys to help with the pigs.

Ike Parson has harbored a passion for fishing from a very young age. To this day, he remains an avid fisherman, possessing an extensive collection of various types of lures.

Hellen Parson fixed Mike's favorite chocolate cake every year for his birthday.

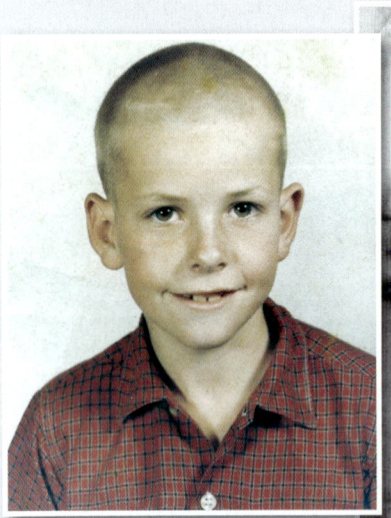

A crew haircut was the norm for Mike Parson as a young boy. His mom liked to keep it short.

The Parson family always had a dog around the farm. Hellen felt dogs were made for the outside and wouldn't let them in the house.

Mike and Ike Parson, dressed in matching attire, were prepared to participate in a school program.

Mike and Ike Parson sat mischievously on their couch, contemplating their next ornery stunt.

GROWING UP: EARLY YEARS AND BEYOND   127

Hellen Parson commonly had the boys dress alike. Often, they were hand-me-downs, but the boys didn't know any different.

Mike and Ike Parson both had a love for vehicles. The cool teenagers posed in front of the vehicle Mike planned to drive when he got his driver's license.

LEFT: Michael Lynn Parson graduated from Wheatland High School in 1973.

BELOW: Mike Parson's dad, Victor, taught his boys much about farming, emphasizing hard work. They focused on raising pigs and tending to a garden that boasted the tallest tomato plants and the largest variety of fresh fruits and vegetables in the area.

Mike Parson grew up in this farmhouse on the "Old Home Place." The floors were uneven and insulation was needed, but it was home to the Parson family.

Victor and Hellen Parson were good, faithful people and parents. They provided for the boys but, most importantly, loved them with all their hearts.

Hellen Parson loved to cook. She could always be found in the kitchen preparing home-cooked meals for the family and any guests at the house.

Victor and Hellen Parson enjoyed relaxing after a hard day's work. It was very common for them to sit outside after putting in the hours.

GROWING UP: EARLY YEARS AND BEYOND 131

Aunt Mabel "Pete" was Hellen Parson's sister. Aunt "Pete" was the second oldest of four girls with a spitfire personality.

A favorite pastime for the Parson family was a good game of cards. A lot of laughing and heckling happened around the table.

The Parson boys helped their mom (Hellen) and dad (Victor) celebrate their fiftieth wedding anniversary.

Mike and Teresa Parson helped celebrate Mike's dad, Victor, on being ordained as a Baptist deacon.

Growing Up: Early Years and Beyond   133

Victor and Hellen Parson were both active church members. Victor was ordained as a Baptist deacon, and the whole family was present for support.

Brothers Kent, Ike, Mike, and Lee Parson posed together after celebrating their dad's ordination as a Baptist deacon.

Victor and Hellen Parson and their boys proudly served their Lord while members of the First Baptist Church in Wheatland.

Victor and Hellen Parson posed with sons Ike, Kent, and Mike.

GROWING UP: EARLY YEARS AND BEYOND 135

Mike Parson spent his early years growing up in this old house on a farm known as the "Carpenter Place."

Current photograph of the "Carpenter Place" where Mike Parson spent most of his childhood. Only a few outbuildings that surrounded the location of the house remain where Mike and his brother Ike spent countless hours.

The old water tower still stands high over Wheatland. This same tower got Mike Parson in a little trouble during his teenage years.

ABOVE: The current Wheatland R-II School District "Home of the Mules" marquee sits out front of the school where Mike Parson graduated from high school.

LEFT: A sign displayed above the current entrance of Wheatland High School identifies a man forever proud to be an alum.

GROWING UP: EARLY YEARS AND BEYOND

Sheriff

Mike Parson served as a deputy sheriff first in Hickory County and later in Polk County.

Being elected sheriff of Polk County was one of the most important elections in Mike Parson's career. The people that put their trust in him as sheriff were the people he would see at church, the store, and around town. He wanted to ensure their safety while making them proud.

Sheriff Parson's investigative skills were perfected while on the job. Investigations were the most challenging yet intriguing part of the position. The experience he obtained investigating crimes paid dividends for the rest of his career.

Elected Official

Governor Parson's brother Kent stood by Mike and gave him big brother advice when needed.

Representative Mike Parson spoke on a proposed bill on the House floor in 2006. (Photo credit: Tim Bommel.)

Representative Kenny Jones, Representative Steve Tilley, NASCAR great and Missouri native Carl Edwards, and Representative Mike Parson enjoyed a moment on the House floor in 2008. (Photo credit: Tim Bommel.)

Elected Official   139

Senator Mike Parson and wife Teresa posed for a photograph on the opening day of session when he assumed the role as a Missouri senator.

Senator Mike Parson took the floor to introduce a bill to his Senate colleagues during the 2015 legislative session. (Photo credit: Harrison Sweazea.)

Kent, Mike, and Ike Parson posed in Senator Parson's office after Mike assumed the role of senator of Missouri District 28.

Lieutenant Governor Parson presented a declaration to his brother Kent.

ELECTED OFFICIAL 141

Marriage, Family, and Fatherhood

ABOVE: Mike and Teresa Parson took every opportunity to teach their children. They taught them how to work, farm, cook, and even play the piano.

RIGHT: Mike Parson has had a front seat watching his and Teresa's children, Kelly and Stephanie, grow up into amazing adults.

Jonathan and Stephanie House celebrated their wedding on May 24, 1997.

Kelly and Tara Parson celebrated their wedding on July 5, 2003.

Marriage, Family, and Fatherhood 143

Governor and First Lady Parson displayed the "57" ties symbolizing Mike Parson being the fifty-seventh governor of Missouri. Kent and Ike Parson proudly wore theirs.

Mike and Teresa Parson love being grandparents. They have enjoyed their grandchildren at every stage of their lives.

ABOVE: David House, Governor and First Lady Parson's oldest grandson, graduated from Drury University in law enforcement. Public service runs in the family.

LEFT: David House, Governor and First Lady Parson's oldest grandson, read scripture during their family Christmas.

MARRIAGE, FAMILY, AND FATHERHOOD 145

RIGHT: Governor and First Lady Parson taught their grandchildren hard work on the farm. Their granddaughters Alicia and Isabella helped with cows any chance they got.

BELOW: Granddaughter Michaela was a cheerleader for the Sparta Trojans. She was proud to have Gramps at her games.

146   Marriage, Family, and Fatherhood

First Lady Parson enjoyed watching her grandchildren in extra-curricular activities. Her granddaughter Michaela competed in cross country for Sparta High School.

Governor Parson gave his granddaughter Michaela a good luck hug before she competed in her cross country meet.

Governor and First Lady Parson's grandson Benjamin posed on one of the big hay bales.

MARRIAGE, FAMILY, AND FATHERHOOD 147

Governor and First Lady Parson's grandson Benjamin played with the Sparta band and choir during the Christmas candlelight tours.

Granddaughter Isabella wore Gramps' hat as she cheered on her older siblings.

Granddaughter Isabella and Governor Parson enjoyed lunch together. Governor Parson looks forward to spending more time with his grandchildren.

148   MARRIAGE, FAMILY, AND FATHERHOOD

Governor and First Lady Parson love all their grandchildren. Pictured are the House grandchildren from youngest to oldest: Isabella, Benjamin, Michaela, Alicia, and David.

After the Joint Session Address in June 2018, the first photograph of the First Family was taken.

MARRIAGE, FAMILY, AND FATHERHOOD 149

Of all the roles Governor and First Lady Parson have endured, being grandparents is a favorite. Pictured with Governor and First Lady Parson are their five House grandchildren, Stephanie (their daughter) and Jonathan's children.

Faith and family are the driving force for Governor and First Lady Parson. They are joined by Kelly and Tara Parson as well as Stephanie and Jonathan House and their five children.

150   MARRIAGE, FAMILY, AND FATHERHOOD

Running a campaign was a whole family endeavor. The House grandchildren were prepared to do what was needed to get their gramps elected.

Jonathan and Stephanie House; Governor and First Lady Parson; and Kelly, Tara, and Sophie Parson enjoyed seeing the Christmas lights at Silver Dollar City in Branson.

MARRIAGE, FAMILY, AND FATHERHOOD 151

ABOVE: Governor Parson, also known as "Gramps," has always known Sophie to be a special little girl.

RIGHT: Granddaughter Sophie used Governor Parson's desk as a tunnel after the 2021 Missouri Bicentennial Inauguration.

152   Marriage, Family, and Fatherhood

Governor Parson showed granddaughter Sophie how to write his signature.

Granddaughter Sophie, the chef, pretended she was baking Gramps some cupcakes.

Governor Parson loves to treat his grandchildren. Granddaughter Sophie received a special cupcake from Gramps.

MARRIAGE, FAMILY, AND FATHERHOOD   153

Granddaughter Sophie checked on the cows with Gramps.

Kelly, Tara, and Sophie Parson took a photo in the governor's office before being introduced at the 2021 Missouri Bicentennial Inaugural Ball.

154   Marriage, Family, and Fatherhood

Granddaughter Sophie enjoyed when Governor and First Lady Parson watched her at gymnastics. She loved to show off her tricks.

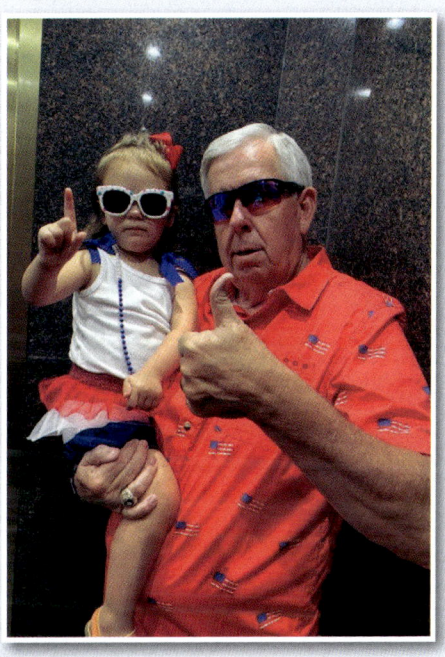

Granddaughter Sophie got to attend the Independence Day celebration at the capitol with Gramps.

Governor and First Lady Parson bought granddaughter Sophie a John Deere. She enjoyed riding it on the farm.

MARRIAGE, FAMILY, AND FATHERHOOD   155

Governor and First Lady Parson welcomed their first great grandson Urijah to the family. Posed is Tyler, Alicia, and Urijah Mendoza.

Photographed are Governor and First Lady Parson's granddaughter Michaela and her husband Gabriel Foskett.

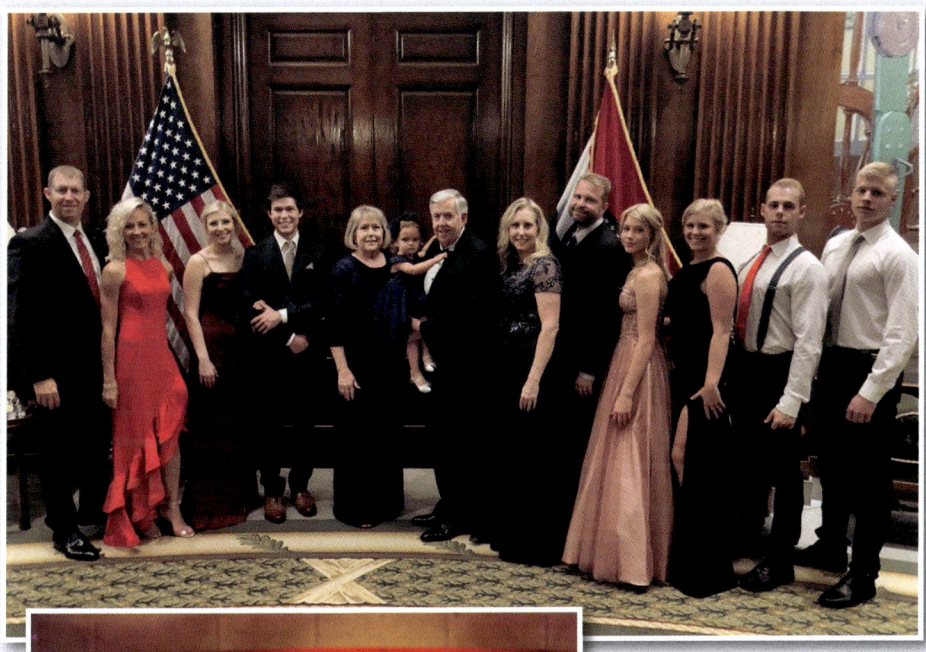

ABOVE: At the 2021 Missouri Inaugural Ball, the entire family was present to support Governor and First Lady Parson: Kelly Parson, Tara Parson, Alicia Mendoza, Tyler Mendoza, First Lady Parson, Sophie Parson, Governor Parson, Stephanie House, Jonathan House, Isabella House, Michaela House, David House, and Benjamin House.

LEFT: Jonathan and Stephanie House, Governor and First Lady Parson's daughter and son-in-law, enjoyed the 2021 Missouri Inaugural Ball

MARRIAGE, FAMILY, AND FATHERHOOD   157

RIGHT: Five generations are in this photo: Bob Seiner (Teresa's dad), First Lady Teresa Parson, Stephanie House (daughter), Alicia Mendoza (granddaughter), and Urijah Mendoza (great grandson).

BELOW: First Lady Parson's parents, Bob and Darlene Seiner, celebrated their seventy-third wedding anniversary in December 2023.

First Lady Parson's parents, Bob and Darlene Seiner, enjoyed visiting the Missouri Governor's Mansion during Christmas.

RIGHT: Governor Parson's nephew Jeff Parson (son of Lee Parson) used his artistic talent to create a portrait of his Uncle Mike.

BELOW: Governor Parson's nephew Jeff Parson used his artistic talent to create this portrait of Parson brothers Lee (his father), Ike, Mike, and Kent.

Marriage, Family, and Fatherhood 159

Governor

In Bolivar, Mike Parson announced his first bid for the Republican nomination for governor. He later would change course and run for lieutenant governor.

Governor Parson's oldest brother Kent brought some advice from the Holy Bible during a prayer service just hours before Governor Parson was to take the oath as the fifty-seventh governor of Missouri on June 1, 2018. Reverend Parson reminded everyone in attendance that this was indeed a huge moment in the life of his brother and soon-to-be governor, but it paled in comparison to the moment he accepted Christ Jesus as his Lord and Savior.

Kent Parson gave his little brother Mike a meaningful hug minutes before he was sworn in as governor on June 1, 2018.

First Lady Teresa Parson beamed with pride as her husband Governor Mike Parson addressed the general assembly for the first time as governor on June 11, 2018.

Governor and First Lady Parson posed for a photograph in the governor's office with Governor Parson's brothers Kent and Ike after his first address to the general assembly on June 11, 2018.

GOVERNOR 161

Governor Parson and newly assembled Team 57 gathered for a photograph in the governor's office shortly after he addressed the general assembly for the first time as governor on June 11, 2018.

The grandfather in Governor Parson can never be denied. It was never more evident than his first bill signings as governor in 2018. A young Missourian took the pen to write her name on a bill in the governor's office on June 22, 2018.

A young Missourian took the pen to write his name on a bill in the governor's office on June 29, 2018.

Governor Parson entered the House of Representatives chamber to give his first State of the State Address as governor to the members of the general assembly and special guests on January 16, 2019.

Governor Mike Parson acknowledged the general assembly after being introduced by Lieutenant Governor Mike Kehoe for his first State of the State Address on January 16, 2019.

Former secretary Ben Carson of the U.S. Department of Housing and Urban Development joined Governor Parson in St. Louis to focus on new opportunity zones in Missouri, created in 2017 under President Trump's Tax Cut and Jobs Act. They ensured the zones were working to bring economic growth and job creation to communities that needed it the most.

Governor Parson got a firsthand look at some of the challenges and opportunities that existed across Missouri as part of his Focus on Bridges program on February 2, 2019.

Governor Parson took an aerial tour of the 2019 northwest Missouri flooding. He was able to see firsthand the severity of the floods.

Governor and First Lady Parson attended a Christmas event with United States President and First Lady Trump.

GOVERNOR 165

U.S. Marines and the Clauses posed for a photograph during the Candlelight Tours and annual tree lighting ceremony at the Missouri Governor's Mansion.

Governor and First Lady Parson hosted an annual Mansion Candlelight Tour during the Christmas season.

Communications team members Kelli Jones and Johnathan Shiflett helped prepare Governor Parson for his State of the State Address.

Governor Parson gave the 2020 State of the State Address to the Missouri General Assembly, highlighting the state's successes and setting the agenda for the upcoming legislative session. Seated behind Governor Parson are Speaker of the House Elijah Haahr and Lieutenant Governor Mike Kehoe.

Governor Parson and his brothers Ike and Kent enjoyed lunch before the 2020 State of the State Address.

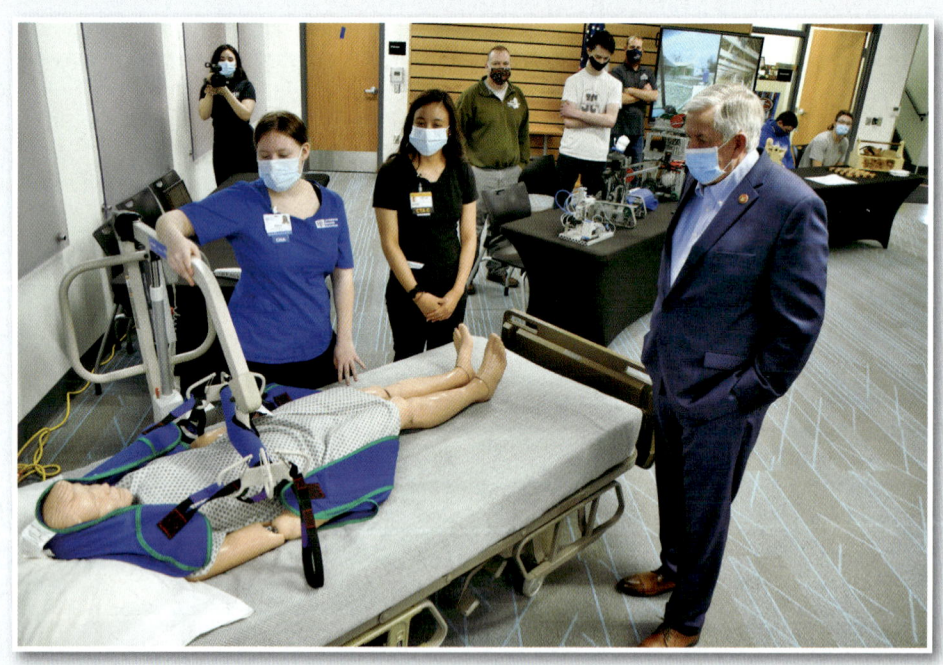

Nichols Career Center students showed Governor Parson around the facility in Jefferson City. Governor Parson enjoyed seeing good-quality career readiness programs, like this one, around the state.

The State of the State went on as planned! Governor Parson and Team 57 pulled off what some wanted to be impossible when at the eleventh hour House leadership denied the governor access to the House chamber for the address. Adversity may build character, but it definitely reveals it! The State of State Address was given in the Senate chamber for the first and only time in Missouri history on January 27, 2021.

Governor and First Lady Parson hosted the Missouri Bicentennial Inaugural Parade on September 18, 2021. The nearly one-hundred-piece parade was emceed by Ned Reynolds of southwest Missouri and Kermit Miller of central Missouri. Edith Harrington, a World War II United States Cadet Nurse Corps member, was the grand marshal.

GOVERNOR   169

Governor Parson was joined by fellow state elected officials as the U.S. Postal Service unveiled the official Missouri Statehood Day stamp commemorating Missouri's bicentennial.

Governor and First Lady Parson posed for a picture with members of the governor's Security Division at the 2021 Missouri Bicentennial Inaugural Ball.

Governor Parson participated in a ceremony signifying the start of construction of a new I-70 bridge (Rocheport Bridge) over the Missouri River near Rocheport on October 12, 2021.

Governor Parson toured the construction of the new terminal at the Kansas City International Airport on April 26, 2022.

GOVERNOR 171

Governor Parson spoke at the National Sheriffs' Association Annual Conference held in Kansas City, Missouri. Governor Parson was Polk County sheriff from 1993 to 2004.

On August 8, 2022, Governor and First Lady Parson unveiled the first lady's official portrait that will join twenty-eight other portraits of Missouri First Ladies displayed on the first floor of the Missouri Governor's Mansion.

Governor Parson met with FIFA representatives to confirm Kansas City, Missouri, as a host city for the FIFA World Cup 2026.

Governor Parson took part in the groundbreaking of the Kansas City Current Stadium, the first stadium built for a professional women's sports team in the world.

Governor Parson participated in a ceremony to signify the start of improvements to the I-270 corridor in St. Louis on September 12, 2022.

Governor Parson joined a construction crew in southeast Missouri to celebrate the completion of the double bridge project near Portageville. The bridges helped to showcase the administration's focus on Missouri infrastructure.

Members of local St. Louis communities welcomed Governor Parson to their Grill to Glory events. These local churches have become beacons of hope in their communities.

Many pieces of legislation and historical documents were signed at the governor's desk in his office.

Governor Parson enjoyed having the Freedom of Road Riders at the capitol.

Governor Parson welcomed World War II Veteran Woodrow Boulware to his office for a visit.

Following Attorney General Eric Schmitt's election to the United States Senate, Governor Parson appointed Andrew Bailey, his trusted general counsel, as the forty-fourth attorney general of the State of Missouri. Andrew was sworn into office on January 3, 2023, swearing to defend the Missouri Constitution and protect the rights of Missourians.

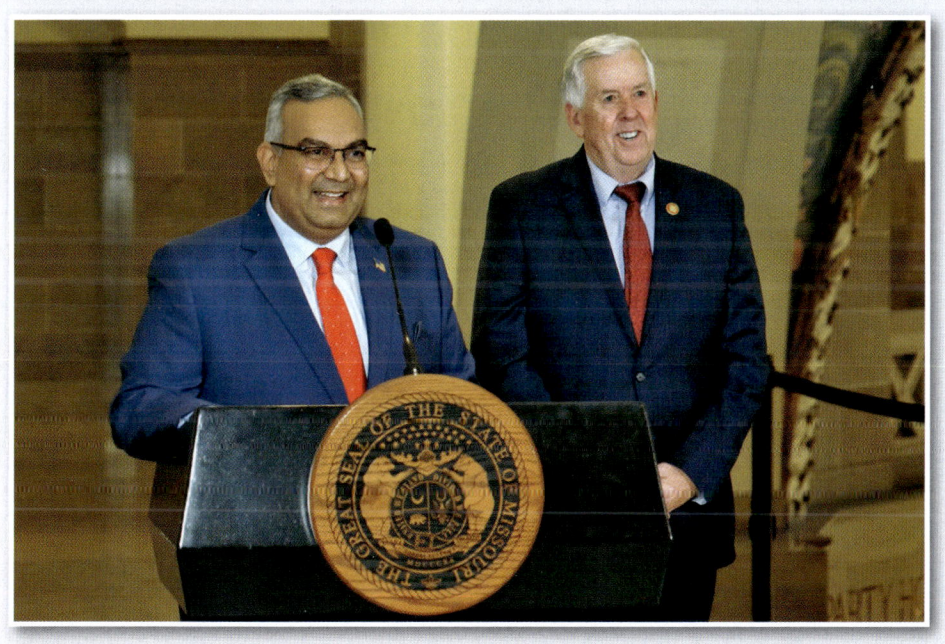

Governor Parson appointed Vivek Malek as Missouri's state treasurer to succeed Scott Fitzpatrick, who was elected state auditor. Vivek's inspiring American story and strong conservative values made him a great candidate. He was sworn in on January 28, 2023, to become the forty-eighth treasurer of the State of Missouri.

On February 27, 2023, Governor Parson signed HB 14 into law at the Harry S. Truman State Office Building, securing a historic 8.7 percent cost-of-living pay increase for all state workers. Since the start of his administration, Governor Parson improved state team member pay by more than 21 percent through targeted and across the board pay plans.

Governor and First Lady Parson hosted a reception for students in the Jobs for America's Graduates program (JAG-Missouri) at the Missouri Governor's Mansion on April 3, 2023.

LEFT: Governor Parson toured the cattle barn at the Missouri State Fair in Sedalia on August 17, 2023, to visit with some proud young Missouri farmers.

RIGHT: Governor Parson went to the state fair as a child and continues to go. Governor Parson was joined by Missouri Department of Agriculture Director Chris Chinn while visiting with a young farmer.

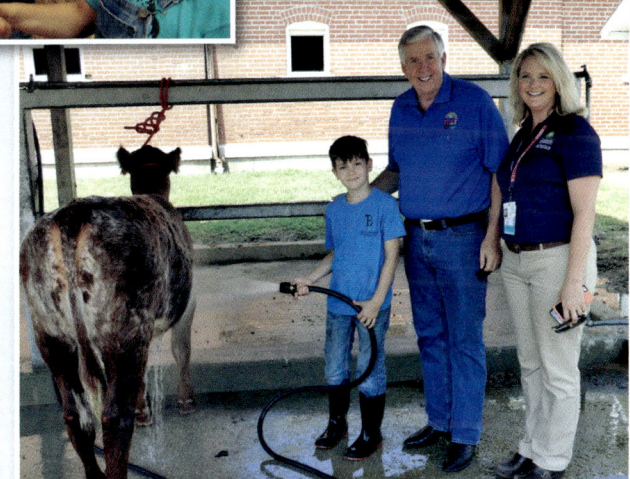

Governor Parson was joined by U.S. Army soldiers at the Missouri State Fair.

Stephanie Whitaker, Governor Parson's communications team member, brought her daughter Ella to help Governor Parson practice for his State of the State Address.

Team 57 posed in front of the Missouri Governor's Mansion after the competition between the East and the West wings.

Governor and First Lady Parson hosted the Wheatland High School Class of 1973 on August 27, 2023, celebrating their fiftieth reunion.

Governor Parson attended a ceremony to name the Kansas City River Port Terminal in his honor on November 14, 2023.

Governor Parson joined the leadership of the Missouri National Guard for a tour of the historic Jefferson Barracks on December 12, 2023.

Governor Parson enjoyed spending time with young Missourians across the state. The governor does his best to find a few minutes for children visiting the Missouri capitol.

Governor Parson was welcomed by members of Meadville R-IV FFA as he traveled to the school to talk about Missouri's new baseline salary grant, which increased the baseline pay of Missouri's teachers.

Governor Parson posed with Truman the Tiger as he and First Lady Parson attended Mizzou Football's Military Appreciation Day.

Governor Parson is proud of Missouri's flagship university—University of Missouri. He has participated in bill signings, half-time recognitions, and ceremonies for various occasions. One of his favorites was when he was able to hit "Big MO" before a game.

Governor Parson was joined by state legislators and members of Mizzou Athletics at Mizzou's Faurot Field for a ceremonial signing of HB 417, Missouri's Name, Image, and Likeness Rights for College Athletes.

Governor Parson attended "It's On!," an event hosted by Missouri State University, Missouri's second largest public university.

Governor Parson exited his favorite kind of tractor—John Deere—in front of the Missouri capitol. Every year as governor, he drove his tractor to work to kickoff FFA week.

Governor Parson participated in the Chiefs Super Bowl Parades. He will never forget the multitudes of people lining the streets of downtown Kansas City to see the parades. The sea of red was definitely a sight to see.

Governor Parson's senior staff gifted him a tailor-made Chiefs jacket for Christmas.

Governor Parson made a wager with Pennsylvania Governor Josh Shapiro for Super Bowl LVII. Needless to say, Governor Shapiro hung a Chiefs flag with Governor Parson's signature in his office for a day and posted on social media.

Governor Parson enjoyed every opportunity to meet Andy Reid, head coach of the Kansas City Chiefs.

Governor and First Lady Parson met with Pennsylvania Governor Josh Shapiro, his wife Lori, and their family to exchange flags as part of their friendly Super Bowl wager. After the Chiefs' victory, Governor Shapiro had to fly the Kansas City Chiefs flag in his office!

As lifelong fans, Governor and First Lady Parson were thrilled to cheer on the Chiefs at Super Bowl LVII.

Governor and First Lady Parson have been longtime Chiefs fans. They were thrilled to help celebrate at Super Bowl Parades in Kansas City, Missouri. The Kansas City Chiefs played in six AFC championship games and four Super Bowls during Governor Parson's six and a half years as Missouri governor.

Governor and First Lady Parson showcased their matching Chiefs jerseys.

Governor and First Lady Parson enjoyed their encounters with Patrick Mahomes, the Super Bowl winning quarterback for the Kansas City Chiefs.

Chiefs Training Camp was held in St. Joseph at facilities on the campus of Missouri Western State University. Governor and First Lady Parson have gone several times. One of the most memorable ones was on Veterans Appreciation Day when they got to meet Chiefs tight end Travis Kelce for the first time.

Governor Parson was granted the opportunity to speak at the Super Bowl celebrations in Kansas City in front of millions. A congratulatory speech to his favorite team was an easy task.

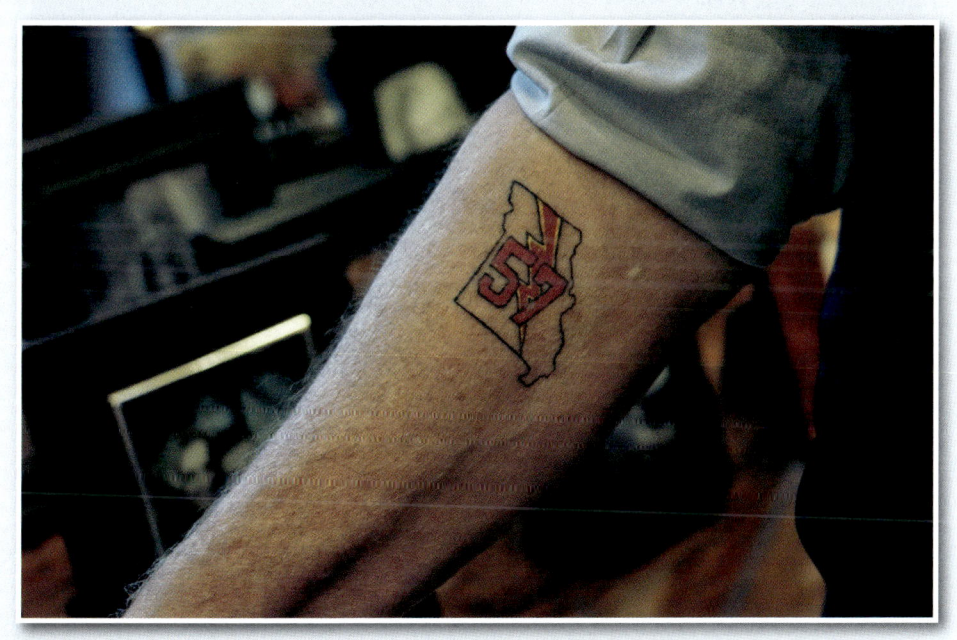

Governor Parson's tattoo, designed by his granddaughter and inked by Josh Braig, paid homage to his terms as Missouri's fifty-seventh governor and his affection for the state. Moreover, during his tenure as the fifty-seventh governor, he earned 57 percent of the vote during the 2020 election and the Kansas City Chiefs clinched the fifty-seventh Super Bowl.

Governor and First Lady Parson were fortunate enough to have had every national champion professional sports trophy in the capitol during the governor's tenure. However, being the fifty-seventh governor of Missouri and having the fifty-seventh Vince Lombardi Super Bowl Trophy was a special one.

Governor Parson grew up listening to the St. Louis Cardinals on the radio. He and his family are big Cardinal fans. He had the honor of throwing the ceremonial first pitch in a couple of games while he was governor. (Photo credit: William Greenblatt.)

Governor Parson was joined by First Lady Parson after he delivered his final State of the State Address to the general assembly and special guests on January 24, 2024, with the themes "No Turnin' Back" and "Putting People First."

Kelly Parson and Stephanie House are proud of their dad. They have been by his side through all his elections.

Chapter 9

Taking Its Toll
Life as the Forty-seventh Missouri
Lieutenant Governor (2017–2018)

"Now you said there was good and bad news, what is the bad news?"

When Senator Parson kicked off his campaign for lieutenant governor, he vowed to run a positive campaign for the position. Mike's positivity was going to have to find a way to overcome a substantial shortfall in campaign finances, as his lead competitor had a nearly two to one advantage with the backing of Rex Sinquefield, the St. Louis financier and conservative political donor. In the primary election on August 2, 2016, Mike edged Bev Randles receiving 51.5 percent to 43.9 percent of the votes. Bev, a Kansas City attorney, was slated as a new and up-and-coming force in the Republican party. After winning the primary election, there was no time to waste.

Senator Parson capped off his campaign for lieutenant governor with a historic victory on November 8, 2016. Mike had never been afraid to put in the work, and his and his team's tireless work during the race led to Mike receiving the most ever votes received by a lieutenant governor candidate in Missouri history. Mike received 1,459,392 votes in the 2016 general election to 1,168,947 votes for Democrat challenger Russ Carnahan, a member of one of Missouri's well-known political dynasties. It was another big night for Missouri Republicans. Governor Eric Greitens, like Lieutenant Governor Parson, won 111 of the 114 Missouri counties. Both candidates dominated across the state, falling short in only the historically Democratic strongholds of Boone, Jackson, and St. Louis Counties as well as St. Louis City.

Throughout his life, Mike had prided himself on always putting everything he had in whatever he was doing. His drive was less about doing what was good for Mike but rather what was good for all people he served. Serving others was his only focus, but to have the right and responsibility to serve others, one must first earn their trust and support. Regardless of the task at hand, Mike Parson has been forever committed to putting in the work. This type of commitment often comes with a cost. Farming, military service, operating service stations, law enforcement, and elected duties can take an emotional and physical toll on a person. No one is exempt!

On the campaign trail, Teresa had observed Mike physically laboring. Shortly after winning the lieutenant governor race, Teresa recommended to Mike he schedule a doctor's appointment. In December, Mike had a routine medical exam at Citizens Memorial Hospital in Bolivar. Following the exam, Dr. John Best immediately referred Mike to Cox Medical Center in Springfield for additional testing on his heart. Doctors at Cox informed Mike that multiple arteries moving blood to his heart were blocked. One of the these causes the heart attack commonly referred to as the "Widow Maker." Mike had not experienced a full-blown heart attack because smaller arteries developed to allow some blood flow to still pass through. The flow was minimal but enough to sustain life.

After a successful election for his first ever statewide elected office, this was not the news he wanted to hear. Inauguration was just over a couple of weeks away, and this direly needed procedure during the Christmas season was not in his plans. "I thought it was going to be the only chance I would ever have in my life to take the oath. I really wanted to be there," he recalled. He wanted to get in and out of the hospital and attend Eric Greitens' inauguration ceremony that would include the swearing-in of the other statewide officials. Mike was determined to do everything possible to be there with his family. He was scheduled to have his quintuple bypass open-heart surgery on Friday, December 23, but the physicians postponed the surgery by a day after similar procedures on other patients had gone longer than expected. He and the family were anxious because of the urgency the doctors expressed upon receiving the test results. Terms like "you can't go home . . . you can't get in the car . . . going to take you by ambulance" really had gotten everyone's attention. Mike recalled the doctor coming into his hospital room saying, "Hey, we have already done two surgeries today. My team is pretty worn out. I think everything is going to be okay. We would like to do your surgery in the morning." Reflecting, Mike was glad fatigued doctors didn't want to open his chest and operate on his heart. At the time, however, the urgency expressed upon arrival consumed his mind.

Mike remembered the doctor's words "I think" gaining his attention the most until early the next morning when the doctor returned to his room. The entire family was present when the doctor sat at the edge of the bed, put his hand on Mike's leg, and said to him, "There are a few things I need to go over with you." Mike remembered looking up and seeing tears in the eyes of his daughter, Stephanie, as the doctor began to discuss the odds and risks involved in the procedure. The doctor continued in a very professional manner as he stated, "But there is some good news and some bad news." This statement, especially the latter part, really got Mike's attention. The doctor began with the good news. "Normally this is very successful. I have one of the best teams for doing this type of surgery . . . the survival rate is very high," the doctor expressed to an attentive Mike. The doctor followed up the positive statements with a moment of hesitation and appeared to be preparing to exit the room. Mike anxiously asked, "Now you said there was good and bad news . . . what is the bad news?" He and the entire family took a deep breath as the doctor settled back on the bed and continued. "My whole surgical team are democrats." Mike remains convinced he had taken hook, line, and sinker as the doctor had drawn his fullest attention for the punchline. He still recalls with laughter the light moment provided by the doctor during a very serious moment in his life.

Just a few weeks before he was to be sworn in as the forty-seventh lieutenant governor of Missouri, Mike was undergoing quintuple bypass surgery. Many doctors and nurses worked relentlessly to save Mike's life. He and Teresa give so much gratitude to the entire medical team and to their Lord and Savior for Mike's successful surgery.

Mike vividly remembers two special female nurses who came to his room shortly after his surgery and told Mike he needed to get out of bed and walk. Mike initially thought these nurses were kidding, but they were not. Although tiny, they were mighty. They got on either side of Mike, hoisted him up, and made him walk. Mike thought these two nurses were trying to kill him at the time, but they were trying to get him healed and strong enough to make it to the inauguration.

Inauguration Day is a big day for all statewide elected officials, especially the governor. Governor Greitens took the Oath of Office as Missouri Governor on Monday, January 9, 2017, on the steps of the state capitol with huge signs reading "Eric Greitens – The Inaugural" framing the scene. In his inaugural remarks, the former U.S. Navy SEAL vowed radical changes were coming to Jefferson City. Governor Greitens pledged to bring an outsider's perspective to the position and end what he viewed as political corruption. Within an hour of taking the oath of office, Governor Greitens acted on his campaign promises by issuing an executive order on ethics reform. With the Republicans as the supermajority, he committed to the passage of major legislation he felt would support Missourians, including "Right-to-Work" and charter school expansion. Supporting his stance as a political outsider, Governor Greitens stated, "There are big fights ahead for big things, and our new administration won't back down because of political pressure or political correctness."

Also taking the oath of office that day were Lieutenant Governor Mike Parson, Attorney General Josh Hawley, State Treasurer Eric Schmitt, and Secretary of State Jay Ashcroft. The entire group was a product of the Republican Party. The day was significant for the party and all those sworn into their new statewide offices, but all of them were shadows to the fanfare surrounding the newly elected governor.

Sure enough, Mike's determination won, and he was sworn-in on that cold winter day. Mike was literally still on the mend from his surgery, so he told Teresa and his children to stand close just in case he collapsed.

Due to his recent surgery, Lieutenant Governor Parson was unable to participate in all the inauguration day events, but once the inauguration was complete, he was adamant on holding a reception in his office. Many friends and families from all over the state came by the office to shake the new lieutenant governor's hand. Seats were available, but Mike was strong willed and stood, determined to shake everyone's hand even though he was exhausted and still recovering. It was important to him to show appreciation to the people who supported him. It was a long day, but one Mike, Teresa, and their family will never forget.

Mike and his family were excited about this new role. This was the office Mike believed to be his final political position. He just knew once his days as lieutenant governor were over, he and Teresa would retire and head back to the farm. Mike looked forward to the days he could escape the chaos and spend more time with his family.

The first year as lieutenant governor was an honor for Mike to preside over the Senate. He was very familiar with the Senate, so this new role was easy for him to manage. Agriculture, veterans, tourism, and seniors were priorities for Lieutenant Governor Parson, and he worked hard to ensure these folks were well taken care of.

The lieutenant governor's office was very different from Mike's former positions. It was an office that didn't have much direction or a lot of power, and it was a much slower pace. It was also made clear early on that little partnership would exist between the governor's office and the lieutenant governor's office, something a future Governor Parson would change.

Lieutenant Governor Parson had created relationships with many in the capitol during his tenure in the House of Representatives, Senate, and now as lieutenant governor, but he never felt a solid relationship ever existed between the governor and lieutenant governor. When asked about the relationship, Mike answered, "It was nonexistent when I was there." He declared it had nothing to do with efforts on the part of him or his office and added, "They did not want anything to do with us. They did not want anything to do with me because I had been around." Seeking political input or advice from those within the walls of the capitol was not the way Governor Greitens operated. He was true to what he promised on the campaign trail.

Nonetheless, Mike set out to make his time in the lieutenant governor's office the best it could be. He wanted to remind Missourians this office was important and played a significant role in Missouri government. Like in everything he had done before, Lieutenant Governor Mike Parson wanted to set a high standard for himself and those to come after him.

Mike traveled throughout the state developing great relationships with everyone he came across. From South West City in McDonald County to Athens (Revere) in Clark County, Watson in Atchison County to Tyler (Cooter) in Pemiscot County, Lieutenant Governor Mike Parson traversed the state primarily by car promoting causes critical to the position. Being a veteran himself, Lieutenant Governor Parson enjoyed the relationships he developed throughout the state with fellow Missouri veterans. Also being a farmer, Lieutenant Governor Parson could easily speak the language of the challenges and successes of farmers across Missouri. As a former sheriff, Lieutenant Governor Parson was quick to partake in conversations with law enforcement personnel about their vital role and encouraged them to stay the course in serving Missourians.

During Lieutenant Governor Parson's tenure, he created the "Buy Missouri" economic initiative to actively promote the products grown, manufactured, processed, and/or made in Missouri. The program is intended to promote tourism, business, and economic development by showcasing and promoting Missouri-made products and businesses. "Buy Missouri" also took Lieutenant Governor Parson across the state where great relationships were formed.

Mike's love for his country is no secret. No matter what position he has held, veterans are dear to his heart. In 2017, Lieutenant Governor Mike Parson held a press conference in Jefferson City to discuss allegations of mistreatment at the St. Louis Veterans Home. He called for the removal of the leadership at that home due to a number of concerning issues. Several months later, the investigation revealed Missouri's heroes were not receiving the attention and care they deserved at the St. Louis facility.

While lieutenant governor, Mike and Teresa immersed themselves in several initiatives they felt were important to the future of Missouri. One such initiative was the Jobs for America's Graduates (JAG) program. He and Teresa have always believed in the young people of Missouri. JAG positively affects Missouri students, both rural and urban, and they wanted more students to have this opportunity. They both worked aggressively to make JAG-Missouri known and respected across the state.

JAG is a nationally based program which initially came to Missouri during Governor Kit Bond's administration. In a nutshell, JAG is both a school-dropout prevention program and a school-to-work program. JAG-Missouri is dedicated to helping students who face significant barriers during life overcome these barriers and place them on a trajectory for lifelong success. Intermediate goals include graduation from high school and entry into the workforce. At first glance, the program is one Mike Parson himself may have benefitted from as a student. The ability to change the trajectory of people's lives in a positive direction has always been a passion of Mike and Teresa. This program may not have existed during Mike's youth, but it would give he and Teresa the opportunity to give back the support and encouragement Mike once received.

JAG-Missouri has made a significant difference in the lives of students in many schools across the state. When Mike transitioned from lieutenant governor to governor, the JAG program made the transition as well. As governor, Mike would not have the same amount of time to dedicate to the program, but since he and Teresa valued the program at such a high level, Teresa assumed the lead. Thanks to their combined efforts, the program has drastically grown over the years from six programs in 2017 to 112 and counting in 2023.

Meeting Missourians where they were, promoting Missouri businesses and Missouri-made products, seeking economic opportunity and prosperity for all Missourians, and always supporting the American Dream for the next generations was who Lieutenant Governor Mike Parson was, and it's who a Governor Mike Parson would continue to be when, like he had always done before, he answered a higher calling to serve.

The Parson family posed for a photo used for Mike Parson's run for lieutenant governor.

The staff of Lieutenant Governor Parson assembled for one last picture together outside the door of the lieutenant governor's office shortly after Governor Parson took the oath on Friday, June 1, 2018, as Missouri's fifty-seventh governor.

CHAPTER 9   201

Jonathan, Stephanie, Michaela, Benjamin, Alicia, and Isabella House didn't get to the capitol too often, but when they did, they stopped by to see Mike and Teresa. This particular visit was at the lieutenant governor's office.

Many people wondered what Mike Parson was doing when he learned he would be the fifty-seventh governor of Missouri. Lieutenant Governor Parson was in the process of sorting cattle the moment he received the call. This photograph shows Governor Parson close to that very spot just a few days prior.

CHAPTER 10

He Answers the Call
Whirlwind Transition from Lieutenant Governor to Governor (2018)

"All of the sudden you realize that this is one of those moments in history that you are a part of."

On Wednesday, January 10, 2018, Governor Eric Greitens delivered his second State of the State Address in front of a full House of Representative chamber. Shortly after the address, stories aired about an affair the governor allegedly had with his former hairdresser. The stories also spoke of potential blackmail relating to photographs that were reportedly taken. Over the ensuing months, Governor Greitens continued to push forward with his political agenda while addressing the allegations that began to include campaign finance concerns. On March 1, the Missouri House of Representatives unanimously voted to create a special committee to investigate. On April 11, the special committee released its report that Governor Greitens stated was "a political witch hunt." Within a week, Attorney General Josh Hawley released the findings of his investigation into potential campaign finance violations. Attorney General Hawley's report concluded there was evidence of wrongdoing and potential criminal acts related to his investigation of the nonprofit the Mission Continues. Throughout February, March, and April, Governor Greitens continually vowed he would not resign in the face of multiple calls for him to do so from both elected officials and citizens across the state.

With limited communication between the governor's office and lieutenant governor's office throughout his tenure, Mike was receiving information about Governor Greitens' increasingly troubling scandals through the media just like most other Missourians. The only direct contact Mike recalls with Governor Greitens was a brief conversation the evening following the State of the State Address. In the days and weeks that followed, the rumors escalated. Through the tumultuous spring, Mike stayed focused on the work of the lieutenant governor, but as the days continued, it was natural for everyone to begin questioning the accuracy of the claims. Is this true? Is this not true? Are some of the ethics violations real? The House Committee began having their hearings, and as the investigation began to heat up so did the Jefferson City rumor mill. Mentions of Lieutenant Governor Parson someday becoming governor began to emerge. At first, it was almost jokingly. Many others began telling him, "You may become Governor." Few were taking it seriously at that point, including Mike himself, but at some point, in the back of his mind, he honestly thought, "What would happen if that did happen?"

As conversations surrounding Governor Greitens' situation continued, Mike began to discuss it with Teresa. "I honestly felt very comfortable. I had been around . . . I had experience . . . I knew how the building worked, so it wasn't like I was a rookie trying to make the team. It is like, you put me in, (and) I will just have to figure out how well I play. That is just how I looked at it," Mike summarized. As time passed, it was a roller coaster of emotions for him and Teresa. Things heated up even more, and many were saying Governor Greitens was in trouble as the House hearings revealed things may be looking worse. Governor Greitens, however, continued to declare he would not resign.

"I am Lieutenant Governor. That is what I need to focus on," Mike reminded himself. As time passed, people called him with several opinions of what might happen. "It never got to the point that you really thought Greitens would resign until about May," Mike admitted. He heard the rumors like all other Missourians that Governor Greitens was going to resign, but Governor Greitens adamantly declared he was not about to resign. Mike remembers living in that world for about sixty days. Mike knew it was not a good look for Missouri, but he focused only on controlling the controllables. Governor Greitens' situation was not one of those. Mike accepted the fact, "I honestly didn't think it was going to happen."

Although he kept his distance from the controversy surrounding Governor Greitens, Mike again reached out to Aaron Willard who had provided a valuable strategy in winning the lieutenant governor's race. Both Mike and Aaron thought it was unlikely it would happen, but it could. Neither presumed it would happen, but Mike wanted to get Aaron's thoughts on what would need to happen if it did. He expressed to Aaron that he needed to be prepared. He then asked Aaron if he would have any desire to help him prepare in the event Governor Greitens resigned. Aaron initially thought this had never happened in the state's history. This was an anomaly. It may or may not happen, but it is better to be prepared for a situation that does not come than to not be prepared if it does. Aaron knew this would be a monumental task, but he had a wide range of political experience and connections to call upon.

Aaron Willard wasn't looking for a job when Mike asked for his thoughts, but it was an honor to be respected enough to be asked. He subsequently took him up on the voluntary offer and went to work. He immediately identified that this would be a tall task. No one knew if and when anything might happen. Aaron put his political mind in governor mode. Data and direction are critical to Aaron. If there were to be a resignation, what would need to be the plan of Governor-to-be Parson? He set his sights on developing a comprehensive plan. What needs to happen the first day? What needs to happen the first week? What needs to happen the first month? What needs to happen in the first year? Each of these components required flexibility because there was no first day, week, month, or year defined at that point in time. Aaron created a plan and put it into a three-ring binder. This playbook would guide the entire state of Missouri if called upon.

Aaron Willard emphasized that if Governor Greitens resigned, a command and control approach would be critical early on. Missouri employs over forty-eight thousand people in the state workforce. It would be important to bring stability to the state workers providing crucial services to Missourians. The state was heading down a path it had never been before. The unknown is never a comfortable feeling. Aaron went to work to develop a framework to provide Missourians with the reassurance that all would be well. Lieutenant Governor Parson was no outsider to the political process. If a resignation occurred, it would be important that Missourians immediately learn the new governor's experience would help Missouri land on solid ground.

The playbook included a system to triage critical functions of the state. The transition needed to be as seamless as possible. The plan identified critical tasks that would need to be completed at various stages. Not knowing if and when a resignation might occur, the playbook included bill review of legislation they did not propose, budget review of a budget they did not write, and staff review of an administration that could potentially be in disarray.

When May came around, the thought that "something was going to happen" was a continued and repeated torment in the capitol. Lieutenant Governor Parson never believed Eric Greitens would resign. The last Missouri governor to resign the office was in September 1836 when

Governor Daniel Dunklin had resigned, and Lieutenant Governor Lilburn Boggs assumed office.

Tuesday, May 29, 2018, started much like any other day for the lieutenant governor. Little did he know when he awoke that morning, this would be a historic day for Missouri, himself, and the Parson family. On this morning, Mike needed to attend to some tasks on the farm and then planned to visit with some political colleagues about ways he could support them in the next election. Mike always found time to help others. Teresa decided to head to Battlefield Mall in Springfield to shop for a new pair of shoes for an upcoming event. On that day, Teresa was laser focused on getting some new shoes. She had become nearly immune to the daily conversations about Governor Greitens in the media and had resolved herself to the fact Mike would be the lieutenant governor, nothing more.

For several months, Governor Greitens consumed the time and thoughts of many people. Anticipation over what was going to happen kept everyone in limbo, and just about the time everyone was finally able to shrug off the rumors, they soon became the truth. On May 29, Eric Greitens announced he would quit his post effective at 5:00 PM on June 1, 2018; he was to be the second governor to resign in Missouri history.

Many people were curious about where Mike was and what he was doing on Tuesday, May 29, when he learned he was going to be the governor of Missouri. Mike had just pulled up to the gate after driving his son's truck with the stock trailer on it. "I was actually out in the pen sorting cattle," Governor Parson shared about the exact moment he heard Governor Greitens was resigning. "I remember receiving a call. The person on the other end said, 'You are going to be receiving a call . . . get ready' . . . that is all they said," Mike recalled. It was at this instant Mike came to the realization this may be the real deal. He thought the person on the other end may know, but it wasn't real until it happened, so Mike continued about his business in the pen. The cows in the lot did not care if he was governor or not, but Mike continued to process what he had heard. Hearing he would be governor at this moment and in this location is not a typical political "Watch Party" but rather a "Watch Where You are Stepping Party."

Mike verbalized the happenings saying, "I am out there trying to sort cattle and trying to process what I just heard . . . is this really happening? 15–20 minutes later, my phone rings again. It is Colonel Sandra Karsten. She says, 'Well . . . it looks like you are going to be the next Governor.

Congratulations! I assume you are going to be coming back to Jefferson City fairly quickly.'" It was the real deal. Things proceeded quickly from that point on. "You will now have security. We can come get you. I can send them down for you. Moving forward you will have security 24-7," Mike recalled of the call from Colonel Karsten.

The cows were not moved by the recent happenings. It was all status quo in the Parson corral. Mike maintains there was no fanfare or celebration at that moment, and to this day doesn't remember if he closed the gate. Mike's first phone call was to Teresa. His first words when she answered were, "You need to come home." Teresa's immediate thought was something may have happened to one of her parents. Mike went on to provide additional clarification. Like Mike couldn't remember if he closed the gate, Teresa couldn't remember if she bought any shoes.

Immediately after ending the call with Teresa, Mike went down to a corner post nearest the gate and made the most important communication he needed to make. When he got settled against the post, Mike prayed. With this being the will of God, Mike asked Jesus Christ to walk along with him, his wife, his family, and his state during this time. The power of Jesus is a mystery, but it is miraculous. God had put Mike Parson in this place at this time. God had called on him to serve as the fifty-seventh governor of Missouri. His Lord had called his name. There was no turning back. Someday when Mike meets Jesus face to face, he may have all the answers, but at this moment, all he knew was he was called to serve the people of Missouri. Amen!

Back to the phone Mike went. He called into his lieutenant governor's office to touch base with Marylyn Luetkemeyer, his executive assistant, and Kelli Jones, his communications director. Kelli remembers Mike asking, "Do you got your pretty dress on? Well, you better cause you're going to need it. It's about to get crazy." He knew they needed to be ready. Media had already flooded the lieutenant governor's office. They wanted to speak to anyone willing to talk. This story was the headline for every media outlet across the state and country.

Governor Parson had spent a few minutes in prayer speaking with the One who had inspired the words of the Holy Bible, but soon after he wanted to talk to the person who had drafted the guide to making a governor transition if and when needed. The author of that guide, Aaron Willard, remembers getting that call. Mike started by asking what he had going on the next few days. He initially perceived this as a request to meet about his draft plan. Aaron opened his calendar and asked, "What day are you thinking?" Mike responded, "No, Aaron. I just got the call from the Highway Patrol. They are coming to pick me up. I am headed to Jefferson City."

Both Mike and Teresa were happy in the position of lieutenant governor and would have been content to finish their political careers that way, but it was not God's will. There was more work to be done. When God calls, there is no turning back. Colonel Karsten had indicated in their initial phone conversation that the Governor Security Detail (GSD) was prepared to come get them and bring them to Jefferson City that night, but Mike and Teresa wanted to make the trip the same way they always had. That night they drove themselves from Bolivar to Jefferson City. They remember the vehicle being half filled with conversation and half filled with silence. They had made this trip many times over the years, but this was not just another trip. "Mike, how do you think this is going to change our life?" First Lady Parson asked Mike as they entered Jefferson City. She remembers Mike answering, "I have no idea."

Since he was lieutenant governor, he had a reserved location in the capitol parking garage. When they got out of the vehicle, they made their way to the elevator as they had done hundreds of times. The ride was quiet as it had been many times before. The silence continued when the doors opened. After Mike and Teresa exited the elevator on the second floor, they proceeded to walk towards his office. When they turned the corner, the silence would be forever broken. Mike and Teresa were quickly consumed by the masses of media assembled outside his lieutenant governor's office awaiting his arrival. The lieutenant governor paused briefly near the door for a few moments with the media.

Later that day, Mike and Teresa had a meeting with the Missouri State Highway Patrol and the security detail. Teresa remembers hearing from them "the things that would be changing in our life." The meeting was not a question and answer session. The GSD did most of the talking. Mike and Teresa learned they would no longer be driving themselves. They would not be going anywhere without someone. Going to church alone was over. Going to the store alone was over. They explained the reasons and provided examples. Teresa concluded that they kindly stated that "your life is going to be changing." And it has! It was a learning experience for everyone. Even the people of Bolivar! Everyone knows when the Parsons are home. The members of the GSD are strictly business when it is business time, but when the group is spending that much time with Missouri's First Family it is hard not to become an extension of the family.

When asked where they spent the night on Tuesday, May 29, 2018, Mike had little recollection and stated it was like a blur. It was a whirlwind of activity. Teresa helped fill in the blanks. While lieutenant governor, Mike and Teresa had purchased a one-bedroom condominium on the southeast side of the city. After Teresa retired from the bank, she and Mike would stay at the condo on occasion during the week. Before taking the oath, Teresa had an event in Bolivar on Thursday night, so she went home and picked up more clothes. Mike stayed in Jefferson City and focused on making the governor transition as seamless as possible. He needed to complete in a few hours what most governors complete in three months after being elected.

Missouri Lieutenant Governor Parson officially left his old office and became Missouri's governor on Friday, June 1, 2018. The day of the swearing-in was a day that will never be forgotten by the ones who experienced it. His staff had him well prepared for the day, beginning with a prayer service at 4:00 PM at the First Baptist Church in downtown Jefferson City. This event was closed to the public but open to the media. At the prayer service, shortly before going to the capitol to take the oath, Reverend Kent Parson, the oldest brother of Governor Parson, reminded all those gathered that the most important event to ever happen in his brother's life was when he accepted Christ as his Lord and Savior. Second was when he made Teresa his wife. Reverend Parson continued that the third most important event would occur later that day when he would take the oath as Missouri's governor. He concluded by telling his brother and soon-to-be governor to "never be afraid to ask God to help you with the decisions you are going to have to make."

The Greitens team provided the Parson team with a specific time they could gain access to the governor's office complex in the late afternoon of Friday, June 1. Those Parson team members unable to attend the prayer service only had a few minutes to prepare the governor's office for the transition ceremony and press conference. The governor's office complex resembled a ghost town upon entry. Desks were emptied; people were gone. Eric Greitens and his team had abandoned Missouri. Aaron Willard remembers putting his head into the complex that afternoon and struggling to find a piece of paper to write on. The lieutenant governor had a skeleton staff in comparison to the governor, but when the Parson team members entered to prepare for the ceremony and conference, the task was completed and successful. In less than thirty minutes, the capitol staff and the Parson team had the governor's office prepared.

The swearing-in was held in the governor's office on the second floor of the state capitol. Supreme Court Judge Mary Rhodes Russell presided. This was one of the highest profile stories going on in the nation let alone the state. The governor's office was full of media from all over the state and country. Members of the media proclaimed this was the most media ever in the governor's office at once. Lights were bright; cameras were flashing. The governor's office was packed. It was quite a sight.

Governor Parson has a vivid recollection of that day. It will be etched into his memory forever. It was a moment carved in Missouri history when Governor Parson stepped through the doors of the east office complex into the governor's office and behind the podium. "The clicks of those cameras to me were just deafening . . . it was like holy crap . . . I had never seen the likes of media and cameras and clicks and flashes . . . all of the sudden you realize that this is one of those moments in history that you are a part of . . . a kid from Wheatland, Missouri, is standing in the center of this gaggle of reporters and people gathered there . . . it was just an unreal moment," Governor Parson recalled. He remembered a few moments in his life that he had stood in front of large gatherings of media, most following major cases while sheriff, but never anything quite at this level. When Mike stepped through the entrance of the office of the governor into the blinding flashes of the multitude of media, there was "no turning back."

Governor Parson owned it. He walked out to the podium and gave a very short, strong, powerful message to Missourians:

> Public service is a privilege and it is truly an honor to serve as Missouri's 57th Governor. My pledge to all Missourians: to work hard each and every day, to bring honor, integrity, and transparency to the Governor's Office. We have an opportunity again today to have a fresh start in state government. I believe now is the time for Missouri to come together. To work together and help one another. I will always be ready and willing to listen to ideas on how the state government can better position itself to serve our families and our communities. I am optimistic about the future of our great state and look forward to the work ahead.

After recalling the emotional magnitude of the initial entry, Governor Parson detailed the comfort he had in those first moments and subsequently in taking over the helm of Missouri. "I thought we had a good plan . . . I think Aaron . . . I think Kelli . . . the staff we had at that time had a very good plan . . . you had to stay on script . . . we knew what we were going to say . . . that is what we did," Governor Parson recalled of the critical nature of carrying out a smooth transition. This was indeed a big day in the life of the governorship and all Missourians. Now, years later, when asked what Governor Parson wanted all Missourians to hear, he stated, "Three things . . . first . . . stability . . . second . . . we are going to be fine . . . Missouri is a great state . . . third . . . I am not coming in here as a rookie . . . experience matters . . . we are going to right the ship . . . we are going to get back to doing the right thing."

Following the transition ceremony and press conference, the Parson family had their first opportunity to tour the place they would call home for the next six and a half years. Both Mike and Teresa had been on the first floor of the Missouri Governor's Mansion but had never been on the other floors that serve as the living quarters. The Parson family and guests, many from Bolivar, had their first meal at the mansion that night. After dinner, Mike and Teresa got a chance to go upstairs and make plans with the staff on the arrangement they desired. Having no children at home, they had some flexibility for designations and purposes of the rooms. They did not stay at the mansion that night. Just as Governor Parson had limited time to complete the transition of Missouri's highest political office, the governor's mansion staff had an equally tight timeline. What they typically complete in a month, they had to complete in a weekend. They proved there is no task or timeline too great for the mansion staff. Mike and Teresa spent their first night in the governor's mansion on Sunday, June 3, 2018, just two days after being sworn in.

Governor and First Lady Parson vividly remember meeting the staff of the mansion and learning how their life would be changing whether they liked it or not. On Monday, Shari Childs, the executive director, got the staff together to meet Mike and Teresa. It is not a true home without meals. Immediately, they learned processes were not going to be the same. Mike and Teresa identified the foods they liked and disliked as the staff collected the details. The days of going to the store to buy groceries were over. Meals would be prepared for them on the first floor in the commercial kitchen and delivered to them on the second floor. When they were traveling, meals would be boxed up to accompany them on trips. The staff made the commercial kitchen available to Mike and Teresa. Mike could not identify a good reason to decline any of the options offered. Teresa remembers the commercial kitchen having little resemblance to her kitchen at home in Bolivar.

There was a small kitchen on the second floor that did have the resemblance of a residential kitchen with basic appliances. Teresa asked the staff what she needed to do if she wanted to cook in that kitchen. The staff informed her she would need to give them a list of the groceries she wanted. Teresa did do a little cooking, but Mike and Teresa quickly learned that life as the governor and first lady moves fast. When asked what the governor does if he wakes up in the middle of the night and needs a glass of milk, First Lady Parson said the small kitchen they use on the second floor is stocked with the basics. The governor loves to start each day with a glass of orange juice he pours in his own glass from his own refrigerator. When the governor gets a hankering at the mansion, he is quick to make his "go to" sandwich—bologna and cheese and when really feeling bold with a hint of onion.

When Mike and Teresa informed their children the next day about the new meal preparation arrangement there were mixed reviews. Stephanie, their daughter, viewed the arrangement as an opportunity to relieve her mother of a responsibility she had her entire life. Stephanie said, "Oh Mom . . . you have cooked for nearly 50 years . . . why would you want to cook . . . let them help take care of you." Kelly, their son, viewed the arrangement as a threat to the great meals he had come accustomed to growing up and now at holiday gatherings. Kelly said, "Mom . . . if you don't keep cooking . . . you won't be worth a darn when you get home."

Governor Parson also learned that lawn and grounds maintenance would not be a part of his routine at the mansion as it was at their home in Bolivar. Things were changing. Since Mike and Teresa would be spending a considerable amount of their time in Jefferson City, they had to arrange many of the routine tasks at their home in Bolivar to be addressed by others. Mike and Teresa have no shortage of family and friends in Bolivar and Polk County, so finding others to support efforts was not difficult. Kelly, who lives in rural Bolivar himself, took the lead attending to the cattle and farm. Mike's brother Ike assists with needs around the farm and home as well. Ike was called on to assist with any task when the governor was away. Ike has fixed ailing water heaters, broken vehicles, and anything that's ever needed for the kids or grandkids. Governor Parson has been so grateful for Ike's help "to hold the fort down while he's in Jefferson City."

When at home in Bolivar, Mike liked taking care of the unexpected needs of his children and grandchildren when available. Being a father and grandfather does not stop even when he is the governor of Missouri.

Governor Parson maintains that if it weren't for family and good friends, they could have never made it. Because just as they were adjusting to the dos and don'ts of their new life, state government continued, and things were moving fast. There was no time to rest once Governor Parson became governor. He had about thirty hours to make the transition where most governors get three months. At 6:00 AM Saturday morning, Governor Parson and his limited staff from the lieutenant governor's office went to work to make something out of the governor's office complex.

Thirty hours certainly isn't much, but timing is sometimes everything. Not mortal timing, but rather God's timing. In early 2018, the State of Missouri was in what might be best described as political disarray. During this period, Lieutenant Governor Parson still considered Missouri to be one of the greatest, if not the greatest, states despite the negative attention it was receiving. He continued to do what he had always done—put his head down, work hard, and make a positive difference.

God knew the critical role Mike would play in the future of Missouri. God knew the events Mike would be facing long before Mike encountered them. God knew Mike and Missouri would face floods, droughts, tragedy, civil unrest, and even an unprecedented global pandemic. A man of faith does not walk with blinders on but rather a trust that the Lord's work will be done through him. Mike was that man. In Luke 10:2–3 (King James Version), Jesus addressed some of his loyal followers who extended past his twelve disciples: "Therefore said he unto them, The harvest truly is great, but the labourers are few: pray ye therefore the Lord of the harvest, that he would send forth labourers into his harvest. Go your ways: behold, I send you forth as lambs among wolves."

Mike answered the call. He, Teresa, and the entire Parson family trusted in God's plan for Missouri. The Parsons were equipped to be who God wanted them to be for Missouri. When Kelli Jones first interviewed with the then lieutenant governor in 2017, she described him to be "a God-Fearing man who wants the best for Missouri." He understood it is always the right time to do the right thing. Where politicians sometimes misstep is narrowing the definition of right to self rather than to state and country. Although there is both agreement and disagreement on some of the decisions made by Governor Parson and his administration during his tenure, the steadfast intent to do the best for Missouri was his calling.

When it comes to making noise, Governor Parson and his administration appear to be almost boring in comparison. Maybe this is exactly what God had planned for Missouri. Being people with tremendous faith, Governor and First Lady Parson know God's hands are in control of all things. God's will is God's will! "Sometimes I think if God actually let us know what was going to happen in our lives, we might tuck tail and head in a different direction," First Lady Parson responded. When Mike took the oath to be lieutenant governor, he knew part of that oath meant stepping up as governor if ever called upon, but he and Teresa still never thought it would happen right up until the moment it did, and he got the call standing there in the barn lot. What Governor Parson wouldn't fully realize until it was much too late was working cattle on the farm wasn't the deepest shit he was stepping into that day.

Governor and First Lady Parson's son, Kelly, worked hard on the farm. Kelly currently serves as a president at a bank in Bolivar but also continues to spend many hours on the farm.

214 No Turnin' Back

Missouri Supreme Court Judge Mary Russell administers the oath of office as governor of Missouri to Michael L. Parson on June 1, 2018.

Governor Mike Parson spoke to what some reporters considered the largest gathering of media ever assembled in the governor's office immediately after he took the oath on June 1, 2018.

CHAPTER 10   215

Senator Ron Richard introduced Governor Parson before he addressed the general assembly on June 11, 2018.

Governor Parson delivered a Joint Session Address to the general assembly on June 11, 2018.

Chapter 11

Open for Business
Governor Completes His Term (2018–2020)

"If everything was a priority, nothing was a priority."

Governor Parson began putting his team together. Aaron Willard was officially named chief of staff on June 4, 2018. Just a few days later, Governor Parson's first round of senior staff was announced. Governor Parson announced Marylyn Luetkemeyer as executive assistant to the governor, Robert Knodell as deputy chief of staff, Justin Alferman as legislative director, Steele Shippy as communications director, Kelli Jones as press secretary, and Chris Limbaugh as general counsel. He then quickly met with his cabinet to reassure them he was not planning to make any abrupt changes. His goals were to stabilize the office and begin working on priorities benefitting Missourians.

The governor's office was filled with nervous anxiety the first time the cabinet convened. The environment had been filled with tension during the spring of 2018. Some of the cabinet members were concerned for their own positions with the unprecedented change in leadership. The governor's goal at the first meeting was to bring the same stability to the cabinet he wanted for the state. He started by informing the group that all their positions were secure. A sigh of relief and peace came across the room. He also notified the members there would be no pressure to stay. If a member wanted to move in a different direction, they needed to meet with him in the days ahead, but at this moment in time he requested all their help.

Governor Parson informed the cabinet members that Aaron Willard would serve as his chief of staff. He asked each of them to schedule a meeting with him soon to upload him on the past, present, and future as it related to their specific department. Aaron addressed the cabinet at this time to create credibility with the group. He had most recently served as the deputy chief of staff for the United States Director of Commerce in Washington, DC. He wasted no time in defining the processes moving forward. He told the members they would find a message in their inbox with a template defining the process for decision requests moving forward. The same process remains in place today.

The Greitens administration had the appearance of being very "closed door." The media felt they had limited access to the operations of the governor's office. Public access was even limited in comparison to past administrations. Facebook videos and other social media platforms became the primary means of public communications. When Governor Parson took the reins, he and his team immediately instituted some profound changes. One could say, "There was a new former Sheriff in town!" The first optical change was removal of the lock on the front door of the governor's office. The doors were opened for the first time in decades. Governor Parson and his communications team used this physical access point to signify a new level of accessibility now available to all. For the first few weeks of his administration, Governor Parson made himself available to the media often through these doors. When he met with a group of Missouri leaders, Governor Parson would offer a preview and a summary to the media. Missouri and Governor Parson were "open for business."

Governor Parson and his team knew "you do not get a second chance to make a first impression." A great relationship with the media would be a step in the right direction. Daily, Mike executed the steps defined in the playbook. Between tasks he would call key people and leaders across Missouri in an effort to bring stability back to Missouri and create confidence moving forward.

Governor Parson knew it was important to appoint a lieutenant governor soon after he took office. This was the first time in Missouri history that a governor would appoint a lieutenant governor. On June 18, 2018, Senate Majority Leader Mike Kehoe was appointed as the lieutenant governor by Governor Parson. There was scrutiny around the appointment because some thought Governor Parson didn't have the constitutional authority to appoint a lieutenant governor.

Looking back at his history in the Senate, the governor's appointment of Mike Kehoe to the position of lieutenant governor might have been considered a surprise selection. When Mike was in the Senate and ran for majority floor leader, there was an unexpected shift in support by several senators who had pledged their support for him. Mike Kehoe was one of those senators who shifted his support to Ron Richards who eventually won the leadership position. That moment was very painful for Senator Parson. This appointment speaks to Governor Parson the man. What is best for Missouri is what is best for Missouri. Governor Parson understood the governorship was much bigger than himself. The right thing is always the right thing.

Several hours after Governor Parson announced the appointment, the Missouri Democratic Party and lead plaintiff Darrell Cope of Hartville filed a lawsuit asking a judge in Cole County to block the appointment. The case was later dropped. It was determined Governor Parson had the authority to make the appointment. So, in just a few days, the State of Missouri had a new governor and lieutenant governor.

The transition of Lieutenant Governor Parson to Governor Parson was bringing some calmness and stability back to Missouri and the office of the governor. Due to the timing of the transition, Governor Parson had to thoroughly review the legislation that had made its way to the governor's desk from the recently completed legislative session. Former governor Greitens had advanced a few pieces of legislation he viewed as favorable with his signature, but any that were potentially controversial or needed further review remained.

As a state representative, state senator, and lieutenant governor, Governor Parson was able to observe from a close distance the responsibilities of the governor, but until one sits in the actual seat, they do not fully understand the roles and responsibilities that accompany the title. One of the first priorities the governor and his team, limited in number, had was to prepare for the unexpected. Near the top of this list was natural disasters. Governor Parson quickly met with the leadership of the Missouri State Emergency Management Agency (SEMA) to clearly understand the roles and responsibilities of all parties in the event of a natural disaster. These types of events can occur with little, or no, warning across Missouri. Weather-related emergencies and other moments of crisis often do not wait for a new leader to learn all the ends and outs of management of these situations but learn he and his team did.

There was no major frequency of crisis related to weather when Governor Parson took the reins, but when Mother Nature inflicted her wrath in July 2018, she didn't hold back. Branson and all its tourist attractions were bustling on what began as a beautiful summer day in the Missouri Ozarks on Thursday, July 19. What started as a gorgeous day would turn tragic. One of the amphibious boats of the popular "Ride the Ducks" attraction encountered large waves generated by winds from a severe thunderstorm as it approached the area while the vessel and its thirty-one passengers and crew were on Table Rock Lake. The resulting waves inundated the vessel and caused it to sink resulting in the loss of life of seventeen passengers on the boat including nine individuals in one family.

With the incident occurring late in the day, darkness set in as emergency personnel worked the scene. Being a former sheriff, Governor Parson knew of the difficulties all those at the scene must be facing. He also learned over the years that political leaders can serve as a distraction to the important work being done at a moment like this. Chief of Staff Aaron Willard remembers Governor Parson asking him for advice on many occasions over the years, but on this occasion the roles were reversed. Governor Parson informed Aaron and the team that he needed to go to Branson. Aaron remembers a composed governor telling him he needed to go not because he was the governor, but because he was a father, grandfather, and a person who loves and cares about people.

On Friday, Governor and First Lady Parson were in Branson. Governor Parson met with Stone County Sheriff Doug Rader and others leading the recovery operation. Governor and First Lady Parson then traveled to Cox Medical Center Branson to meet with survivors and some of the medical personnel who helped treat the injured. The governor met with the civilians and emergency responders who helped with rescues and with the loved ones of the victims.

During a nationally broadcasted press conference, after reviewing the facts as he knew them and thanking all those who had heroically responded in a time of need, an emotional Governor Parson emphasized "right now . . . our main focus should be . . . thoughts and prayers with the family members involved . . . those in the hospital . . . those traveling to be reunited with loved ones." Governor Parson declared he and Missouri would exercise all available resources in support of all. Numerous local, state, and national agencies facilitated in addressing the needs of all who were affected.

Over the years, Governor Parson had dealt with many tragic events, but there is no training course that could adequately prepare a person to stand before a national audience to address an event such as this, but speaking from the heart is all Mike Parson knows. His experiences in life have proven he loves God and loves people. As sheriff, he had to look many parents in the eyes, and even the wife of one of his young deputies, telling them their loved ones would not be returning home. Governor Parson has the gift. The gift to let his heart provide the words to speak. Like others, Kelli Jones, his press secretary at the time, being a former English teacher, may question the verb tense of some of the words he selects to use but claims no one can ever debate the heartfelt intention of them.

Also in the summer of 2018, Missouri was experiencing one of the worst droughts in history. On July 18, Governor Parson issued an executive order, which declared a drought alert for forty-seven Missouri counties. Governor Parson called upon the Missouri Department of Natural Resources (DNR) to activate the Drought Assessment Committee and the associated drought impact teams. By August 2018, every county in Missouri had been affected by dry to exceptionally dry conditions, and eighty-six counties were considered in drought alert. Governor Parson announced the creation of a lottery for farmers interested in haying, free of charge, on almost nine hundred acres of Missouri State Parks. The drought was one of the first natural disasters for Mike to have to face as governor. As always, Governor Parson faced the challenge and provided solutions to the problem. Eventually, Missouri found relief with some rainfall.

During his first one hundred days in office, Governor Parson met with leadership across the state. He wanted to reassure them that they needed to work together to determine the best methods to address Missouri's top concerns. He organized and led many roundtables addressing the opioid crisis and crime in Missouri. He began to stress the importance to his cabinet and to the state workforce that everyone comes together, stays focused, and works for Missouri people. This was just the beginning of how Governor Parson planned to change the negative perception around the state workforce.

Some may define Mike Parson as being a "horse trader." If defining a horse trader as someone who negotiates in a clever and skillful manner, one may be defining Mike Parson. Others may just define Mike Parson to be a "tight ass." Governor Parson grew up with little. He learned he had to make a little go a long way. If defining a "tight ass" as someone who is prudent with finances and all other assets, one may be defining Mike Parson. Sometimes it is difficult to clearly see a return on investment in state government on an initial glance, but Mike Parson is not a leader who leads on gut feeling or initial glance.

Soon after the governor took office, he and his team immediately initiated a "whole government approach." Under previous administrations, departments within state government had often operated in silos. Departments were sometimes hesitant to assist other departments and were protective of the resources they had been allocated. As a result of this approach, departments would sometimes miss opportunities to be more efficient with state resources. Governor Parson knew the state had ample resources to call upon. The walls of the silos needed to come down. All the departments needed to work together to develop effective and efficient solutions for Missourians. In the eyes of Governor Parson and his team, there was no other way to responsibly govern.

Soon after taking office, Governor Parson and his team began charting a path to go big for Missouri. The governor and his administration started to develop the priorities they would have for moving Missouri forward. The list of priorities in and of itself became extensive in initial discussions. The governor and his team concluded that where many administrations had made mistakes in the past were "if everything was a priority, nothing was a priority." Priorities were not going to just be talked about but rather moved upon. Missourians deserved to know what their leaders truly believed in. Simplicity and consistency would create priorities all Missourians could understand. They didn't need to necessarily be political or partisan. The priorities needed to mean something to all citizens of the state.

When Governor Parson took office, there was a gas tax initiative on the ballot (Proposition D) for voters to decide on Tuesday, November 6, 2018. If approved, the tax on fuel would increase to seventeen cents the first year then incrementally increase over the next five years until it was fully phased in to twenty-seven cents. The increase in revenue would be used for road and bridge construction and maintenance across Missouri. There were also provisions to move funds to local projects across the state. It was obvious to all Missourians that the fundamental road and bridge infrastructure across the state was depleting. The gas tax initiative was ultimately voted down.

Although Mike Parson was not the governor when the gas tax was put on the ballot, he knew something needed to be done to improve the transportation infrastructure across the state. Governor Parson and his team determined it was time to go a different route. If the transportation infrastructure was truly a problem, it was time to double down and determine an alternate solution. On the heels of the failed ballot measure, Governor Parson and his team went to work. The result was a proposed $350 million in the governor's budget for the 2019 session for bridge improvements across Missouri known as the Focus on Bridges Program.

In Governor Parson fashion, the extensive list of priorities was whittled down to two all Missourians could personally relate to. Upon establishment, it was not known whether the administration would have two and a half or six and a half years to advance the priorities. Workforce development and infrastructure were identified by Governor Parson and his team to be the signature priorities of his administration not only in his first proposed budget but in the years that would follow. Missouri One Start and Apprenticeship Missouri were big players in the initial workforce development effort, but the hallmark piece was Fast Track. The Fast Track Workforce Incentive Grant was and continues to be a program designed to provide adults with the education and skills needed to enter the workforce in fields that are in high demand. The scholarship program was geared to working adults and how to provide training to them. Working adults had the opportunity to retrain into a different job category with better pay. The second concentrated area was in the high schools. Apprenticeships connected to career and technical education were introduced.

On the infrastructure side, the bonds needed to fund the Focus on Bridges Program were sold at historic lows. Not every state is fortunate like Missouri to have a AAA bond rating. The rating is a product of responsible bonding practices in Missouri. To maintain the superior rating, two things must be done: responsibly meet repayment obligations and responsibly use bonds. The first set of bonds that were a part of the project were sold at eighty-nine basis points (eighty-nine cents) and the second set of bonds were sold at forty-nine basis points (forty-nine cents). It will likely be a significant time, if ever, for rates to be this low. As a result, Missourians saw a tremendous return on investment.

A third, less flashy but equally important, priority is the governor's commitment to deferred maintenance across the entire state. This obligation to take care of the things Missouri already has is just a way of life for Mike Parson.

One major change came on August 27, when Governor Parson announced his first appointment to his cabinet. Colonel Sandra Karsten was appointed as director of the Department of Public Safety. The governor knew this position was a very important one to fill. Sandra Karsten's qualifications spoke for themselves, and she proved to be the right person for the job. She would be the first female to assume this position.

With a statewide official winning election to the United States Senate in November 2018, the governor was required to appoint a replacement. The appointment process ultimately created a domino effect. When Attorney General Josh Hawley won the U.S. Senate election, his office became vacant. On November 13, Governor Parson appointed Eric Schmitt to attorney general. Once this transition took place, this opened the state treasurer position. On December 19, Governor Parson appointed Scott Fitzpatrick to state treasurer. Rarely does a governor appoint even one statewide elected official, and now Governor Parson had appointed three statewide officials.

On May 24, 2019, Governor Parson joined with House and Senate members and pro-life coalition leaders to sign House Bill 126, known as the "Missouri Stands for the Unborn Act." This bill prohibits an abortion in a non-medical emergency past eight weeks of gestational age and ensures the protection of women's safety. HB 126 prohibits an individual from performing or inducing an abortion solely because of a diagnosis of potential for Down Syndrome in an unborn child or because of the race or sex of the unborn child. This bill was one of the most aggressive pro-life bills in the country. Governor Parson wanted to send a strong message to the nation that, in Missouri, residents stand for life, protect women's health, and advocate for the unborn.

Droughts were an issue in 2018, but both the Mississippi River and Missouri River experienced flooding in 2019. The flooding in the lower Missouri River basin was historic in multiple states. What was most historic in northwest Missouri was not just the water depth but the duration. The levee system in Missouri, Kansas, Iowa, and Nebraska was put to the ultimate test and failed on multiple occasions. These four states are the lowest in the basin with Missouri being the lowest.

This was one of the numerous occasions Governor Parson exercised the thought to begin with the end in mind. It was one of those moments when how to get there was less important than just getting there. Governor Parson could care less who got the credit, he just had his eyes on the goal. Since the mouth of the Missouri River is in Missouri, there is no way to avoid its power. Leverage with the United States Army Corps of Engineers was critical to creating a long-term solution to a problem that may persist forever. The four governors and states joined forces to work together on a solution.

They entered a memorandum of understanding (MOU) setting the stage for historic solutions. The component of leverage was not necessarily intended to strong arm the Corps of Engineers but rather create an unprecedented relationship with them. That is exactly what it did. Maybe not a perfect relationship but an improved relationship. The states, especially Missouri, wanted to be a part of the solution. Since Missouri can never hide from the Missouri River, it was critical to be realistic and practical. Raising the height of the levees everywhere was not a practical long-term solution. Solutions resulted, but it must be remembered that the state's two largest rivers are called "Mighty" for a reason.

Governor Parson faced many challenges, some expected and others unexpected, during his first year in office. Stress was just a way of life. Governor and First Lady Parson decided in June 2019 to inflict some additional stress on themselves. They considered themselves stewards of the state and the Missouri Governor's Mansion. When a governor wins the office, the governor and governor's family take residence there. The mansion has a basement and three floors. The living quarters are on the second and third floors. First Lady Parson coined the term the "People's House" for the "Governor's Mansion" immediately upon taking residence in June 2018. Governor and First Lady Parson decided, although an obvious inconvenience, there was no better time than the present to complete needed renovations on the structure. The renovations were extensive and included improvements to the flooring, ceilings, windows, security system, insulation, heating, air conditioning, electrical, plumbing, sewer, and fire alarm systems as well as general structural improvements.

   In June 2019, Mike and Teresa relocated to a small white house on the grounds of the Missouri National Guard–Ike Skelton Training Center east of Jefferson City. The governor's staff ultimately coined the temporary residence the "White House." After five months, in October 2019, Governor and First Lady Parson returned to the "People's House" just in time to entertain the kids and community at the annual Halloween event.

   Despite the circumstances that led to Governor Parson getting to the top political office of the state, the political process is a perpetual machine with a life cycle. The governor had concentrated his focus on helping Missourians. In 2019, both Republicans and Democrats were looking to the future and the 2020 elections. Where did Governor Parson see himself in the future of Missouri? Mike and Teresa thought for many months on whether it was the right choice to run for governor in 2020.

   The requirements needed to be a quality governor are demanding. This job was stressful for the governor as well as his family. Mike and Teresa both disliked missing quality time with their family. Time with kids and grandkids was very limited for the state's top executive. However, Mike was a public servant and knew there was more he could do for Missouri and for its people. He really wanted an opportunity to finish what he had started. Missouri was moving in the right direction. He was poised to leave the office and state in a better place than he found it. Governor Parson did not just want to get things accomplished for Missourians while he was governor, but he also wanted to provide a solid foundation for his eventual successor. The office had some resemblance of sinking sand when he arrived. His goal was to create a solid foundation moving forward.

After a lot of praying and getting the blessing from his family, Mike sat down to discuss the possibility with two key team members. He knew he needed committed, loyal, and quality people who would stick with him until his final term was over. He called Aaron Willard and Kelli Jones into his office for a meeting to confirm their support for another run as governor and to see if they would remain on his team if victorious. After getting a commitment from them and support from his family, Mike internally announced he would run for governor in 2020.

Governor Parson knew that a run to be elected to a full-term would be challenging, but he was up to it. He understood while leading the state, he would have to raise money to run a successful campaign. When Governor Parson assumed the position, he dedicated himself to working hard for Missouri. A second term and the related fundraising needed to win a second term were never much of a thought for the governor.

Typically, when a politician sets course to win the governorship, he or she develops a chest of financial resources often through PACS to support election and/or reelection efforts. Governor Parson had not set course to win the governorship when he assumed the position of governor. He would be starting at ground zero. The work began. Governor Parson hired Steele Shippy to be his campaign manager. To assume this role, Steele made the tough decision to depart the Parson administration, where he was communication director, to take the helm of the Parson campaign team.

Some things are indeed "Made in America!" The song of the same name recorded by Toby Keith and released on June 13, 2011, tells a story very similar to that of Mike Parson. There was a man "born in the heartland," who "raised up a family," who lived by the "King James" Bible, and who served his country and respects "Uncle Sam!" The song was debuted by Toby Keith on June 8, 2011, at the CMT Music Awards in Nashville. There have been few events that have ever exemplified "Made in America" any more than the day a man from Wheatland named Mike Parson took the oath to serve as the fifty-seventh governor of the Great State of Missouri on Friday, June 1, 2018.

"Made in America" became the theme song of Governor Mike Parson, and he wanted to make his big announcement in his hometown of Bolivar. On the stage of the performing arts center at Bolivar High School on Sunday, September 8, 2019, Governor Parson declared his intent to run for governor of Missouri. This event occurred only miles from Wheatland, the community where he grew up, and even fewer miles from the businesses he had previously owned and operated in Bolivar. Many of those in attendance were also residents of Polk County where Mike had served for years.

Surrounded by many people that had been influential in his life, a confident and composed Mike Parson took the microphone to address all those in attendance declaring his future intent:

> There's only one place in the world where someone from a small rural town with modest means could have the opportunities I have had. To serve my country in an Army uniform. To serve my community in a Sheriff's uniform. To complete my dream of starting and owning a small business. To enter public service and serve my community and state. These experiences are only possible in this country under the red, white and blue of the United States of America. Our state is abundant with people pursuing the American dream. Dreams we have for ourselves, our families, and our children. We believe that everyone should have the opportunity to pursue the American dream. If you are willing to work, that dream should never be out of reach for anyone, regardless of what their background is or where they came from. That's why I feel the call to serve again. I want to continue to do the hard work. To make sure everyone has the chance to pursue the American dream. To move Missouri forward with common sense, with honor and integrity. And that's why I am here today, in my hometown of Bolivar–to announce that I am running to be your Governor of the great state of Missouri.

Between primary and general elections in his career, Governor Parson had eighteen victories on his resume without a defeat. This would be his first race for the highest position in Missouri state government. Governor Parson's path to the position of Missouri's highest political office was not the typical route, but he was poised to continue his service to the state he loved. This time it would not be under unprecedented circumstances. This time it would be for a regular, full, four-year term following an election of Missourians.

Mike's address and declaration to the people finished with his commitment and declaration to the people of Missouri: "I've never been afraid of hard work and nobody is going to work harder than I will in this campaign. We are at a critical moment. Now is the time to defend who we are. Now is the time to come together. Now is the time to stand up for Christian and family values. Now is the time to lead with honor and integrity. Now is the time to stand up for the American Dream. Now is the time to get to work and to win this election."

Former state representative Steve Tilley regards the introduction video of Governor Parson narrated by First Lady Teresa Parson first shown at the campaign kickoff event in Bolivar to be "the best commercial he has ever seen in politics." Following is a transcript of the narration by First Lady Teresa Parson on the campaign kickoff video and political advertisement.

> It all started on a farm
>> where long days and hard work go hand and hand
>> where friends and neighbors are like family
>>> and where lifelong values are learned at an early age
>> Mike and I both grew up on farms
>> we didn't have much
>> but it always seemed like enough
> Like a lot of us
>> Mike learned some lessons the hard way
>> about doing right
>> that school was important
>> and through it all
>> he worked
>> he learned
>> and he grew
> Those lessons moved Mike
>> giving him a strong desire to serve and give back
>> so after graduating high school
>> he joined the army
>> serving his country
>> and seizing on every opportunity the army would give him
>> he became an MP
>> pushing himself after long days to take classes at night
>> to do more
>> to do better
>> and when he was done
>> he came back home to serve the community
>> eventually becoming Polk County Sheriff
>> where he was trusted to keep our families safe

    modernized the department
    and he led by example
That same work ethic drove him to start a business
    running a local service station
    where he treated customers like family and friends
    always there to lend a helping hand
    touching the lives of those around him
Mike and I raised our family with the same values and hard work
    sacrifice and service that were instilled in us growing up
They are the same values he took with him to the state house
      and senate
    where he continued to serve by focusing on helping all
      our communities
And now as Governor
    he is working hard to move Missouri forward
    using those same values of hard work and education
      for Veterans who need a voice
      to high school students that choose a difference path
    his workforce development initiative is empowering us for the future
Mike is doing what he does best
    rolling up his sleeves and getting to work for those people he serves
These days his work may take him away from here
    but the values and work ethic he learned growing up have never
      left him
To think
    it all started on a farm
    and as a husband
    Father
    and grandfather
    a Veteran
    who proudly served our country
    a sheriff
    who protected our communities
    and now as Governor
    the one thing that doesn't change.
Mike Parson works for Missouri!

If one has had an opportunity to spend a few minutes with Mike Parson, learning about his past, his present, and his vision for the future, they understand the value he brings through these words that accurately describe him. Immediately, the unofficial and official sides went to work. Under the slogan "Parson Works for Missouri," he began campaigning job creation, workforce development, and infrastructure.

Governor Parson is who he says he is. Following the suicide of Missouri State Auditor Tom Schweich in early 2015, Mike vowed to denounce negative campaign tactics and big money in politics. Regardless of one's position on campaign contributions, there is no way to win an election for governor in any state without some campaign finances. Soon after being sworn in as the fifty-seventh governor of Missouri, Governor Parson told friend and Republican colleague Steve Tilley that he "was not doing any fundraising . . . I need to focus on the state," Steve recalls. Governor Parson put all of himself into leading the state as its governor, but Steve knew if he later decided to run for a second term, he would need to have more than a love for Missouri to do it.

People who know how the political game works know it cannot be done on love alone. With the governor's focus on Missouri, others would need to lead the fundraising charge. He would need to have at minimum a small base to get started. In July 2018, Steve Tilley reached out to Governor Parson. Steve volunteered to be that person. At this point, Governor Parson had only expressed his intent to run, but Steve knew waiting too long to get started could be disastrous to a reelection campaign.

Steve said he would do his best to stay out of the way of the day-to-day activities required of the governor, but if Mike was indeed interested in running for a second (and final) term as governor the team would need to start raising some money. Governor Parson concurred with Steve but remained committed to not allowing fundraising to be a distraction to his role as governor. Steve received blessing from Governor Parson to explore campaign fundraising opportunities for a second term as governor and immediately went to work to make that happen. In August 2018, the PGA Championship was slated for play in Missouri at Bellerive Country Club in suburban St. Louis. Anheuser-Busch reached out to Steve and made their suite available on the final day of the tournament for a fundraising opportunity.

Steve went to work to make the most of this occasion. He contacted twelve of the biggest donors and business leaders in St. Louis. He offered them an opportunity to view the final day of the major golf event from the Anheuser-Busch suite at $25,000 a piece. It was a great opportunity to see some great golf in a PGA major and be joined by Governor Parson during the afternoon of play. That is where the smiling Steve Tilley says people get to really see a special side of Governor Parson. Steve worked extremely hard to get the event organized. He requested Mike show up about 1:00 PM on Sunday. He recalls showing up shortly after noon that day to put the final touches in preparation for the event. Steve knew the day would provide Governor Parson with an afternoon with some of the key people in St. Louis. Steve recalls everyone enjoying the sights and sounds of the final round of a major tournament.

When the clock showed 1:00 PM, there was no Governor Parson. Still no Governor Parson at 1:15 PM. Steve still thought "no big deal." He must be running a little late. At 1:30 PM, he started to feel it was becoming a little bigger deal. At 1:45 PM, Steve started reaching out to the governor. He started texting him with no reply. Irritation turned into embarrassment as time continued to pass. With each text and no reply from the governor, Steve's language on the text got more aggressive and more aggressive. He recalls, "By this time I am mean texting . . . I was talking to the Governor like you should not talk to the Governor . . . I was irritated . . . it was embarrassing." The clock passed 2:00 PM, then 2:15 PM, then 2:30 PM. By this time, the guests started asking if the governor was coming to the suite. Steve remembers the repeated questioning coming his way. "Steve . . . why isn't the Governor here?"

Around 3:30 PM, Steve's phone begins to ring. It was the governor. The reaction he got from the governor was a testament to the kind of guy he is, but at the moment, it did little to relieve his irritation. Steve vividly remembers the phone conversation that ensued. The first sound he heard from the governor was uncontrollable laughter. Steve said, "He sounded like a kid in a candy store." He remembers not being in a laughing mood and really desiring an explanation, and the governor offered one even before he asked. He recalls Governor Parson saying, "Let me explain. Number one: I apologize. Number two: They bring me into Bellerive Country Club, I get out; they welcome me, and the first thing they ask is 'Would you like to walk inside the ropes with Tiger Woods?'"

The governor, instead of coming to the fundraiser, walked inside the ropes for nine holes with Tiger Woods who was in the hunt in the major. After the brief explanation by the governor, Steve did his best to try to understand the predicament the governor had been in. Steve had personally invited a dozen St. Louis donors and leaders to the suite who expected a visit from the governor. He remembers his response to the governor, "Here's what you have got to do . . . you have to call all twelve of these people and explain to them why you did not show up."

In the days that followed, Governor Parson reached out to all donors and business leaders in attendance that day. Steve remembers the governor responding back to him after making all the phone calls. With a grin Steve now recalls, "The funny thing is . . . he called all twelve of them . . . and all twelve said 'you know what Governor, I would have done the same thing.'"

Steve recalls it being comical that the first event done for the governor's race, the governor does not even show up. Not exactly the first impression he envisioned the governor making, but it was Governor Mike Parson being Mike Parson.

Steve says Governor Mike Parson is like no other politician. He has observed many politicians being like chameleons as they travel about the political landscape. Some politicians fail to be themselves and try to adapt to the expectations of others from location to location. Steve declares that is not Mike Parson, "You put Mike Parson at a sale barn in Polk County, or you put him at the Log Cabin Club in Ladue, and you get the same person. That shows that he is confident in who he is."

Governor Parson and his official team were working tirelessly to govern Missouri and take care of six million Missourians. At the same time, Governor Parson's campaign team was preparing for an election that would potentially give Governor Parson four more years as Missouri's fifty-seventh governor. When Governor Parson assumed the position, he and his team used the playbook developed by Aaron Willard to guide the way. The three-ring binder was as detailed as it could be, but one pending situation not addressed was the unexpected challenges to be presented by a pandemic. At the end of 2019, the coronavirus (COVID-19) started garnering considerable attention worldwide and Missouri was no exception.

During his campaign kickoff in Bolivar in September 2019, Governor Parson promised all Missourians he was equipped to lead the state through whatever challenges that might be faced in the future. No one knew the exact challenges on the horizon, but Governor Parson emphasized, "We can do all of this with a servant's heart, with the American values of which we were raised: love of country, love of family, Christian faith, common sense, and conservative principles." Little did he know at the time, but the characteristics he mentioned that day in Bolivar in 2019 would soon be put to the test in March 2020.

After his initial announcement on his intent, many in the Parson camp were excited about him running for his first full-term as governor of Missouri, but during this same time Governor Parson was monitoring, like most Americans, the pandemic taking aim on the United States as it traversed countries around the world. It was only a matter of time before it reached American soil and that of Missouri. Like many challenges faced by political leaders, there are often responses from previous events that could be called upon when comparable trials are faced. That historical perspective may work in most situations, but COVID-19 was unlike any situation faced in recent memory. Governor Parson, like the rest of the world, quickly realized there would be no previously created playbook to reference during this pandemic. Through the start of the 2020 calendar year, Missouri had not been impacted, but the governor knew it was just a matter of time.

Governor Parson and his team began making preparations for Missouri. His leadership during the challenges presented during the pandemic speak for themselves. He faced trials no Missouri governor may have ever faced in the past and may never face in the future. He will be forever recorded as the governor of Missouri who led his state through one of the most unprecedented periods in Missouri history. A book could be written about Governor Parson and his leadership of the state during this period, but the account in this book will highlight key moments during the unprecedented journey through the pandemic.

At the beginning of 2020, campaigning for governor and normal operations of government slowed considerably to devote nearly full attention to the global pandemic that was making daily strides toward Missouri. The governor and his office began receiving regular updates on the COVID-19 pandemic by Missouri Department of Health and Senior Services (DHSS) Director Dr. Randall Williams on January 29.

Governor Parson and his team, like all Missourians, "kept their ear to the rail" listening and learning as much as possible about the global pandemic. Although Missouri had not yet been directly impacted, Governor Parson and his administration did not sit idle. On March 3, Governor Mike Parson was joined by his team, his cabinet members, external stakeholders, and Missouri State Emergency Management Agency (SEMA) officials for a briefing at the SEMA facility in Jefferson City regarding COVID-19. Following the meeting, Missourians were updated on the preparedness measures being taken by the state in anticipation of COVID-19 making its presence in the Show-Me State.

Through all the preparation, Governor Parson and his administration knew it was only a matter of time before the first positive case would hit Missouri. Saturday, March 7, 2020, proved to be that time. During the late morning hours of March 7, Governor Parson got a call from Chief of Staff Aaron Willard stating a woman from St. Louis County had tested "presumptive positive" for the virus. He immediately contacted Communications Director Kelli Jones to decide the next move. At that moment, neither Governor Parson, Dr. Williams, Aaron, nor Kelli was in Jefferson City. Governor Parson, Aaron, and Kelli promptly dropped everything and decided to meet in Jefferson City, so they could travel to St. Louis for a press conference to update Missourians on the response they could expect as a result of the confirmed case.

Late that Saturday afternoon in St. Louis, Governor Parson announced in the press conference, along with St. Louis County Executive Sam Page and medical professionals, the first case to test presumptive positive for the novel coronavirus in Missouri. Governor Parson knew how important it was to reassure Missourians that the state was prepared to respond to the challenges ahead.

From this point on, Governor Parson experienced something no other governor of Missouri had ever experienced. He was faced with navigating through a pandemic with no playbook. He was not alone because not one existed across the world. He and some of his senior staff spent forty-two consecutive days from pre-sunrise to post-sunset creating plans for and communicating to Missourians. Since the onset, Governor Parson's administration, Missouri's sixteen executive agencies, and numerous stakeholders from across the state worked together to respond, rebuild, and recover.

It was a very trying time for Governor Parson and his administration. Governor Parson remembers his daughter seeing him on television. She made a quick call and told him, "You need to go home and get some rest. You look like death warmed over." Governor Parson continued, explaining, "People do not realize how many hours my administration put in during these times. A few of my senior staff went home only to sleep for a few hours. Their families' lives were disrupted drastically, so they could serve Missouri. I am so proud of all of them for stepping up during some of the most difficult times."

Like many young men growing up, Governor Parson heard his mother ask him many times, "If your friends jumped off a bridge, would you?" Governor Parson was only focused on doing what was right for Missouri.

To do this, he called on Missouri's best. Governor Parson requested his cabinet members gather their best employees from their agencies. He knew with a pool of over forty-eight thousand state employees he had the best of the best. They would listen and learn from other states, but the focus would be on Missouri and Missourians. If the cabinet members would have asked him the same question his mother did growing up, he would have responded, "You raised a leader, not a follower. If there is a need to jump off the bridge, I will be the first one."

Governor Parson knew open lines of communication would be critical to keeping Missourians informed and updated. These lines needed to be two-way. To make this happen, Governor Parson began putting groups of leaders together, so he could offer updates and learn from the experts in their fields. Governor Parson had groups of pastors, mayors, school superintendents, university presidents, and the list went on. For months, Governor Parson conducted conference calls to inform these leaders about the issues being faced and actions being taken. These calls became very valuable in navigating the path through COVID. He discovered these relationships helped create dialogue important to moving Missouri forward.

After the first positive case, Governor Parson and his administration knew it was imperative for Missourians to hear from the governor daily. Governor Parson remembers the daily press briefings like they were yesterday. Every day his communications team had him ready to face millions of viewers. For months, Governor Parson would do live daily briefings inviting other leaders to join him. Eventually, the press briefings were only streamed due to the health order. This was a unique set-up because the media was not actually present. They would watch via Facebook and then submit questions to Kelli. She would read them aloud to the governor, and he would answer them. The press briefings were draining, but they were necessary for Governor Parson to be seen and heard by Missourians. Governor Parson wanted to be the one to deliver the message to the people of his state.

The media was searching for answers as well. However, it can't be forgotten that there was an election in the near future, and the media was working this angle as well. Some media outlets were trying so hard to turn the pandemic into politics. Governor Parson refused to make the pandemic political, but it was hard to avoid the polarizing effect the pandemic had. He stayed the course and focused on Missourians.

Many challenges were facing Governor Parson and his administration. Personal protective equipment (PPE) was scarce, and Missouri hospitals were filling. Governor Parson and his team continued to lead and solve problems. He still felt communication, both internally and externally, was top priority. "Wash your hands, social distance, and stay home if you are ill" became a common phrase at early press gatherings with the governor.

Though not officially documented, Governor Parson was among the first leaders to coin the phrase "personal responsibility." At first, the governor took a tremendous amount of criticism for these words. Many people and leaders around the nation were reluctant to use them early on. Governor Parson knew the people could not have it both ways. From the beginning, Governor Parson felt the people of Missouri had "the final answer" when it came to controlling the spread of the virus. Government could provide factual data, make recommendations, and provide resources and support, but unenforceable mandates from the government would only create problems. "Why would you make a mandate that you cannot effectively enforce?" the governor consistently reminded his team.

Governor Parson maintained a steadfast commitment to "local control" during the pandemic. Missouri is a very diverse state. There was not a "one size fits all" solution for a state as diverse as Missouri. He realized early that conditions were not the same across the entire state. There was no one who knew the needs of communities across Missouri more than the local leaders of those communities. Local officials were able to make decisions for their community that reflected their conditions. As a result, local jurisdictions (counties and cities) implemented restrictions they felt were appropriate for their circumstances. Since conditions were so different across the state, the governor never felt statewide restrictions were appropriate.

During the daily press conference on March 18, Governor Parson was joined by Dr. Randall Williams, medical professionals from University of Missouri Healthcare, and the mayor of Columbia to announce the first COVID-19 related death in Missouri, which had occurred in a Columbia hospital. This single messaging method became the norm to ensure Missourians were getting all the facts in a complete and timely manner.

Decisions in the governor's office were being made rapidly during the final few weeks of March. Governor Parson would announce that municipal elections set for April would be postponed, would urge gatherings of less than fifty people and later less than ten people, and would close all 555 of Missouri's public and charter schools for a tentative period but later closed them for the remainder of the academic year and transition to virtual learning methods. The governor remained optimistic about the future and consistently reminded Missourians "we are all in this together."

Governor Parson, on Wednesday, March 25, requested a federal major disaster declaration to provide federal assistance for state and local COVID-19 pandemic preparedness in addition to emergency response efforts. President Donald Trump approved the request one day later.

The governor had spent many years as a member of the United States Armed Forces. He knew firsthand that military service members were well trained and efficient and knew how to take orders. During the previous year, Missouri completed a great partnership with the Missouri National Guard in response to flooding. The governor knew he had a great resource that could help respond on a moment's notice. Things were changing quickly and Governor Parson wanted a consistent response across the state. "There is never any doubt in my mind . . . what the Missouri National Guard can do . . . they are mission driven . . . when you tell them to charge the hill . . . they are going to charge the hill . . . right now . . . General Cumpton and his troops have been given instructions to charge the hill . . . at the top of the hill is testing," Governor Parson stated in his briefing on March 27. He also announced he had signed an executive order mobilizing the Missouri National Guard to assist with the state's COVID-19 response, mainly to help with testing and PPE services. The federal CARES Act was also signed into law, allowing state leaders to direct economic relief for individuals, organizations, and businesses in need.

Information was coming in swiftly, but it was always important to send the information received through a filter. It was critical to decipher the facts from the fiction. News outlets and social media were consistently changing the narrative. During the pandemic, Governor Parson got extremely frustrated with communication about the virus and unrealistic response measures being fueled by the media. States needing to "shut down" was a recurring theme being endorsed by many media outlets. Governor Parson and his team did not think the government should or could force people to not interact with one another. Some states across the country started to "shut down." The pressure started to be applied to the governor and his administration as more states made the decision to "shut down."

With the information being all over the board related to the virus, the governor wanted to consider all potential alternatives to safely move forward without a complete "shut down." Governor Parson was not convinced a "shut down" would have a positive effect on a person's mental, social, or emotional health. The one thing he knew for certain was a decision to fully "shut down" the state would be putting many businesses, especially small businesses, out of business. With a clear conscience, Governor Parson could not conclude that state governments should even have this authority.

The governor convened his cabinet and his senior leaders to come up with alternatives. This is where the whole government approach again paid dividends. Important to the team was providing the essentials Missourians needed but doing it in the least restrictive manner possible. There were many state regulations restricting businesses during this period. The cabinet and senior leaders worked together to identify potential waivers of the state regulations that would assist businesses and help them survive. The group ultimately recommended over six hundred waivers of statutes and regulations intended to change practices and procedures. With so many waivers being reviewed and granted, the ability to authorize a waiver was passed down to the directors to expedite the process.

Governor Parson was always a governor focused on doing the best for Missourians. God had put Mike Parson and his team members in this position in less than ideal conditions to make a positive difference for Missouri. The governor's former policy director Kayla Hahn summarized the man, the team, and the mission this way:

> Mike Parson being Governor of Missouri is a testament to him as a person. He has an innate ability to stay focused on the goal, put his head down, and just keep working hard. Governor Parson expects the members of his team to do the same. He secured the title as Missouri's 57th Governor under rare and unusual circumstances, but it was meant to be. The Governor often reminded those in the room that God put us here in this place for this reason. Sometimes we may not fully understand it all, but someday our eyes will be opened fully. I found myself being spiritually and emotionally moved during these meetings. It was a shared feeling among all the team members. He had a really good way of relating to people. He remained in tune with what Missourians were thinking. Sometimes when people get into political offices, they narrow their focus, they do not hear what common people are talking about on their front porch, at their church, with their neighbor, or their friends. Governor Parson never narrowed his focus. He was good at tapping into what Missourians were thinking.

One of the earliest frustrations of the governor and his team was the inability of the federal government and companies outside of Missouri to provide PPE to those Missourians who expressed a need. During a meeting with his cabinet and senior leaders, Governor Parson voiced that being one of the lead manufacturing states in the country, it was time to look from within. It was time for the best leaders in Missouri to develop a solution for the state. The Department of Economic Development (DED) ultimately took the lead. In April 2020, the Missouri DED, in partnership with the Missouri Hospital Association, launched the PPE Marketplace. Governor Parson touted the efforts of Missourians saying, "Manufacturers across the state have answered the call to help protect our health care workers, and we are committed to doing all we can to get this equipment into the hands of those that need it." At the time it was initiated, Missouri was the only state providing this tool. The Missouri PPE Marketplace went from idea to implementation in just two weeks.

The effort of Missourians to take care of Missourians was one of the first of many initiatives to be recognized as models by federal leaders in Washington, DC. At a White House press briefing, Vice President Mike Pence highlighted the Missouri PPE Marketplace stating Missouri "worked with Google Marketplace to create an online portal of more than 200 companies in Missouri who have repurposed their manufacturing lines to create medical supplies to meet their need within the state." The creativity and innovation of the people of Missouri set the stage for a model solution.

The governor and his team started having weekly meetings with doctors throughout the state to keep this critical line of communication open. Hearing from doctors on the front lines was important to getting a medical perspective on Missouri and safely moving forward. These meetings typically occurred on Saturday mornings as a conference call with a group of doctors representing regions of the state.

These meetings would prove to be extremely valuable but were not without some trying moments. Everyone had their own perspective during this time, and those of the medical personnel were critical. One morning a frustrated doctor on the call got aggressive with his opinion about what needed to occur. He declared that a complete shutdown was the best course of action, and the governor had this ability. His final statement to all was a question directed at Governor Parson, "Why are you not doing this?" It took the bold actions of another doctor on the call to bring a level of calmness to the conversation. He understood his colleague was frustrated but wanted everyone to do their best to respect the perspectives of others.

The intervening doctor began by focusing on the fundamental beliefs of physicians. As doctors and healthcare professionals, he first reminded everyone that improving the health of others was their job and the vacuum of decision making they lived in. He then moved his attention to the position of governor stating the governor has a very different set of things he needs to consider and cannot only consider the things they are focused on. He must think about all these things and much more. The doctor brought it all together declaring the doctors needed to understand his perspective on this was different from their perspective and these calls needed to be used to share their perspective but also understand his. When the doctor ended, there was a moment of silence on the call. There was a moment of united understanding. The conversation continued that day and on subsequent Saturdays with a peace which would not have existed without a doctor daring to step out. Being a doctor now was not an easy task. Being the Missouri governor was no easy task either. This group needed to provide information and recommendations to support one another.

Emotions ran high. Even the emotions of those on the governor's team. There were members of the team who were reluctant to come to work because they thought they were being put at risk. Regardless of the level of anxiety, Governor Parson needed the best from everyone especially during their forty-two straight days of service to the citizens of Missouri at the onset of the pandemic. The governor feels he has always been blessed with a tremendous staff.

Governor Parson and his team knew there was a high level of anxiety among most Missourians. They knew if they did not provide timely and accurate information to the public, the information void would be filled by the media. Whether it was their intent or not, the media had the appearance of attempting to control the narrative. The early heroes during COVID in the media were leaders who shut down their states. It is hard not to want to be a hero. Early on, Governor Parson and his team analyzed the potential impacts a statewide shutdown would have on the state. It is natural for people to look at Missouri from their own perspective, their own home, their own town or city, and their own region. The governor always looked at Missouri in its entirety. Missouri is the "Show-Me State!" After analyzing the potential impact of a statewide shutdown, the governor quickly realized Missouri is not a "One Size Fits All State!" Governor

Parson was never afraid to declare a statewide shutdown if it was the right thing for all of Missouri.

Steve Tilley feels he and the governor are great friends, but during the campaign and COVID, Steve remembered being reminded by the governor that Mike Parson was the governor and he was not. Steve remembered vividly being respectfully put in his place by the governor. COVID had placed pressure on people like nothing they had ever experienced. The pressure of being the governor of Missouri was likely greater than a governor had ever felt. Early in the pandemic, Governor Parson committed himself to making the right decisions for Missouri. Opinions and pressure were being applied from every direction. He and Missouri could not go wrong by doing the right thing. Early in the pandemic and campaign, states bordering Missouri were making some radical decisions related to stay at home orders (sometimes referred to as shelter in place orders). As states started closing things down, Steve Tilley reached out to Governor Parson encouraging him to fall in line with the other bordering states. Steve remembers the governor telling him something along the lines of "kiss my ass!" It was not actually those words, but those were the words that resonated. Governor Parson remembered having multiple conversations with Steve about the topic. "It was the safer route politically, but it was the wrong route," the governor emphasized. He knew there were some Missourians who were in favor of a shelter in place order but it was not the sentiment of most Missourians.

Steve was thinking from a political perspective and had been in some of those areas of the state where shelter in place was popular. "Steve . . . it is the wrong thing to do," the governor remembers telling him. "You don't need me to tell you to stay at home . . . if you want to stay at home . . . stay at home." Governor Parson remembers asking Steve a question, "Steve . . . where are you today?" The governor remembers Steve responding he was at home. "I didn't tell you to stay home did I," the governor remembers replying.

It seems everyone is unyielding on the subject of local control unless an unpopular decision needs to be made. During this period, when an unpopular decision needed to be made, it was important someone make it above them on the organizational chart. Leave the popular decisions to the local leaders and pass the responsibility and blame of unpopular decisions to those at the top. Being a leader is being a leader. Governor Parson was not afraid to lead. Leadership is about leading, not making orders or mandates that are unnecessary and unable to be enforced. Leadership has its boundaries.

The governor was getting input from every direction. He remembered getting a call from a pastor at home encouraging his intervention. The governor responded, "I can't do that . . . you have to make that call . . . if you do not think it is safe for the congregation to go to church . . . find an alternative way . . . you are not going to keep people from praying . . . you are not going to keep people from worshiping . . . I am not going to do that from the Governor's seat."

Looking back, it is evident God had placed Mike Parson in that seat at that moment. Mike was a part of God's plan. When First Lady Teresa Parson reflected on this she concluded, "It is important that God not reveal his plan for us in advance . . . we may not feel worthy to accept his will for our lives . . . knowing what we know about the challenges of that period." Advice was coming from every angle. "There was a tremendous amount of pressure to do so many things . . . you got to do this . . . you have got to do that . . . your friends are calling . . . your pastors are calling," the governor spoke of the personal struggles during the pandemic. There was no shortage of advisors. The governor's focus was on doing the right thing. With the advice from one person being the opposite of the next person, the governor had to lean on the Lord to filter the clutter and reveal the truth.

Governor Parson understood a complete shutdown of Missouri was not the right answer for Missouri. Throughout the pandemic, Governor Parson was consistent with his messaging and beliefs. No matter what political advice he was getting, he always stayed true to what he felt was best for Missourians. He knew Missouri would need to take a balanced approach. A complete shutdown order from the state level was never issued by Governor Parson. The governor focused his attention on consistently providing Missourians with the essential products and services they deserved. He wanted alternative methods to be considered and put in place when needed to avoid a complete shutdown. Governor Parson knew people still needed their livelihood, and residents would eventually work their way through the pandemic.

Governor Parson and his team did their best to focus on the data and not be influenced solely on the responses of others. After thorough consideration, on Friday, April 3, Governor Parson issued the statewide "Stay Home Missouri" order effective Monday, April 6, until Friday, April 24. The governor maintained that "personal responsibility" would remain the key to seeing Missouri through. "First and foremost, I want everyone to know that I love this state and the people of this state," Governor Parson said. The order stated individuals currently residing within the state of Missouri shall avoid leaving their homes or places of residence unless necessary. The governor felt the order would not last long. He added, "The people of this great state clearly define who we are in Missouri, and as Governor, I have no greater responsibility than to protect the health, well-being, and safety of all Missourians." On Thursday, April 16, the governor extended the order through Sunday, May 3. He also announced the state's initial framework, the "Show Me Strong Recovery" Plan, to help Missouri safely and gradually move into the recovery phase of COVID-19.

Governor Parson on Monday, April 27, highlighted data supporting the state's "Show Me Strong Recovery" Plan outlining how Missouri would gradually begin to reopen economic and social activity on May 4. The plan rested on four essential pillars designed to give Missouri a benchmark for moving forward. Governor Parson recognized the efforts of all Missourians saying, "Because Missouri took aggressive actions to combat COVID-19 from the start, we are in a good place with each of these pillars and confident that we are ready to move forward into the recovery process." Over time, the state used multiple Missouri specific sources to monitor these pillars and inform its decisions.

The global pandemic had created a stressful situation for all Missourians. Additional stress occurred as result of an incident that did not occur in Missouri but touched the lives of Missourians. On Friday, May 29, hundreds of protesters in Kansas City marched from the Country Club Plaza to Westport during the evening. Some of the protesters sat in the middle of the street, closing several streets and intersections. These protests were in response to the death of George Floyd in Minneapolis, Minnesota, on May 25. Subsequent protests were expected across the state in the days that followed. On Saturday, May 30, Governor Parson took proactive measures to protect and support Missourians. "We are deeply saddened by the tragic death of George Floyd. We are also saddened by the acts of violence that have transpired across our nation and state in response to this event. At this time, we are taking a proactive approach to protect Missouri and its people," Governor Parson said. Spending much of his life in law enforcement himself, Governor Parson understood well that citizens had the right to peacefully assemble and protest, and the State of Missouri was committed to protecting the lawful exercise of these rights. Despite the many peaceful assemblies, there were other events occurring throughout Missouri that had created conditions of distress and hazards to the safety, welfare, and property of residents and visitors. The governor activated the Missouri National Guard to assist local authorities across the state if needed.

Missouri's cutting-edge wastewater research for identification of potential COVID hotspots was the second initiative garnering national attention. Some states were beginning to see COVID frequency spike in congregate-care facilities. To be proactive in finding a solution, Governor Parson called on a group of people he often turned to during the pandemic, his cabinet and senior leaders. At one of the whole government department meetings, the topic of COVID detection through wastewater sampling came up. The Department of Natural Resources (DNR) was ready and willing to answer the call.

Missouri DNR partnered with the Missouri Department of Health and Senior Services, Missouri Department of Corrections, Missouri Department of Mental Health, Missouri Department of Public Safety's Missouri Veterans Commission, and researchers from the University of Missouri–Columbia to create Missouri's Coronavirus Sewershed Surveillance Project. By September 2020, sampling and testing were being completed across Missouri. In June 2022, Governor Parson awarded this team a Pinnacle Award for their efforts on this groundbreaking project— the first and one of the largest scale projects of its kind in the United States. Missouri was one of the first states to initiate this testing. Once again, Missourians were finding solutions for Missourians.

Mask on or mask off! In early July 2020, the St. Louis region adopted the first mask mandate in Missouri. Dozens more counties and cities followed suit by issuing similar mandates throughout the course of the pandemic, though the State of Missouri never required masking statewide. Missouri is one of only eleven states that never issued a statewide mask mandate.

Governor Parson traveled to Washington, DC, on July 7 to join President Trump, the First Lady, Vice President Pence, the Second Lady, healthcare professionals, educators, students, and others in a summit to discuss the reopening of schools across the country. At the press conference that followed, Governor Parson, after thanking the president and vice president for their leadership, spoke to the critical importance of getting students back in school. He spoke from the heart, as a father and grandfather, not just about learning but the other essential functions schools serve to students and families. From nutrition to mental health,

Governor Parson referred to schools as a "safety blanket" for many students. Schools provide students with a safe ride to and from school, a breakfast and a lunch and in some cases a dinner, social experiences with peers, supervision including counseling when needed, and some quality learning along the way. Schools were a safety blanket for students and a safety net for parents and families.

During this time, Governor Parson was doing multiple interviews with both local and national news networks on almost a daily basis. One interview that will never be forgotten during the pandemic was one with Marc Cox on the *Marc Cox Morning Show* on July 20. At the time, children were getting COVID, but most were fully recovering unless they had underlying health conditions. Governor Parson was adamant at the beginning of the school year kids needed to be in school.

When asked by the reporter about the upcoming school year, Governor Parson stated children who get the coronavirus when schools reopen will "get over it." He went on to say, "There's data out there, there's scientific evidence now on who this affects and who it doesn't, and kids are the least likely to have a problem with this. These kids have to get back to school. They're at the lowest risk possible, and if they do get COVID-19, which they will – and they will when they go to school – they're not going to the hospitals. They're not going to have to sit in doctor's offices. They are going to go home, and they're going to get over it."

For several weeks, Governor Parson faced terrible backlash. The politicians and the media went crazy with this interview. Claims were made that Governor Parson was trying to kill kids. Critics called him "a sociopath" and even "pro-death." They even accused him of wanting the kids to spread the virus to their parents and grandparents. His intentions were never to underestimate the power of the virus. However, he did know healthy kids were not the most vulnerable. Ironically, several months later, Governor Parson would be as accurate as any doctor or scientist. Most kids, in fact, went to school, got the virus, got over it, and went back to school.

Governor and First Lady Parson did their best to observe the COVID-19 guidelines, but what they were not going to do was be hostages from living and serving Missourians. They and other members of the governor's team traveled to Big Cedar Lodge and Payne's Valley Golf Course on September 22 for the official debut of the course. This course was the first public-access course in the United States designed by Tiger Woods' TGR Design. Tiger Woods was joined by Justin Thomas, Rory

McIlroy, and Justin Rose in what was declared the Payne's Valley Cup. The governor enjoyed his time that day with Woods, Thomas, McIlroy, and Rose. He considered any event hosted by Bass Pro Shops founder and friend Johnny Morris to be a first-class occasion. The day also included an event in northwest Missouri, so the travel schedule was demanding.

Travel on the official and unofficial side had taken its toll on the entire team. They were hitting it hard. Everyone was cautiously following COVID-19 guidelines, but they all knew Governor Parson needed to be out in Missouri and seen. So far, Governor and First Lady Parson had escaped from being infected by the virus. However, Teresa began to start feeling a little run down. It wasn't certain if she was just exhausted from all the travel, or she was getting sick.

The next day, they both decided it was best to be tested in case Teresa did have COVID. She had mild symptoms, but they wanted to be abundantly cautious. Governor Parson requested Dr. Randall Williams send a couple of people who could administer the test at the mansion. The third floor of the mansion quickly turned into a testing site. Minutes later the results came back, and Governor and First Lady Parson had tested positive for COVID.

Governor Parson immediately called Chief of Staff Aaron Willard and Director of Communications Kelli Jones to report to the mansion. He knew this was going to garner tremendous media attention and would require a strategic plan. As a precautionary measure, all in the governor's administration were tested. Several tested positive. The biggest hurdle at that moment involved the Missouri Press Association who was downstairs at their annual conference waiting for Governor Parson to address them. Aaron had to go downstairs to address them because Kelli had tested positive for COVID. Once the Missouri Press Association was told Governor and First Lady Parson had COVID, the news spread like wildfire. Within minutes, Kelli had over one hundred inquiries wanting all the details. She worked hard to provide information but also to protect people's private information.

First Lady Parson traveled home to Bolivar, but Governor Parson, Aaron, and Kelli agreed the governor must stay in Jefferson City at the mansion so business could be conducted, and he could continue to lead Missouri. At the time, this was the best decision made. Missourians were scared and needed to know their leader was alive and well.

All official and campaign events were canceled. Governor Parson never displayed any symptoms, and the First Lady had mild symptoms.

Proper safety protocols were implemented, and they were both put in isolation for two weeks.

During this time, Governor Parson continued to conduct and fulfill all roles of business for the state from the Missouri Governor's Mansion without interruption. He did live videos of himself, so they could be posted to social media. The goal was for Missourians to know he was healthy and would continue to lead the people of Missouri. Governor Parson described those days of isolation as frustrating. He was isolated in the mansion and had to conduct all business via phone and computers. He had no face to face contact with people, including the first lady.

A third effort garnering national attention was the Missouri COVID Dashboard. The governor and his administration from the beginning wanted to do everything possible to be transparent with the collection and communication of COVID numbers in Missouri. The governor's office worked closely with the Missouri Hospital Association and all the counties across the state to collect data summarizing COVID positivity. It was like a double-edged sword. Sometimes the data did not trend in a positive direction, so the media would take statistics and use them against them. Despite the negative attention the numbers would draw periodically, the goal never changed. The focus was on transparency to all Missourians.

As time passed, Governor Parson and his administration thought the Missouri COVID Dashboard could be even better. To make this happen, members of the team participated on a conference call with other states to brainstorm methods to improve reporting. When the call started, the Missouri participants were quick to present what the state was already doing and thoughts about improving the model. After a few minutes, the conversation stopped. No one had requested an introduction of those on the call. "What states besides Missouri are on the call" was requested by the leader. Silence! Missouri thought they had assembled a posse of states to assist. At this moment, the team came to the realization they were going it alone. Missouri thought they were going to draw information from multiple resources throughout the other states. It was not to be. Press on was exactly what they did. It was an unprecedented period. With the assistance of the data companies, Missouri created a dashboard that was ultimately considered a model across the country.

Missouri submitted its vaccination plan in October to the Center for Disease Control and Prevention (CDC). Missouri received national recognition on its COVID-19 vaccination plan which was used as a framework by other states in developing their own plans. Governor

Parson's team worked diligently for months to ensure they were prepared to execute the plan once the vaccine arrived. This was an incredible collaborative effort. The agencies and partners were so dedicated and committed to the people of Missouri.

One of the key partners in the vaccination effort was the research facility of Pfizer located in St. Louis. The Food and Drug Administration (FDA) issued an Emergency Use Authorization (EUA) for the Pfizer vaccine on Friday, December 11. Governor Parson announced on December 14 the first shipments of the Pfizer COVID-19 vaccines had arrived. "Today is an exciting day for Missouri as we have received the first of many shipments of the COVID-19 vaccine. We have been preparing for many months and will soon begin administering vaccines according to our COVID-19 vaccine plan," Governor Parson said.

Two days later, Missouri DHSS administered the first COVID-19 vaccines in the state primarily to patient-facing healthcare personnel, long-term care facilities, high-risk EMS workers, and healthcare providers. Shipments of the Pfizer COVID-19 vaccine continued throughout the next week to each of Missouri's twenty-one initial vaccination sites. These sites included hospitals and healthcare facilities across the state. As each vaccination site received its shipment of vaccines, implementation of phase one of Missouri's COVID-19 vaccine plan began. Governor Parson reminded Missourians that although a COVID-19 vaccine was now approved for use, it was important to continue practicing preventative measures.

While all of this was happening, Governor Parson was vying for a subsequent full four-year term as governor of Missouri. The Republican primary election would occur in August, and if successful in the primary, the general election would occur in November. Usually, on the campaign trail, candidates are spending financial resources from their campaign coffers to do messaging through various sources. The Governor Parson campaign team did not have to spend a penny to get the governor's picture and comments in front of Missourians daily. There has never been and will never be a candidate for the position of governor that has been under such a scrutinized political microscope as Governor Parson.

Governor Parson had spent nearly all of 2020, the main campaigning year, focused on navigating Missouri through the challenges created by the global pandemic. The response to the virus in the United States had a polarizing political effect across the country, and the same occurred in Missouri. The national media put the virus front and center. The media put it in the front, but there was not much of a center. In political terms, there was a response by many that resembled a far left or a far right approach. Governor Parson committed himself and directed his team that the Missouri response would value its people over politics.

When Governor Parson committed to the people of Missouri, he did not turn his back on the people that make Missouri great. Polarization was taking over. Finding unity in the United States of America was no easy task. Crisis affects people in different ways. A person's physical being is a product of what he or she physically consumes. A person's mind is a product of what he or she hears and reads. Missouri and its people were not exempt from the information bombarding them from every angle.

One thing Governor Parson initiated immediately upon being sworn in was making the governor's office accessible to the people of Missouri. To make this happen, people needed to be on the ground communicating with the people. These communications typically come by phone or electronically. During the pandemic, the Constituent Services Team (CST) of the governor's office was inundated with correspondences. Stephanie Whitaker and Johnathan Shiflett, members of the governor's communications team, remember it was "all hands on deck" during the pandemic. Everyone would assist in taking calls. "Kelli . . . the Governor's Director of Communications was not above taking calls to assist during this time," Johnathan added.

"What surprised me was the amount of hate people had," he recalled. "They hated this man that they had never met . . . whether by their political views or the news they watched . . . people had been turned around or twisted so much . . . some thought that the decisions this Governor was making were purposefully trying to kill them . . . it is hard to wrap your head around the fact that people can actually think like that."

"I want more regulations . . . you are going to kill everyone . . . we need a mask mandate . . . we do not need a stay at home order . . . quit infringing on my rights . . . send everyone back to work . . . this is just fake news" are a few of the phrases Stephanie and Johnathan recalled. When taking calls, the next caller often had the exact opposite viewpoint of the previous caller. The members of the CST lived with these phone calls for months. The governor knew these individuals were catching the wrath of haters all day long. There was little these team members could say that would help the callers, but the team members kept picking up the line, call after call, day after day! Kelli remembers the governor reaching out to the team on a periodic basis to check on their physical, mental, and emotional well-being. The governor always emphasized the importance of each team member to all Missourians but also requested each of them look after themselves as well. It was difficult to be respectful to those who demonstrated no respect, but the governor did not want the mental well-being of his staff to be collateral damage of hate. He knew the CST members were going through some trying times during the pandemic.

Governor Parson told his team they would utilize a balanced approach in Missouri. The wellness and safety of all Missourians would be the focus when making all decisions, but all decisions would be made in a way that would allow Missourians to still live their lives. He did not want people to live in fear, but he did not feel taking rights away from Missourians was the answer. Governor Parson emphasized he was going to concentrate on doing what was best for Missourians by concentrating on Missouri.

"In the day and age we were in . . . you always expected someone to have the answer . . . there is always an expert out there that has the answer . . . the reality was . . . none of that existed," Governor Parson said of the challenges created by COVID-19. The greatest think tanks in the world had their opinions and theories, but no one spoke with certainty. With no clear-cut answers and states doing countless things in response, the governor kept his focus on Missouri. "I put the brakes on everything," Governor Parson said. "I asked that we bring the best we have in state government . . . directors and top leaders . . . we are going to build a plan around the borders of Missouri," the governor ordered his staff. "One of the most powerful lessons I have learned . . . within 48,000 state employees . . . the answers were there . . . every one of them was there . . . we have some smart people that work in this state . . . you had to depend on them to do their part," the governor proudly proclaimed. Through his experiences in life, he felt confident in what he could do and what he could not do. He summarized the realities he discovered through the pandemic:

> You soon learned that you cannot control a mom and pop store in Bolivar or Fair Play . . . you cannot shut a convenience store down when someone utilizes it for necessities . . . you cannot tell superintendents how they are going to set up a classroom . . . it was not my job before COVID hit and it is not my job now . . . nowhere in the guidelines for communities with a local elected board does it say that the Governor gets to step in when the shit hits the fan . . . I had to trust

in the fundamentals that we have learned all our life . . . to trust that people are going to do their jobs . . . and they did.

When it came to the Republican primary election in August and the general election in November, the results would be left in the hands of the voters of Missouri and the "Will of God." There was and will never be another candidate for governor of Missouri that could be evaluated on the job like Mike Parson. Everyone in Missouri knew who Governor Parson was and had an opinion about him and his leadership of Missouri. Governor Parson always felt his election to the position of sheriff of Polk County was most special because those were the people that knew him best. The end of 2020 would be the ultimate litmus test by the people of Missouri. Whether his constituents loved him, hated him, or fell somewhere in the middle, it was time to cast their vote and make their voice heard.

Governor Parson was joined by Director Todd Richardson, MO HealthNet, and Director Dr. Randall Williams, Missouri Department of Health and Senior Services, during a press conference to provide updates regarding COVID-19 in Missouri.

Governor Parson was sworn-in on the steps of the capitol at the 2021 Missouri Bicentennial Inauguration by Judge Sarah A. Castle on January 11, 2021. Governor Parson was joined by First Lady Teresa Parson, daughter Stephanie House, and son Kelly Parson.

Governor and First Lady Parson joined the governor's office staff to celebrate the Super Bowl LVII Lombardi Trophy coming to the Missouri State Capitol.

CHAPTER 12

Appropriate Reaction
Governor Earns Four More Years

"Parson Works for Missouri! It is not just a tagline. It is my dad!"

In the Republican primary, Governor Parson defeated State Representative Jim Neely and U.S. Air Force veteran Saundra McDowell on August 4, 2020. Governor Parson received 74.9 percent of the votes cast in the Republican primary compared to 12.4 percent being received by Saundra McDowell who finished a distant second. This was only the beginning. The work was not done. Mike Parson, the common man with common sense, forged ahead.

Although pleased with the outcome during a pandemic, there was no time to enjoy the primary election victory. In the election process, this was but an intermediate goal. Governor Parson stayed the course. He maintained his focus on being a winner for Missouri over being a winner in an election in the weeks ahead.

On November 3, 2020, Governor Parson defeated the Democrat nominee, State Auditor Nicole Galloway, in the general election. Governor Parson received 1,720,202 votes to the 1,225,771 votes received by his challenger. He received 57.1 percent of all the votes cast for governor in the election. He was the first Republican governor to be elected by a double-digit margin in Missouri modern history. It was only fitting the fifty-seventh governor received 57 percent of the votes. The number fifty-seven became a recurring theme during the tenure of Governor Parson.

After he was declared victorious, Governor Parson told his supporters in Springfield, "People believe in common sense, and I think they want leaders that believe in common sense." He further summarized, "They don't want government to tell them what to do every day. They want to live their lives in peace."

When Governor Parson was elected by the people to the highest office in the state, it validated a commitment by himself and his team to support all Missourians. His undefeated record in elections by the people continued. This election occurred during the most tumultuous period in the history of Missouri and the United States. While guiding the state through the challenges of a global pandemic, Governor Parson and his team had to navigate a polarizing environment. During the election cycle, 99.9 percent of Missourians wanted to tell the governor how to govern and an equal percentage were glad they were not actually the governor themselves. Everyone had the answers, and they aggressively expressed them. Governor Parson was pleased with the overwhelming support he received in the election. He was excited to continue to move Missouri forward. He committed to staying true to Missouri and his supporters but, more importantly, Mike Parson was staying true to himself.

After the election, Governor and First Lady Parson as well as their family were able to take a deep breath and reflect on life's journey. There was no script for this. A boy who grew up in Wheatland in Hickory County was elected by the people of Missouri to its highest political office. With this election victory, Governor Parson had the ability to approach the next four years with the mindset he could "begin with the end in mind." This state of mind may have been different than after previous election victories, but term limits this time would likely put a finality to his political journey. Governor Parson had spent almost all his life in public service.

Mike Parson has forever had a deep commitment to the service of Missourians. Mike's daughter, Stephanie, summarized her observance of his passion this way: "My dad really wanted to serve the people of Missouri. I never really understood why, but he has a genuine love for serving people. From Polk County Sheriff to Missouri Governor, he has always wanted to be a public servant. He may not have had all the things (like a college degree) that the world says you have to have to be successful, but what he had was a heart that wanted to serve the people."

The moment to reflect with the first lady and his family was indeed just a moment. It was time for Governor Parson to continue his leadership and hard work for Missourians. It was no time for a victory lap, but rather it was time to create more victories for the citizens of Missouri. Mike Parson is Mike Parson. He is a God-fearing man who wants the best for Missouri. When his tenure as the fifty-seventh governor of the Great State of Missouri ends, he will remain a God-fearing man who wants the best for Missouri. Governor Parson clearly understood he could go around telling people Missouri was the greatest state in the United States or he could shut his mouth and show people Missouri was the greatest state in the United States. With the work of the campaign behind him, it was time for the governor to join with Missourians to show the world Missouri was one of the best of the best.

Governor Michael L. Parson, on January 11, 2021, was sworn to a full term as the fifty-seventh governor of the State of Missouri at the 2021 Bicentennial Inauguration. The best of the best in Hollywood would have had difficulty writing the script. Governor Parson's career in public service began with six years in the United States Army and over twenty-two years in law enforcement, including serving as sheriff of Polk County from 1993 to 2005. Governor Parson served as the forty-seventh lieutenant governor of Missouri and was a member of the Missouri General Assembly. He now had earned the title of the highest office in the state.

Governor Parson was sworn in by Judge Sarah A. Castle. Judge Castle was appointed by Governor Parson as circuit judge for the Sixteenth Judicial Circuit on October 20, 2020. At the time of her appointment, Judge Castle was serving as associate circuit judge of Division 27, having been appointed by the governor to the bench on January 29, 2020. Judge Castle at the time was the only judge to be appointed twice by Governor Parson. The Bible used by Governor Parson during the swearing-in ceremony was a gift given to him by First Lady Teresa Parson. Also sworn in during the inauguration ceremony were Lieutenant Governor Mike Kehoe, State Treasurer Scott Fitzpatrick, Secretary of State John Ashcroft, and Attorney General Eric Schmitt.

Dr. Jonathan House, son-in-law of Governor Parson, and Alicia House, granddaughter of Governor Parson, performed the National Anthem. Musical selections were performed by the 135th Missouri Army National Guard Band and Missouri State University Chorale, and the Pledge of Allegiance was led by former Jobs for America's Graduates (JAG) student and current Missouri S&T student John Sanders. Dr. Ray Leininger, pastor emeritus of First Baptist Church in Bolivar, delivered the invocation, and the Most Reverend Bishop Shawn McKnight delivered the benediction. Scripture readings were recited by Rabbi Yosef David and Pastor John Modest Miles of Morning Star Baptist Church in Kansas City. A nineteen-gun salute was also performed by the Missouri National Guard during the inauguration ceremony, which concluded with a special salute to Missouri signifying its entry as the twenty-fourth state into the United States two hundred years ago.

A common man, with common sense, who grew up in Wheatland was now the elected governor of Missouri. Those who thought the office was gift wrapped for him had to rest their case. Governor Parson had navigated Missouri through one of its most difficult periods. The leadership of Mike Parson had earned him four more years as governor. The election victory was not the end of the story but a resurgent beginning. Missouri had spoken. It was time for Mike Parson to continue his hard work for Missouri and that is what he did.

Mike Parson and hard work go hand in hand. Mike's son, Kelly, compared the two this way: "It doesn't matter what he does. Whether he was working on the farm, pumping gas, running his own small business, being sheriff, a state representative, a state senator, or the governor, there is not a single person that is going to outwork my dad, no one. Parson works for Missouri! It is not just a tagline. It is my dad!"

Sometimes politics is politics! In some cases, the governor of Missouri is not exempt from the political games that are played. Back in the day at Wheatland High School as a young basketball player, Mike Parson could expect members of the opposing team to attempt to block his shot during a game, but one thing he never had happen was one of his own Mule teammates block his shot. As a matter of fact, one Mule blocking another Mule's shot would be seen by most to be an ass move. On Wednesday, January 27, 2021, Governor Mike Parson woke up excited to deliver his third "State of the State Address" from the House of Representatives chamber as it had been traditionally done each year. Governor Parson had delivered his first two State of the State Addresses to a packed House chamber and saw no reason why his third address wouldn't be the same.

It appeared everything was going as planned again in 2021 until a mere four hours before the address was to be delivered. It was at this moment the House leader informed the governor's office that if the governor wanted to give his address in the House chamber, he would be doing it in an empty chamber. Yes, just four hours before the largest, most highly anticipated political speech of the year, one that had taken place in that same chamber for over one hundred years, the House leader made the communication to the governor's office that it wasn't happening. Suddenly, months of planning, logistics, speechwriting, and statewide communication and coordination came to an abrupt standstill. Speaker of the House Rob Vescovo, also a Republican and by title and position would be considered the ultimate decision maker related to House operations of this magnitude, chose to wait until just four hours before the event to communicate the change. In the political arena, this stunt would be like Chicago Bulls player Scottie Pippen blocking a breakaway dunk attempt by Michael Jordan in the old Chicago Stadium. An unprecedented event Bulls fans would likely regard as the most classless move of all time.

Since Scottie Pippen thought better of ever blocking a Michael Jordan shot, it will never be known how Michael Jordan would have reacted, but since someone felt compelled to block Governor Michael Parson's State of the State Address, Missouri got to witness how this Michael would react. Maybe a reaction is exactly what someone was looking for. Speaker Vescovo had actually conducted House business in the chamber during the morning of the scheduled address. He saw firsthand the work that had gone into preparing for the State of the State Address. Multiple pieces of technology (cameras, microphones, teleprompter, etc.) with associated wiring were in place in the chamber to do a live broadcast and stream of the address. Being the larger of the two general assembly chambers, the address had always occurred in the House chamber. Members of other state agencies along with other outside vendors had spent multiple days preparing for the event. All their hard work and dedication would have been in vain thanks to one ill-intended leader if it had not been for the quick wit, cool resolve, and true leadership of Missouri's fifty-seventh governor.

In football terms, the Parson team, with the support of other key personnel, had to initiate their two-minute offense. There was no reason to watch the clock because time was not on their side. The governor's team first had to gain permission from Senate leadership to use the Senate chamber for the address. After gaining authorization, it was time to begin transitioning the equipment across the capitol to the Senate chamber. One of the greatest challenges to be overcome was the fact the Senate chamber did not have many of the technological capabilities the House chamber did. The State of the State Address had never been done before in this chamber, but it was going to happen now, adding yet another first for the State of Missouri under the Parson administration. It was all hands-on deck. All the technology intended for use, from the House podium to the satellite truck parked outside, was disconnected and prepared for transit. When the job was complete, there were even wires running through interior windows in the Senate chamber to make it all work. Like a well-executed football two-minute drill, with a catch and toe-tap in the back of the end zone, the winning touchdown was secured just as time expired. It is disappointing to think a competition even existed, but it did.

Team Parson would not be denied. The one absolute throughout the day was the remarkable composure shown by Governor Parson. When last-minute communications were made about the location change, inquiries from media outlets quickly followed requesting a comment from the governor on his feelings about the unexpected and untimely change of location. On this day, Governor Parson remained focused on the address. When Director of Communications Kelli Jones was posed the question by an in-state media outlet, her "off the record" comments were quoted in the days that followed. Kelli, who was frantically working at the moment, told the reporter the governor was fine and ready to go, but his communications director's blood pressure was extremely high.

The State of the State Address is one of the marquee events of the political year. It is an opportunity for the governor to provide an annual summary of the condition of the state and is defined in the constitution. Contained in the address is typically a look back at the successes over the last year, a report on the current pulse of the state, and a look forward to the processes the governor has defined to address the challenges and opportunities the state has in the next year. Months of preparation goes into putting the content of the speech together. The State of the State Address is a celebration of sorts. Numerous Missourians are invited to the event to be recognized for their contributions to the state over the last year. The invitations to special guests are extended in some cases multiple months in advance. The recognition of the guests is woven into the content of the address.

It is often a time for the governor, and in this case the Republican Party, to celebrate the successes of the last year, making the decision by the House leadership even more disturbing. Hours of research goes into making sure the address has all the facts related to its content. Multiple media advisories and press releases are issued to make sure everyone is prepared for the event. The address itself is practiced numerous times even in the chamber it will be presented. The content of the speech represents a capstone to a months-long process building out an entire $50 billion budget spanning seventeen state agencies and impacting all 6.2 million Missourians. It was not like the State of the State Address had come out of nowhere. Despite the challenges of COVID-19 over the last year, there were multiple things to celebrate including the responsible way the governor and his colleagues directed the state through the pandemic.

Governor Mike Parson handled the situation like Mike Parson handles all situations. One does not overreact! One does not underreact!

One appropriately reacts! When the communication reached the governor and his staff, there were 240 minutes until the event would begin. Invited guests were already en route to the state capitol.

Missouri is the Show-Me State. The governor and his staff were in a Show-Me Moment. In less than ideal conditions, the governor and his staff pulled off what most would regard as impossible.

When the governor's address was completed, and the dust settled, it was time for the governor to go to work to determine the intended result of the last-minute disruption. The governor quickly learned the actual decision to not allow an audience in the chamber had been made the previous day, but leadership had directed no one to contact the governor's office until the day of the event. One does not have to be a certified investigator to conclude that the decision was purposeful and made with ill intent.

Governor Parson decided in the days that followed to issue a written response to the events which occurred resulting in the moving of the State of the State Address. The governor and his staff, with the assistance of multiple agencies, had worked tirelessly in preparation for the event. Multiple official communications had been made by the governor and his staff. It was critical to Governor Parson that the words and communications made by the governor's office be of high regard.

The letter written by Governor Parson was addressed "To the Republican Members of the General Assembly." In the letter, the governor said the State of the State was an opportunity to "share our successes and vision for the future" but due to the orchestrated actions taken, he concluded, "It is hard to see this as anything other than a purposeful and disgusting scheme to embarrass me and the Office of the Governor." He stated the day became "an insider stunt and petty show of arrogance and political power."

This was definitely a defining moment, but Governor Parson did not let the actions of others define him and his administration. There was no time to sweat the small stuff; it was time for Governor Parson to roll up his sleeves and continue his work for Missourians. Governor Parson and his team faced many challenges over that year, but there was some faint light at the end of this tunnel and it was only going to get brighter. Thanks to Governor Parson's balanced approach and the efforts of millions of Missourians, incredible progress was made in a short amount of time, and the data showed Missouri was winning the fight.

As vaccines increased and more Missourians became eligible, Governor Parson announced that local pharmacies across Missouri would receive prioritized shipments of the COVID-19 vaccine through a new state pharmacy program. Missouri also continued to partner with health centers, local health departments, hospitals, and other community providers to ensure equitable distribution among the state's nine regions.

To reach areas with limited access to healthcare, the state partnered with local healthcare agencies to host mass vaccination events in each of Missouri's nine regions as well as targeted vaccination events in St. Louis and Kansas City. As of March 7, 2021, 108 mass vaccination and fifty-five targeted vaccination clinics had been completed with more than one hundred thirty thousand total doses administered.

Missouri held a mega vaccination event in the parking lot at GEHA Field–Arrowhead Stadium in Kansas City on Friday, March 19 and Saturday, March 20. Two Missouri National Guard mass vaccination teams and personnel from the State Emergency Management Agency (SEMA) and Department of Health and Senior Services (DHSS) partnered with the Jackson County Health Department, Truman Medical Centers/University Health, Kansas City Chiefs, Kansas City Royals, Urban League of Greater Kansas City, Kansas City Area Transportation Authority, numerous volunteers, and other local leaders. Governor Parson remembers vehicles being lined up for miles to get into the stadium. He had seen this scene for a Chiefs game but never for a vaccine. The collaborative effort led to more than 7,250 Missourians being fully vaccinated with the Janssen vaccine during the event at Arrowhead Stadium alone. This far exceeded the state's and local health department's earlier expectations of vaccinating six thousand Missourians over the two-day event.

The level of coordination among the hundreds of professionals and volunteers at the mega vaccination event allowed people to be vaccinated and drive away within twenty-nine minutes after their arrival, including the mandatory fifteen-minute observation period. This time dropped as low as twenty-five minutes during the day on Saturday. The event was well-organized.

This event sticks out to Governor Parson of all the vaccine clinics and events coordinated by the state. There were so many well-run vaccine sites across the state, but since this was at Arrowhead Stadium, he knew it would be massive. He also was a bit skeptical it could be successfully completed. Governor Parson considered the vaccination of over seventy-two hundred people to be a lofty goal in two days. It was amazing to see how well orchestrated everything was and went.

During this period, Governor Parson had to respond to repeated questions about vaccine equity across the state. The governor continually emphasized his desire to make the vaccine accessible to all Missourians who wanted to take it, especially the state's two largest cities. "We cannot thank our partners enough for their efforts in making this event possible for the people of Kansas City. We far exceeded expectations, and the success of last weekend's events show just how much we can accomplish when we work together to find solutions that better serve the people of Missouri," Governor Parson concluded. In the week that followed, a similar mega vaccination event was held in St. Louis. Vaccines, testing resources, and treatments were now readily available for all Missourians, and much of the population had some immunity to the virus.

The governor looks at Missouri in its entirety, a view most will never have. Missouri has fundamentally operated much differently than many states across the country. The first difference is Missouri believes one should operate within their means. One should not spend money they do not have. The budget needs to reflect this annually. The second difference is Missouri pays its bills and it does it on time. This has been the focus for years. Governor Parson committed himself to running a fiscally responsible and efficient operation. When COVID-19 hit the country and state, it was a challenge to all. At that time, federal financial assistance was critical to Missouri and all Missourians. The unprecedented challenges required uncommon practices by all. Unanticipated expenses were being faced while revenues were declining. This trend was faced at both a state and a personal level. Federal assistance was required to help ends meet.

Governor Parson is proud to be a Missourian himself but what speaks volumes about him is the respect he has for all Missourians. He understands the pride Missourians have in themselves and their state. No line emphasizes this more than when Governor Parson says, "Missourians are not looking for a handout, they are looking for a hand up." Handouts and hands ups come in various ways. During the pandemic, states and citizens across the country needed a financial hand up to make ends meet. The expectation that these resources would last forever turns those into a handout. That is not Missouri. Missouri and its citizens were extremely grateful for the financial hands up, but when Missouri and Missourians had regained their footing, it was time to part ways with unnecessary aid. When it was time to get back to work, Missourians responded.

On May 11, Governor Parson announced Missouri would no longer be participating in federal pandemic-related unemployment benefit programs. Data showed Missouri was "back on its feet again." Governor Parson further drew this conclusion from conversations he was having. "From conversations with business owners across the state, we know that they are struggling not because of COVID-19 but because of labor shortages resulting from these excessive federal unemployment programs," Governor Parson said. He further recognized that the hands up was necessary and appreciated, but it was turning into a handout and it was time Missouri moved forward. "While these benefits provided supplementary financial assistance during the height of COVID-19, they were intended to be temporary, and their continuation has instead worsened the workforce issues we are facing," the governor recognized. It was time Missouri ended these programs that had ultimately provided incentive for people to stay out of the workforce.

Despite the challenges presented by COVID during his early tenure, Governor Parson was able to celebrate the two-hundredth anniversary of Missouri becoming a state in August 2021. Missouri Statehood Day, August 10, 2021, marked the milestone since the Missouri Territory became the twenty-fourth state to enter the Union.

Governor and First Lady Parson celebrated the pride they have in Missouri by recognizing the commitment of all Missourians to making the Show-Me State such a special place by declaring it was time to celebrate the past, present, and future issuing the following statement. "As we approach the 200th anniversary of our state this August, we are reminded of the dedication, passion, and love so many people have for Missouri. Missourians work hard every day to continue building on our strong foundation that has made our state a great place to live, work, and raise a family. From our rural areas to the big cities, Missouri offers so much to so many, and the story of our state is one to be remembered, shared, and celebrated."

As part of Missouri's statewide bicentennial celebration, the governor's office hosted a parade in Jefferson City on Saturday, September 18, to showcase Missouri's past, present, and future. The Bicentennial Inaugural Parade celebrated the history and significance of the state of Missouri and celebrated the swearing-in of Missouri's elected officials from the Bicentennial Inauguration in January.

During the day, the Missouri State Capitol featured various community engagement items including the Missouri Bicentennial Quilt, the Missouri State Parks Quilt, and the Missouri Bicentennial Mural. These items were joined on display by the Kansas City Chiefs Super Bowl IV and LIV Trophies; the St. Louis Rams Super Bowl XXXIV Trophy; the Kansas City Royals World Series Trophies from 1985 and 2015; the St. Louis Cardinals World Series Trophies from 1967, 1982, 2006, and 2011; and a St. Louis Blues 2019 Stanley Cup Replica Trophy.

During the evening, the Bicentennial Inaugural Ball was held on the north portico and lawn of the Missouri State Capitol. All of Missouri's state legislators and elected officials were introduced during the grand march at 6:30 PM. This was the first and only time the Inaugural Ball had been held outside. The Lord blessed all the events of the bicentennial celebration with beautiful weather. Governor and First Lady Parson danced to the "Missouri Waltz" to launch the night on the dance floor.

On March 30, 2022, just over two years after his first press conference on COVID-19, Governor Parson put a "so called" end to the pandemic in Missouri and likely two of the most trying years for a Missouri governor and his staff. "Over the past two years, we have learned a lot that will help us respond to future outbreaks and challenges that may come our way," Governor Parson said. "We don't know if this virus will ever completely go away, but we do know that there is no longer a need to live in crisis mode and that we can shift our response to meet the current needs of Missourians. The COVID-19 crisis is over in the state of Missouri, and we are moving on," the governor proclaimed. During the press conference, Governor Mike Parson announced the state would be shifting to the endemic phase of the pandemic on Friday, April 1. The governor applauded the efforts of all Missourians in response to the pandemic. He emphasized the COVID-19 emergency response in place for more than two years had accomplished many positive results in the face of unprecedented challenges. Two of those results were the fact the response addressed the needs of all Missourians during the global pandemic and sustained state operations as more was learned about the novel virus.

There is only one Mike Parson in the world. All Governor Parson wants is the best for Missouri. To make that happen, Governor Parson stayed true to himself and Missouri. He is indeed a special breed. Governor Parson is masterful in the creation of positive relationships. When asked what First Lady Parson sees in her husband that makes him so successful, she had no hesitation in revealing his God-given abilities. First, Governor Parson wants the best for everyone. There is no way he can do everything for everyone, but he wants the best. Second, Governor Parson is willing to listen to everyone. Communication with the ears can be more powerful than communication with the mouth. He will take time to listen and try to deeply understand where they are coming from. Listening leads to understanding but does not always lead to agreement. Lastly and most importantly, Governor Parson wants to do the right thing. He has always had the ability to get people around the table to hear and understand the perspectives of others to create unified solutions. At every stage of his political career, these would be some of the same features identified by his colleagues to be who Mike Parson was and is.

Governor Parson was excited to join local churches across St. Louis for their Grill to Glory events. Every Saturday, these local churches hosted cookouts to feed the community and help get neighborhoods on a path toward stabilization.

Governor Parson and Chief of Staff Aaron Willard were on the King Air to an event.

Governor Parson signed a bill on August 14, 2023, in St. Louis to expand I-70. Senator Lincoln Hough, chairman of Senate Appropriations Committee, joined him.

Governor and First Lady Parson were greeted by Fredbird after Governor Parson threw the ceremonial first pitch at the start of the St. Louis Cardinals baseball game.

Chapter 13

Making the Right Call
Life as Missouri Governor
Stories from Behind the Scenes

"Everything he has ever done has prepared him for where he is."

When looking at a political figure, one sometimes sees a person who is bigger than life as they know it. If they slowed it down, they would observe Governor and First Lady Parson and the Parson family are like many Missourians and Missouri families. The bottom line: they are human! They experience the same emotions as everyone. They experience the same challenges as everyone. The Parson family has had a memorable journey to the highest political office in the State of Missouri, but it must be remembered they are people, too.

THE GOVERNOR DOES GET PISSED

Governor Parson always seems to have a consistent appearance of being cool, calm, and collected. It is important to remember Governor Mike Parson is human just like the everyone. The one significant difference is Mike Parson is the governor of Missouri twenty-four hours a day, seven days a week. Although he always looks happy and cheerful, there are moments when events related to his position just flat out "piss him off." Throughout his life experiences, Governor Parson has learned that how one chooses to react to a situation is the most critical component when addressing a challenge. To identify those moments on the job where the governor's proverbial "blood starts boiling," go to those around him on an almost daily basis. Stephanie Whitaker works as a member of the communications team for the governor. She summarized his unique talent this way:

> When others may just throw a straight up fit, he will just talk through it. Usually with one of his senior staff. He doesn't necessarily want someone to respond. He just wants to talk through it. But by the time he reaches the next event, he knows the time and space to rant is over, and he will get right back on topic. For the Governor to have the special ability to get that done is not the norm. I have worked for

others who would have had their days ruined repeatedly. When a rant is done, it is done! Few have the ability to do that. He knows he has to get the Governor's face back on for the public. When he is upset, he will just talk through the situation. He will seldom raise his voice or curse. He will verbalize why a person or a position is wrong and why he and his team are on the right track. Most often Governor Parson goes to his Director of Communications, Kelli Jones or his Chief of Staff, Aaron Willard. He has a special talent. I want that talent.

SPEAKING FROM HEART: ONE CAN NEVER GO WRONG
One characteristic all those who work around the governor is clearly aware of is one can measure the level of someone's education by degrees but often unmeasurable is the level of impact personal experience can have on making a real difference in the lives of others. It is unfortunate some of these moments of deep impact come in response to tragic events. One of those events occurred on Monday, October 22, 2022. During the morning hours of that day, a nineteen-year-old former student at Central Visual and Performing Arts High School opened fire at the St. Louis school, killing two and injuring several others. The shooter, who also died during an exchange of gunfire, graduated from the high school at the end of the previous school year.

First and foremost, Governor Parson loves all Missourians. When tragic events occur, Governor Parson is personally affected. He understands the most important response during and following the tragic event needs to be the most appropriate response to support all involved. Governor Parson can look at events through lenses few, if any, governors have had the opportunity and responsibility to wear. The governor's primary goal is to provide support for those affected. Some think it would be best for the governor to get to the location of the tragedy as soon as possible. Although this is always considered, it is seldom part of the best and most appropriate response. People and agencies across Missouri are equipped with the expertise and personnel to respond to specific events. Sometimes it is important to stay in one's lane. Many people view the role of the governor as encompassing all lanes. The governor himself agrees with this viewpoint but being responsible for all lanes does not mean one has to micromanage or provide obstacles for those with the expertise who are specifically responsible for overseeing a lane.

Rushing to the scene of a tragic event can sometimes cause more harm than good. These are important considerations when determining when the time is right for the governor to be on the ground supporting the response. When the governor travels, he does not do it alone. Typically, a large number of media outlets cover a governor visit. The governor never wants the logistics surrounding a visit to have a negative impact on those with the specific responsibility to provide for the needs of Missourians. There is a time and place that is best and most appropriate. Although some leaders have and will see these moments as a great photo opportunity, Governor Parson puts all his attention and responses toward supporting those most in need.

Based on his experience in law enforcement, he realizes how distracting a politician and a media entourage can be to an effective and appropriate response during a crisis. Although maybe not perfect all the time, Governor Parson and his team always do their best to be where their value can be most impactful for others and not for him. Following the school shooting in St. Louis, Thursday, October 22, was determined to be that moment. Stephanie Whitaker remembers that day vividly. The shooting had occurred on Monday, so tension from a political perspective remained. Emotions were high related to gun violence and the direction a political response should take. The St. Louis media outlets were seizing this opportunity to bring the debate front and center. The governor had a couple of visits earlier in the day in north-central Missouri to celebrate education successes. In planning the visit that day, the governor and team knew the schedule was going to be tight. It was important to prioritize the visit. Although the media is always a priority, it sometimes does not always get top billing. Numerous communications had taken place by phone in the days following the shooting, but where was the right place and who were the right people needing the governor's support at this moment? Since the St. Louis visit would occur late in the day and the school was still considered a crime scene, the decision was made to go to the St. Louis Metropolitan Police Department and visit with those that responded first to the school shooting.

Stephanie remembers entering a somber room in the police station filled with numerous law enforcement personnel. Unfortunately, moments like this seem to happen too often. It is important for elected officials to show their support for those who did what their job required of them at the most challenging time. In this meeting, the governor was joined by multiple leaders from St. Louis and the St. Louis region. Those leaders addressed the group early in the meeting and thanked the law enforcement officers for a near textbook approach to their response from start to finish in the crisis. An emotional Stephanie remembers vividly, the governor approaching the front of the room to address the officers, spouses, and children that filled the room. She recalls the silence as Governor Parson walked to the front. "You could hear the silence talking as he prepared to begin," Stephanie remembers.

The governor did not say much but what he did say was just what needed to be heard by the people in that room. Stephanie remains moved by his first words, "You made the right call!" "At that moment . . . it was like a wind of relief moved about the room . . . it was like the room shuttered at that moment . . . it was like a weight was lifted," Stephanie continued. Once a law enforcement officer, always a law enforcement officer. One of their own, someone who had been in their shoes, now governor of Missouri, was reassuring them they had done the right thing. Anyone could have said those words, but it was not only the words but rather the heart of the person it was coming from that made the moment. Governor Parson went on to talk about his darkest day in law enforcement. "Only his lived experience gave him the ability to say those words and for that to have any meaning to those officers . . . his words mattered," she concluded. Many important people and leaders said many valuable things that day, but it was the lived experience which mattered most, when it mattered most. When Stephanie Whitaker named a few of her most cherished moments serving Missourians, this moment echoed with great emotion about the heart of Governor Parson.

ALWAYS ACCESSIBLE

After the meeting with the officers and family members, the governor saw a gathering of press members across the street. Governor Parson was on a very tight schedule, but he made time to walk over to the media members, who wasted no time in engaging with him. One of the reporters quickly asked a question through the statement, "Governor . . . many people are blaming the Second Amendment Preservation Act as to why Missouri is absent of red flag laws and cannot remove guns from a household where someone is deemed mentally ill." The governor quickly responded, "That law does not keep them from doing so." Johnathan Shiflett remembers the media aggressively jumping on this statement. "That is not true . . . yes it does," the media retorted.

Johnathan witnessed a complete lack of decorum from the media. "How is he going to recover from this . . . they are just pouncing on him," he recalled asking himself. Based on the aggressive response by the media, it appeared the governor might have said something wrong. Johnathan said the governor had that day, and has always had, the unique ability to bring things back together. "No . . . that law does not prevent that . . . we have laws on the books . . . that allow a judge if they make that determination that someone should not have a gun due to mental illness," the governor explained. The press did not want to hear that. When one thinks there is no way he is going to recover from this, the governor remains calm and answers the questions with the facts as he knows them. He may not know the statute number, but he remains versed in the language primarily due to his experience in law enforcement. He has a special awareness of laws and language many people do not know even exists. The governor is a quick thinker. He always attempts to answer the questions as they pertain to Missouri and Missouri law. Like most, when the governor was able to reflect on his answers, he said he could have done a few things differently by comparing Missouri law to the neighboring state the reporter referred to, but that is not the Governor Parson way.

Those who work closely with the governor soon realize he is a sponge when it comes to the retention of information. This retention, many may regard as unnecessary, has created a special relationship between him and the members of the media. The governor takes a genuine interest in those he interacts with including the members of the press. Sometimes the press tries to create what others may view as an adversarial relationship. The governor knows all people, including the press, have a job to do. The governor remains consistent in his relationship with the press. He takes an interest in the lives of the press members as people and individuals outside of their job. Members of the press sometimes are taken aback by the governor's interaction with them before and after press conferences. He recognizes the members of the press are all people and many of them are fellow Missourians. When a member of the press got married, the governor asked, "How was your honeymoon?" When a member of the press had a child, the governor inquired, "How is that little one?" When there is a new press member, Stephanie Whitaker stated she observes "a what is happening right now moment" when the governor engages in an open personal conversation with members of the press.

THE POWER OF FAITH

Faith plays a powerful role in the lives of Mike and Teresa Parson. Governor Parson understands the power of faith. He does his best to have his ear available to everyone, but the faith community is one he does his best to communicate with on a routine basis. Soon after unexpectedly assuming the role of governor, the faith community served large for the entire state. When civil unrest was threatening Missouri following the death of George Floyd, Governor Parson turned to the religious leaders of his two largest cities. These leaders often bring an unbiased and nonpolitical perspective to situations affecting their communities. Listening, hearing, and understanding were important to Governor Parson. Pro-action over reaction was important when situations allowed. Protecting the lives and the property of Missourians begins with understanding and communication.

The communication with faith-based leaders never stopped. Periodically, the faith-based leaders will stop by the governor's office for a visit. The visits are two-way communication opportunities. Governor and First Lady Parson initiated a monthly faith-based luncheon at the Missouri Governor's Mansion early in his tenure. These opportunities to create open communication have been critical on multiple occasions.

COVID was another time that faith served great value. The faith-based community reached out on numerous occasions while important decisions were being made in the response to COVID. It was only by faith that scriptures shared to the governor would so closely speak to the critical decisions being made at a particular moment in time. Governor Parson read some Bible verses from a card he had received from a young Missourian during a press conference shortly before Easter. The verses were from Esther. The governor held up the card for all to see as he read the contents inside. The communications from people of faith always came at just the right time. This was a God thing, not a governor thing! During this period, encouraging words from the outside were not easy to come by, but when the governor and his team needed a lift, God acted through fellow Missourians to give him that lift.

EXPERIENCE OVER DEGREE

The governor was sworn in as the fifty-seventh governor of Missouri on June 1, 2018. Governor Parson had to hit the ground running. The State of Missouri had experienced a great deal of disorder and embarrassment over the months leading up to his elevation to governor. The turmoil had an impact on all. Repairing and restoring relationships were a must for Governor Parson. These relationships were inside and outside of the boundaries of the state. He understood the importance of the internal relationships that must be mended as well as the ones on the outside.

Within days of taking office, Governor Parson got an opportunity to begin the healing process with the state workers at the Missouri Department of Social Services (DSS). Healing in this case may have been an understatement because the DSS Building in Jefferson City is one of the oldest and had experienced a failure of its air-conditioning system in the days prior to his visit in June. The air conditioning had been restored the day prior to his visit, but the proverbial "heat was on." Governor Parson selected the people who answer the child abuse hotline to be his first to recognize. Stephanie Whitaker remembers the scene clearly. "As we walked into the room, people were clustered together in the back of the room," Whitaker recalled. "It was like those in the room were ready for another contrite politician to breeze in, say thank you so much, get a photo, and leave," she remembers of the vibe she got when entering. The group of people, mostly women, did not expect much.

The governor moved to an area of the room where all could see him, and he began to address the gathering. He did not speak from behind a podium but rather just stood before them. "The work you do answering the child abuse hotline is so critical and I know this because I have been one of the people on the flipside of those calls you have taken . . . I have gone into those homes of those children you have received those calls about," Stephanie recalled him proclaiming. She remembers "the people just being floored and the dynamic of the room suddenly shifting." The governor continued by recognizing their work was hard and often not appreciated at the level it should be by the public. He emphasized his appreciation for the critical nature of their work and for the positive difference they were making for the well-being of those children and all Missourians.

He stressed their interaction with the callers was making a difference in the lives of those children and they often do not get to see the positive difference they are making in the lives of others. Stephanie remembered the governor's closing words being "that what they do is the greatest difference anyone can make in state government . . . they are the rescuers at the most critical moment in a young person's life." Governor Parson was speaking from the heart. "It was evident that hearing the Governor say that their job was meaningful reached their core . . . not because he was the Governor but through his life experience," Stephanie proudly recalled. She remembers that by the end, those in the room wanted a selfie with the governor. His life experiences made him the right person for the moment. "Everything he has ever done has prepared him for where he is," she summarized.

FILLED WITH PRIDE

Governor Parson has experienced many things that have brought him great pride during his tenure as governor. There are moments others witness where there is no denying the pride that filled the governor.

True Difference Makers: Employees of the State of Missouri

Governor Parson is truly about the people of Missouri. He understands it takes all Missourians to make Missouri the special place it is. He knows the whole state is a sum of its parts. He wants all people to understand their worth to the final product. Nothing makes the governor prouder than seeing those that make Missouri great proud of their own contributions. In January 2023, Governor Parson, with the support of the Missouri General Assembly, was able to announce a historical pay increase for all state employees at the Truman Building in Jefferson City. There was no mistaking the pride within the governor as he navigated through the crowd greeting the state employees assembled. Hundreds of state employees stood along the railings of every floor of the building looking down the building's center as the governor began to address the gathering.

State government had come together under Governor Parson's leadership to say thank you for a job well done. Smiles and sounds of appreciation filled the building. The pandemic had made it a difficult time for all Missourians, but together all persevered. A common sense approach was not only the right thing for Missourians as a whole, but it assisted in creating this historical opportunity to reward the employees of Missouri. Making a positive difference for state workers and their families was a special moment for the governor. These employees energize Missouri. The employees of Missouri include both Republicans and Democrats, but that day was not about differences they may possess but rather the pride they had in this great state.

Missouri State Fair

The Missouri State Fair in Sedalia is an annual event where there is no mistaking the governor is full of pride. When Governor Parson walks through the cattle barn at the state fair, he is in his element and filled with pride. There may be no bigger honor for Missouri youth than having the governor ask detailed questions about their livestock as they wash them down for showing later that day. The governor loves when the young farmers "talk shop" with him. There may be no bigger sign of respect than having the Missouri governor stop by and inquire about their livestock and the benefits this experience has had for them.

Election Nights

Election nights are always filled with emotion. November 3, 2020, was Mike Parson's first contested election for governor. There was no mistaking the governor was filled with pride as the election results came in that night. COVID-19 had consumed much of his tenure after being sworn in. The pandemic had a polarizing effect on the political landscape during the preceding months. Voters across the country wanted their voice to be heard through the ballots they cast. The fifty-seventh governor of the Great State of Missouri received 57 percent of the votes cast in the election—the largest margin by any Republican governor candidate in recent history. The election served as a moment of validation for not only Governor Parson but also for his team and for Missouri. Every decision being made leading up to the election was publicly magnified by the media microscope. The voters affirmed that a common sense approach was the right decision for most Missourians.

Young Missourians at Their Best: School Visits

Sometimes "the Grandpa" just comes out in Governor Parson. There is no mistaking the pride he has when making visits to schools across Missouri. When observing a welding project completed by a student or sampling the creation of a culinary arts student, Governor Parson loves to see the pride students have when doing something they may have never envisioned possible. His pride is genuine. Students love when the governor takes time to have a sincere exchange and they appreciate when he takes an interest in what they have invested so much personally.

BUCK SERGEANT PINS A GENERAL

Much like the president of the United States can appoint a general to the United States Armed Forces, the governor of Missouri can do the same for the Missouri National Guard. Regardless of the amount of military service, the president and the governor have this ability and responsibility. Governor Parson served in the United States Army ultimately elevating to the rank of sergeant. A sergeant selecting and subsequently pinning a general is not the military norm unless one happens to be the president or the governor. The president of the United States is the United States Armed Forces Commander in Chief. The governor of Missouri is the Missouri

National Guard Commander in Chief. The governor can promote any officer of rank colonel and above to the position of general.

Being a military man himself, Governor Parson respects the code and honor that is military service. One of Governor Parson's earliest appointments was Brigadier General Levon Cumpton to adjutant general of the Missouri National Guard on August 2, 2019. In October 2020, Adjutant General Cumpton would be promoted to major general. The first ceremony would be the first time Governor Parson would have the opportunity to pin the star on a newly appointed officer. Brigadier General Cumpton was accompanied by his wife and family at the ceremony that took place in the governor's office. Right before the pinning, Governor Parson and then Brigadier General Cumpton had a conversation those in the military will truly relate to. Governor Parson remembers General Cumpton telling him "how humbled and appreciative he was of this appointment." Being the first, Governor Parson had humbling feelings as well and looked at General Cumpton and stated with a grin, "You just got promoted by a Buck Sergeant."

LIFE WITH THE GOVERNOR SECURITY DETAIL

When asked what was one of the biggest transitions, First Lady Teresa Parson said "the constant presence of security." She indicated she did not take much notice of the Governor Security Detail (GSD) surrounding the governor before she and Mike assumed their roles. This observation may be the ultimate compliment to the members of the Missouri Highway Patrol who have served in this capacity. They have a responsibility to be seen while not being seen. Mike and Teresa have a great rapport with the members of the GSD. "They are wonderful people . . . we enjoy them all . . . we have a great relationship with them . . . but to have someone with you everywhere you go was a real eye opener," Teresa remarked of the infusion of the GSD in their lives. The realization GSD would have constant supervision of everything they did was a true indicator that life had changed.

The GSD has a critical role and responsibility in state government. With the critical nature of their work, GSD operations are always well coordinated. The GSD is strictly business all the time. They have procedures and protocols that are non-negotiable, even by the governor. This responsibility is always respected and honored by Mike and Teresa, but they are relationship people. Governor and First Lady Parson spend as much, if not more, time with the GSD than their own family. Over the years, the GSD has become an extension of the Parson family. Spending Christmas Day in Bolivar, away from their own families, to monitor and supervise the activities of the Parson family is a tremendous sacrifice for the members of the GSD. Yes, it is their job, but these members of the highway patrol are people, too. Mike and Teresa do what they can, within boundaries, to make the members of the GSD part of the family.

It was also a transition for the city of Bolivar. Bolivar is proud to be the hometown of Governor Parson. There has never been another governor from Bolivar. When the GSD Suburbans go down Main Street, the citizens of Bolivar know who are in town. At the beginning of Governor Parson's tenure, the GSD garnered much attention. Over time, they became just another part of the great city. Whether it was a trip to the local diner for Saturday morning coffee or to church on Sunday morning, the GSD became a few extra citizens of Bolivar. Some things changed around Bolivar when Mike Parson became governor of Missouri, but one thing that did not change was when Mike Parson was in Bolivar, to them he was Mike.

INTERNATIONAL TRAVEL—NOT A VACATION BUT A BUSINESS TRIP

The perk First Lady Teresa Parson relates most closely to the political responsibilities of the governor has been international travel. The governorship afforded them to travel to numerous countries across the world while in office. These were not vacations but rather business trips. Few Missourians likely have an accurate understanding of the importance trade is to the economic well-being of the state. The Hawthorn Foundation and its investors support the trade mission travel and the diplomatic expenses. These trade missions allow the governor to promote Missouri and Missouri businesses overseas as part of the overall economic development efforts of the administration. People sometimes fail to take the time to realize that most countries of the world are not just like Missouri. On some occasions, members of the House and Senate attend the trips as members of the Missouri delegation. These international trade trips truly serve as an eye-opener for all those who attend. Legislators often have no idea how beneficial international relations are to Missouri when they begin their tenure, but they quickly learn.

The fundamental concept of supply and demand is one Missouri uses to support the state. Missouri has products other countries need. In some countries, they have products Missouri could benefit from. Living in Missouri, it is hard to come to grips with the fact that grain and livestock are totally absent in some countries on the other side of the globe. The ability to negotiate import and export of products is critical to both the state and their country. A second benefit to the economic well-being of Missouri is businesses in other countries often are seeking opportunities to expand in the United States. Missouri has been an attractive landing spot for companies. The workforce in Missouri is among the best in the country. Missouri workers work. Cultivating relationships is one of the specialties of the governor. International relationships can often be as important as those he has with people he grew up with in rural Hickory County.

Governor and First Lady Parson both learned early they do not have much free time on international trips. Despite the time limitations, they have deeply appreciated the opportunity to see the landscapes and enjoy the people they have met. They are grateful for the chance to see many countries they would have otherwise never had the opportunity to see. Those trips were not vacations, but they did give them a sneak preview of places they will likely return to for personal enjoyment after the governor's term is complete.

MAKING THE TOUGHEST CALLS

Being the governor is a tough and a stressful position. The daily decisions of the governor are affecting real people. Everyone can make the statement that they leave work at work, but the only ones they are fooling are themselves. To put some pressure on oneself, be the one person in Missouri that has the final answer on life or death as it relates to the death penalty. The first lady has many initiatives she attends to on her own calendar, so she does not stay fully in tune with the governor and his calendar. This was the situation when the first execution took place during his tenure. About a week out from the execution date, First Lady Parson was still unaware of the scheduled execution, but she was aware she was not seeing the same Mike Parson she saw on most occasions. She saw a man who was "withdrawn." She remembers Mike being eerily closed the entire week. By the day of the execution, she had learned what was consuming him. COVID decisions had weighed heavy on the governor, but decisions during executions made COVID decisions light as a feather in comparison. She never had any details, but she knew the weight was extreme on her husband.

When a person envisions themselves being governor, most likely seldom consider the totality of the decision made in the political office.

Governor Parson is a man of faith. Governor Parson, like any human, fought battles within himself. The governor ultimately understood there was a method in place involving multiple steps and multiple people that led to the recommendation of execution, but a life is a life. If that does not touch the core, one may not be human. Governor Parson loves God and loves people, but he also respects the process.

PASSION FOR THE KANSAS CITY CHIEFS

"It is one of the coolest things you could possibly do," Governor Parson spoke to the close relationship he has garnered with the Kansas City Chiefs. Being governor has allowed Mike Parson to get close to a team he loves as a fan. The experience has been unreal. He has had the opportunity to personally know many in the Chiefs organization including Clark Hunt (chairman and CEO), Mark Donovan (president), Brett Veach (general manager), and Andy Reid (head coach). Governor and First Lady Parson have been lifelong Chiefs fans. Being a Chiefs fan is a title he is very proud of and he had way before adding the title governor.

The Parson family sits on the highest level of the stadium opposite the Chiefs sideline. This is just the vantage point Mike and Teresa Parson desire. "Love going to my seats . . . sitting with the fans . . . outside . . . third, upper level . . . it gets you back to the reality of who you were before you had a title Governor . . . when you are sitting in those seats . . . no one cares who you are . . . we want to wear our Chiefs gear . . . watch the game . . . passionately cheer for a winner," Governor Parson said of his expected experience.

Governor Parson considers himself a passionate Chiefs fan. Although Chiefs Nation is within itself, Chiefs fans do not attend a game at Arrowhead Stadium for the social experience and the governor is no exception. When Governor and First Lady Parson are in their seats at Arrowhead, just like the other seventy-five-thousand-plus Chiefs fans clad in red, they plan to play their role in a Chiefs victory. Disrupting the opposing offense is a must as a Chiefs fan. If one is not going to be a part of the process, they may not be a real Chiefs fan.

When Governor and First Lady Parson get to their seats at a Chiefs game, they stand on equal ground with the other fans in Arrowhead Stadium. For those that have had the opportunity to travel along with them to a Chiefs game, they quickly realize they sit in the same seats when they get inside the stadium, but the way they negotiate the game-day traffic and congested parking lot is not the same. Loyal Chiefs fans must typically find ways to stay positive while waiting in lines at the parking lot gates, at the stadium gates, and even at the portable bathrooms. When the GSD transporting the governor joins local law enforcement near the stadium upon arrival, it is game on. The next thing Governor and First Lady Parson know is the vehicle has stopped, and they are getting out about one hundred feet from the stadium. Out of respect, the Parsons were not asked if they were going to miss this perk of the position after the governor's term is complete, but they will. In a few years, a Chiefs fan will likely see a late model pickup trying to merge into traffic with a silver-haired guy driving and a good-looking lady riding shotgun. If this happens, please take it easy on them, it might just be the former governor and first lady of Missouri trying to get into the parking lot and stadium to support their favorite team.

Governor and First Lady Parson have had the opportunity to be at two of the three Super Bowls the Chiefs have played over the last three seasons. Coincidentally, those were the two the Chiefs won. When in the Chiefs facility during the 2023 NFL Draft hosted by Kansas City, Coach Reid told Governor Parson that based on his undefeated record when in attendance he needed to definitely be at their next Super Bowl. Being lifelong Chiefs fans, Governor and First Lady Parson feel blessed to align a piece of Missouri history with a piece of Chiefs history that will never happen again. On February 1, 2023, the Kansas City Chiefs won Super Bowl LVII defeating the Philadelphia Eagles 38–35 in Glendale, Arizona. Michael L. Parson served as Missouri's fifty-seventh governor at the same time Missouri's only NFL team, the Kansas City Chiefs, were winning the NFL's fifty-seventh Super Bowl. There is the possibility a subsequent Missouri governor will have the opportunity to be in office for more Super Bowl titles, but one thing is certain, the numerical sequence of the Missouri governor and the Super Bowl will never align again. Governor Parson is proud to be an American, a Missourian, and a fan of the Kansas City Chiefs.

In the summer of 2023, Governor Parson boldly acted on this extraordinary occurrence. Unknown to anyone, including the first lady, the governor made the occasion personally permanent by getting a tattoo on his right forearm commemorating the sequence of fifty-seven. The tattoo, designed by one of his granddaughters, included the outline of Missouri with the number 57 and a lightning bolt inside the state outline. He disclosed the tattoo to First Lady Parson first, but the second to see the tattoo were the members of the Kansas City Chiefs following a preseason practice in St. Joseph. It was a special moment for all just to say the least.

When Governor and First Lady Parson are joined by Head Coach Andy Reid and his wife, Tammy, they feel blessed to get to see a side of the Reids few may have the opportunity to see. When asked what they talk about, Governor Parson quickly admitted, "Eventually you are going to talk about football . . . you are not going to pass up that opportunity." The governor is quick to proclaim, "They are just good people." Governor Parson has seen a humorous side of Coach Reid few people get to see. Governor Parson loves the moments talking about leadership, family, and things outside of football. They will forever cherish their times with Andy and Tammy. "There is nothing like having a candid talk with Coach Reid without the lights and cameras," the governor concluded.

THE ICEBREAKER: JUST IN CASE IT WAS MISSED

Most public speakers tend to have a go-to story or joke to serve as an icebreaker when speaking to a large gathering. Governor Parson is no exception. The story of Mike Parson being the governor of Missouri is a special story itself. Governor Parson's story and joke typically begins a public engagement by conveying the honor and privilege it is to be the fifty-seventh governor of Missouri. Whether she is in attendance or not, he follows by introducing First Lady Parson and has a heartfelt expression of how important she is to him and the state. The introduction leads to the governor ultimately asking the first lady the question, "In your wildest dreams, have you ever imagined us being where we are today as the Governor and First Lady?" Governor Parson usually pauses briefly. The crowd at this point is moving to the edge of their seats anxious to hear the answer to a question they would have asked the first lady themselves. The dramatic pause is then followed by the dramatic response. Governor Parson takes a deep breath and then reveals the first lady's answer to him saying, "You might think I would have Mike, but you are not in my wildest dreams." Now that is an icebreaker!

HE MAY NOT ALWAYS READ THE DIRECTIONS
(ONE STORY FROM TIME IN GENERAL ASSEMBLY)

Mike Parson seldom missed a day of work while a state representative or senator. Finding a way to work through times of illness was a Parson requirement. While at home preparing to head back to work in Jefferson City, Mike told Teresa he was not feeling well and thought he may be coming down with a cold. Teresa handed Mike a tablet of cold medicine in a wrapper and told him if he started to feel worse to take the tablet. As Mike neared Camdenton, he started to feel worse. He decided he should take the cold medicine. As he opened the wrapper, Mike's first thought was this tablet was awfully large but if Teresa told him it would help, he was going to give it a shot. Mike proceeded to pop the tablet into his mouth. The next thing Mike knew he was foaming at the mouth. Not a little bit of foam but a lot. Mike was wearing a suit as he was headed to the capitol. The foam just kept coming. To keep the foam off his suit, he leaned forward over the steering wheel as he approached a traffic signal in Camdenton.

At this point, Mike is scrambling when he stops in the lane next to another car stopped at the light. He is trying everything he can to capture the foam before it gets on his suit. At that moment, he looks to his right out the passenger window to see a mother with her son riding in the back peering at him. He feels the mother and son had to have been traumatized by what they saw. They just observed a silver-haired politician headed to Jefferson City to do work for the people of Missouri who was foaming at the mouth. Mike thought he might have smiled at them but felt they did not see his kind gesture due to the foam. When the light turned green, Mike proceeded to the nearest business parking lot to stop and regroup. He immediately called Teresa. Mike asked her, "What did you give me?" Teresa knew he could not have made it all the way to Jefferson City yet. Mike told her he started to feel worse and had taken the tablet she had provided him. He then reported he began foaming from the mouth. Teresa responded, "Good Lord, Mike Parson . . . didn't you read the directions!" Let's just say when taking an Alka-Seltzer cold tablet it is important to read the directions.

Every year, Governor and First Lady Parson hosted a fall festival at the mansion. People from around the state came to enjoy the fall festivities and see the autumn decorations. Governor and First Lady Parson enjoyed seeing all the unique costumes; in 2019, a T-Rex seemingly bit the governor during a photo.

Governor Parson began a tradition to drive his tractor to work in honor of the FFA tradition where students drive their tractors to school during National FFA Week. Every year he drove his tractor to the capitol.

Governor Parson loves his farm. Getting behind the wheel of one of his John Deere green tractors has never gotten old.

Chapter 14

Made His Mark
Legacy of Governor Parson

"He was poised to leave the Office and State in a better place than he found it."

Being the fifty-seventh governor of Missouri was not something Michael L. Parson ever took lightly. He and Team 57 worked hard every day to make Missouri a better place for all. The level of intensity in the governor's office is very different than most places. Governor Parson knows firsthand that to be a good leader he must surround himself with the best and make them better every day.

Looking through the years of this administration, there were so many firsts and so many wins to celebrate. Team 57 is a unique team that truly became a family over the years. From marriages, births, and the happiest days of life to the darker days like a death in the family, they always supported each other and cared for one another just like a family would do. Team 57 was never about egos or advancing their own agendas; all were just simply proud to be part, whether big or small, of the historic work accomplished on behalf of all Missourians.

When it all started, Governor Parson focused on two categories he knew were nonpartisan and could move Missouri forward: workforce development and infrastructure. From day one, he never wavered. Governor Parson and the words "workforce development" and "infrastructure" will become synonymous in the archives of Missouri history.

WORKFORCE

Governor Parson understood the importance of education and workforce development that was needed to meet the demands of the future. Throughout his time as governor, he worked hard to improve education and provide more options for high-demand job training. From early childhood education to post-secondary opportunities, Governor Parson made substantial investments aimed at giving more Missourians the education and training necessary to fill the jobs of tomorrow.

Governor Parson is a firm believer that an education and a job are the game changers for reducing crime and substance abuse. Although many politicians rant about education and reform and never get anything done, Governor Parson and Team 57 moved full force throughout his time in office to reform and improve education and the workforce. He also made historical investments in secondary education and higher education. When the private sector, secondary education, and higher education all work together, transformational opportunity for Missourians is the result.

The foundation formula for the Department of Elementary and Secondary Education (DESE) was fully funded every year under the Parson administration. Governor Parson also funded student transportation at historical highs. This created additional resources for school districts to invest in other needs, like teacher pay. Governor Parson increased the baseline pay for Missouri's teachers by nearly $15,000. Team 57 began early in Governor Parson's administration to reorganize and focus on early childhood development. In 2021, Governor Parson established the Office of Childhood, through Executive Order 21–02, to consolidate childhood programs across the state. This streamlined the process to make all efforts for Missouri children more efficient. He continued this momentum by signing Executive Order 22–01 to further cut bureaucracy, streamline processes, and increase the efficiency of state government. Toward the end of Governor Parson's term, he appropriated the largest increase in funding for early childhood education in the state's history. The focus on early childhood the governor chose to prioritize will pay dividends for decades to come.

Career and technical education (CTE) was also significantly expanded under Governor Parson's leadership. He knew, just like himself, not every person was destined to earn a college degree. Governor Parson knew the world wasn't going to be short of MBAs and attorneys but rather welders, plumbers, and electricians. Hundreds of new CTE programs were created to help thousands of Missourians earn a good living. Businesses worked with educational institutions to train students, so they could get a job after graduation. The Office of Apprenticeship and Work-Based Learning Division was created under the Department of Higher Education, which led to statewide strategies that engaged business and industry stakeholders to develop and implement solutions in partnership with education systems. Missouri soon became a national leader, rising to second in the nation for apprenticeships and creating over fifty-seven thousand new apprenticeships during the Parson administration.

Governor Parson packaged a piece of legislation with workforce development and economic development called "Best in the Midwest" to help give Missouri an advantage when competing with other states. The "Best in the Midwest" created a new statewide strategy for economic development. To complement this new strategy, Governor Parson launched two successful programs that have proven to benefit many Missourians and companies. Missouri Fast Track filled workforce gaps through financial aid for adult learners pursuing education and training in high-demand industries, and Missouri One Start improved Missouri's workforce programs that helped businesses recruit, onboard, and train a large number of job applicants during major expansions. Governor Parson invested every year in these programs to continue the development of employer-driven workforce education and training programs in high-demand occupations. Missouri soon made its way to the top ten in the nation for customized workforce training programs.

INFRASTRUCTURE

Governor Parson knew for people to live and work where they want, they must have quality infrastructure to support them. When seeking the greatest way to improve the lives of Missouri citizens, infrastructure is one of the surest paths. It brings both economic growth and safety improvement to Missouri and its people.

When Governor Parson came into office, more than nine hundred of the state's 10,424 bridges were in poor condition. To start addressing this issue, in 2019, he proposed a plan to repair or replace 250 of the state's worst bridges. As a result, the Focus on Bridges program was launched, which utilized a combination of cash, bond proceeds, and federal grants totaling $350 million to rebuild or replace Missouri's bridges in the worst condition. All 250 were completed. The strategic financial planning allowed Governor Parson to not only fix these bridges but also replace others across the state, including the I-70 Bridge near Rocheport and the Buck O'Neil Bridge in Kansas City and repair the I-270 Corridor in St. Louis. Over one thousand bridges across Missouri have been repaired or replaced.

Governor Parson didn't stop there. He also recognized the need to improve low-volume roads and other long-neglected infrastructure needs. He committed hundreds of millions of dollars in new funding to low-volume roads, levees, water ports, airports, and rail safety through cost-share programs with local communities. During Governor Parson's tenure, approximately seventeen thousand miles of Missouri's roadways were repaired. This is approximately 50 percent of Missouri's entire highway system, and Missouri has the seventh largest system in the United States. The impact has been transformational, having a positive effect on future planning.

Each year in Missouri a Statewide Transportation Improvement Plan (STIP) lays out every transportation project planned to be done over the next five years. When Governor Parson became governor, the five-year STIP included about $2.5 billion in projects. Before Governor Parson leaves office, the STIP will include nearly $14 billion in projects—five and a half times the original size.

When it came to infrastructure, there was no doubt Missourians and the nation were taking notice of the accomplishments Governor Parson was making in Missouri, but he didn't stop there. Governor Parson took on one of the busiest corridors in the country—Interstate 70 (I-70) and made one of the largest infrastructure investments in Missouri state history. I-70 serves as the engine for economic growth and prosperity for Missouri and is a vital supply chain link through America's heartland. It also connects Missouri's two largest cities—Kansas City and St. Louis—and carries more rural daily traffic than any other route in Missouri.

In 2023, $2.8 billion was allocated to rebuild and add a third lane to over two hundred miles of I-70 in each direction across the state. Long after Governor Parson has left office, the economic benefit of this project will still be felt, and the transformation of I-70 will be one of the governor's most remembered legacy items.

It was important to Governor Parson to also improve Missourians' connection to the internet. Governor Parson believed if electricity could be put in every Missouri home, the same could and should be done with broadband in the modern age. When he became governor, many of Missouri's rural and underserved urban communities still lacked access to high-speed internet. In response, Governor Parson invested over $2 billion to expand broadband access to Missouri's rural and underserved urban communities as well as school districts. He knew expanding broadband was essential to Missouri's infrastructure. Nearly one hundred thousand new and improved connections were established in hard-to-reach areas under the Parson administration, and before he leaves office, Governor Parson will have implemented a plan to connect all Missouri residents to high-speed internet within five years. This will complete a decade-long push to connect all Missourians to quality broadband.

Infrastructure was central to the mission of the Parson administration, and tremendous success was achieved. Smooth roads, strong bridges, and fast internet are just a few results of the common-sense Parson priorities that will serve Missourians for generations to come.

BETTER GOVERNMENT

Governor Parson was on a mission from day one on the job to change the perception of state workers for the general public as well as themselves. He wanted his forty-eight-thousand-plus state workers to feel valued and proud to serve Missourians, instead of being just "state workers." He knew how important it was to have and to keep a quality state workforce. He began his cultural transformation and was successful.

The cabinet was a priority. For state employees to feel supported, Governor Parson focused first on his top leaders. He wanted his cabinet members to know they were supported, and they should break down silos in state government by working together as a team. Governor Parson invested in his cabinet, and through the years of his administration, his cabinet became a powerhouse. Being some of the strongest leaders in the nation, their motivation and energy began to filter down to Missouri's state team members. Immediately, a renewed sense of pride in their work and in the people they served was noticed. Customer service improved. Efficiency improved.

While state team member pay was not the only piece that needed to be improved, Governor Parson understood it had long been neglected and was a good place to start. To obtain and retain qualified, hardworking employees, state government had to keep up with the private sector. Since the start of his administration, Governor Parson increased state team member pay by nearly 25 percent, a historical investment, through targeted and across-the-board pay plans, all to ensure continuity of state services, combat inflationary wage pressures, and improve competitiveness with the private market. He improved employee benefits, increased the deferred compensation employer match, and even approved a couple of extra days off during Christmas, the Fourth of July, and a new, permanent state holiday, Juneteenth.

Governor Parson and his administration invested in giving state team members opportunities for professional growth. A Quarterly Pulse Survey (QPS) was conducted four times a year, so state team members could provide feedback on program development and enhancements. Many learning opportunities came to fruition such as MO Learning (teaches more than twelve thousand courses available), Leadership Academy (helps state team members become better leaders), ShowMe Excellence (helps team members continuously improve departments to better serve citizens), Show Me Challenge (allows team members to submit work improvements), and MO Appreciation (builds a culture of meaningful appreciation for team members and their work). After several years of offering these programs, state team members participated and grew in their fields, improving the retention and recruitment of workers.

HISTORICAL FIRSTS

Through Governor Parson's tenure as governor, he experienced many historical firsts that may never be repeated. Just the fact he took over as governor after his predecessor resigned was unique within itself. He then was tasked to appoint five Missouri statewide elected officials: Lieutenant Governor Mike Kehoe, Attorney General Eric Schmitt, State Auditor Scott Fitzpatrick, Attorney General Andrew Bailey, and State Treasurer Vivek Malek who was the first minority statewide official. These appointments opened the door for big opportunities for these five individuals to pursue.

A significant role of the governor is to make judicial appointments. He had the opportunity to set a record of over 160 judicial appointments, over 40 percent of the state's entire judiciary, surpassing a previous record of 132. Under Governor Parson's leadership, he also had the honor of appointing three Missouri Supreme Court judges. It was over thirty years since a governor had named two supreme court judges within the same year and a couple of decades since a governor had appointed three during a single administration. His first was the Honorable Robin Ransom, the first African American woman to be appointed as a judge on the Supreme Court of Missouri. He later had the opportunity to appoint Judge Kelly C. Broniec and Judge Ginger K. Gooch. With these appointments, for the first time in Missouri's history, there was a female majority on the Missouri Supreme Court. The judicial ideology of the Missouri Supreme Court significantly changed when Governor Parson made these three appointments. He truly reshaped and strengthened the makeup of the state's highest court for decades to come.

Governor Parson also pledged to do things differently than administrations had done before, and that included addressing the backlog of nearly thirty-seven hundred clemency applications sitting in the governor's office. He directed his staff to begin reviewing clemency files and getting cases to his desk for a decision as timely as possible. Whether clemency was granted or denied, he and his team were committed—at the very least—to providing answers to as many individuals as possible. The backlog has been depleted. Governor Parson and Team 57 are proud of their commitment to working diligently to address the backlog and grant approximately seven hundred pardons and twenty commutations, denying twenty-eight hundred requests for clemency.

MISSOURI ECONOMY

While Governor Parson was in office and even after facing a pandemic, Missouri's economy boomed. Unemployment fell to its lowest in state history at 2.1 percent under Governor Parson's leadership. At one point, for every unemployed Missourian there were more than two job openings available.

Workforce development and infrastructure priorities are extremely important, and as a result companies wanted to start and continue to do business in Missouri. Partnerships between the state and private companies helped create over one hundred ten thousand new jobs and over $15 billion in capital investments, and that's excluding thousands more jobs and billions invested without state incentives.

Business investments and job creations were accomplishments for Governor Parson and his team. Some of the larger companies investing in Missouri under his leadership were American Foods Group, Chewy, Meta, Ace Hardware, Bayer, General Motors, EquipmentShare, Accenture, James Hardie, Swift Prepared Foods, and Deli Star. Governor Parson knew all along if the focus was on workforce development and infrastructure, businesses would follow.

Trade missions were an important part of the equation when it came to economic development. With Missouri being in the middle of the United States surrounded by waterways, railways, and highways, Governor Parson knew many countries would find this appealing to do business. He and the first lady traveled to France, Germany, Switzerland, Australia, the United Kingdom, Ireland, the Netherlands, Israel, United Arab Emirates, Greece, Sweden, and Japan before entering his final year as governor. In fact, from his trade missions alone, Missouri has been able to achieve over one thousand new jobs and more than $1 billion in business investment for Missouri, and the count will grow as more deals continue to be inked thanks to his efforts.

A booming and thriving Missouri economy allowed Governor Parson and his team to make three separate tax cuts, one of which was the largest income tax cut in Missouri history. Missourians saw their state income tax decrease by over 20 percent while Governor Parson was in office. Missourians work hard, provide for their families, pay their bills, and pay their taxes. Governor Parson believed when the coffers were full, Missourians deserved to keep their hard-earned money and not spend it for the sake of spending. This helped Missouri families make ends meet and maybe save a little, too.

The experience and common sense Governor Parson had used in running a business became very helpful in running a state. While many states struggled after battling the pandemic, Missouri's economy thrived and has done so the entire time he was in office. With his conservative spending and targeted investments, Missouri maintained a AAA credit rating each year and will leave an estimated $1.5 billion surplus in the budget. Missouri is financially stable and better than he found it.

Over the course of his six and half years in office and the thousands of speeches he delivered to audiences across the state, one of Governor Parson's favorite lines to give at the end of each speaking engagement was, "Do you know that when a speaker says 'in conclusion' 85 percent of the audience pays attention?" So, in true G57 fashion, "in closing," being the governor of Missouri was a life-changing opportunity for Michael L. Parson. His story, one of rags to riches, brought him from a small-town farm boy in Wheatland, Missouri, to gas station owner, county sheriff, state representative, state senator, lieutenant governor, and governor of the Great State of Missouri, something he nor anyone else probably ever imagined until it happened.

But one thing that is evident and speaks to the soul of Mike Parson is out of all the titles he has held none were more important than husband, father, and "Gramps." Throughout his career and life, family came first. But it was with the same principled character that Mike Parson would serve as Missouri's fifty-seventh governor. With every decision he has made, he has made it because he truly felt it was the right decision. Just as he has always wanted the best for his children and grandchildren, he fought for the same for Missouri's children and the next generations.

Governor and First Lady Parson have worked their whole lives to help ensure the next generations have the same opportunity at the American Dream they had. They saw it as not only a privilege to do so but a responsibility. To them, the American Dream should be achievable for all and never the exception for some. Each day, they woke up happy to take on the criticism, critiques, and crude comments because Missouri's children, Missouri's families, and Missouri are worth fighting for.

Mike and Teresa lived their American Dream, one of faith, family, and patriotic service. A dream that allowed a rowdy farm boy and a bright and beautiful woman to meet. Together, they would grow crops, grow businesses, and grow a family. Together, they grew a wonderful life.

Life took them from turnin' wrenches to turnin' the key of the Missouri Governor's Mansion. Now, after a lifetime of service, achieving a successful career, and building a beautiful family, they'll return to where it all started. Mike and Teresa will spend the remainder of their lives on their farm in Bolivar enjoying life with family and friends. And while there are sure to be days where they look back on their time in public service with nostalgic pride and critical wonder for what more could be done, for them, just as it has always been, there will be no turnin' back.

From Governor Parson himself, "It was an honor and privilege to have served as the 57th Governor of the state of Missouri. God bless you, God bless the great State of Missouri, and God bless the United States of America."

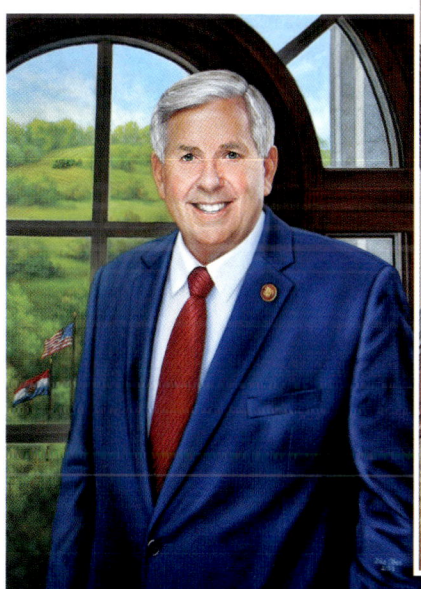

The official painting of Governor Parson by Lisa Ober will be permanently displayed in the Missouri capitol.

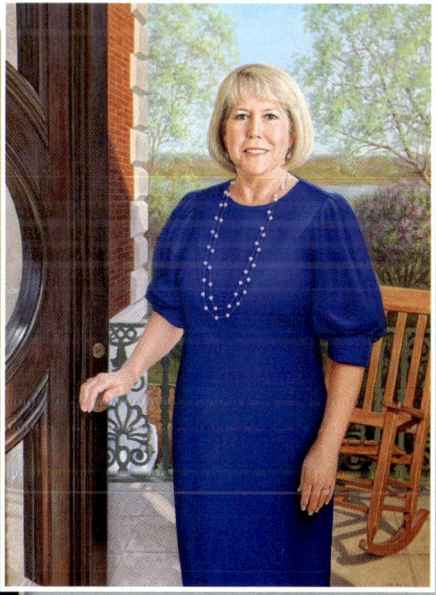

The official painting of First Lady Parson by Lisa Ober will be permanently displayed in the Missouri Governor's Mansion.

A Governor Parson
Thank You to Two Special Team Members

Governor Mike Parson has worked alongside many special people over his career. As he prepares to write life's next chapter, he wanted to pause to reflect on two individuals who have been with him every step of the way during his tenure as the fifty-seventh governor of Missouri. Aaron Willard (chief of staff) and Kelli Jones (deputy chief of staff) have been unwavering allies of Governor Parson even before he was Governor Parson. When expressing his feelings about Aaron and Kelli, Governor Parson emphatically declared, "I will be forever grateful for their unwavering loyalty to not only me but to this great state." Aaron and Kelli have been on the front lines with the governor every day, providing their valuable intuition. Prior to a decision being made by the governor, it must survive thorough examination by Aaron and Kelli. The governor always makes the final decision, but what he said he appreciated most about Aaron and Kelli was that "these two have never questioned a decision, after a decision was made." This type of loyalty is hard to find. To speak to this realization, Governor Parson followed, "I can tell you, not everyone is that way." Governor Parson stressed that Aaron and Kelli were his "go to people" while governor. When looking back, Governor Parson has no hesitation in expressing the level of influence Aaron and Kelli had on him, the governor's team, and Missouri.

Kelli came to the lieutenant governor's office in December 2016 and took on the nickname of "Teach" to Governor Parson. When asked if Kelli was too tough or too soft of a grader of his speeches, the governor responded with the English teacher fearing answer, she is always fair. The speed of operations increased significantly when they were elevated to the governor's office. In the lieutenant governor's office, they were looking for things to do, but in the governor's office, there is never a shortage of things to do. The governor felt Kelli served as an anchor in the transition. Shortly after moving to the governor's office, Aaron Willard was named chief of staff. Governor Parson knew right away that Aaron and Kelli would face challenges none of them could anticipate during the transition. With Aaron and Kelli, Governor Parson immediately realized he had two first-team all-pro players. The important thing then was building the team around them. He reflected that both Aaron and Kelli used their wisdom and experience to move him and Missouri forward.

Kelli served as director of communications for the governor before being elevated to the position of deputy chief of staff in July 2023. As director of communications, she prided herself on creating great and respectful relationships with all members of the media. She learned early on that media reporting is not an exact science. The placement of a few words by these word wizards can quickly turn fact into fiction. When the goal of media outlets was beating their competition to the punch and getting more hits on social media than their rivals, accuracy was sometimes sacrificed. Kelli was always available, fair, and consistent with members of the media. Respect was a two-way process. When a media member would not meet respect with respect, Kelli was not afraid to place that member in the "penalty box." If someone committed an infraction, they faced the consequences.

Governor Parson still cringes at the fact Kelli analyzes every word he says from an English teacher perspective, but he never ignored the guidance, leadership, and advice she provided him and the team. The governor and "Teach" realized quickly it may be a little late to fix the English, but Kelli knew the God-fearing man who only wanted the best for Missouri always spoke from the heart. He may not have gotten straight As in her English class, but he was right on when speaking what he felt was best for Missouri.

When speaking about the importance of communication from the governor's office, especially during COVID, Governor Parson highlighted the commitment of Kelli Jones to the effort. "I will tell you one thing . . . Kelli Jones . . . she is as tough as nails . . . she never wavered one time . . . she said if you need to go on the battlefield . . . I am going . . . that is what her level of commitment was," the governor spoke of her unwavering loyalty.

Aaron was the governor's first hire to his most critical position after being named Missouri governor. Prior to becoming governor, he had the opportunity to witness the political expertise of Aaron from a distance and up close. Aaron had a variety of experiences in the political arena at both the state and federal levels. When Governor Parson made the decision to run for lieutenant governor, he consulted with Aaron as he believed him to have an extremely sharp political mind. Governor Parson would be the first to declare that Aaron may be the smartest person in the capitol.

When there was talk around the capitol that Lieutenant Governor Parson may become Governor Parson, Aaron was approached by the lieutenant governor about assisting in the transition if it occurred. Aaron was humbled by the request and instantaneously put his political mind in governor mode. Lieutenant Governor Parson knew Aaron would have the blueprint. Aaron subsequently developed a comprehensive plan to guide the governor during the transition. Aaron's playbook has served as a beacon for Governor Parson and Missouri.

Governor Parson regards Aaron as a "no nonsense person who is driven by the numbers." Aaron has data and statistics that support every decision he recommends. If a decision cannot be supported by the facts, it is not a decision worthy of being made. Aaron knows the political landscape as well as anyone in the capitol. One does not have to read between the lines to determine where Aaron stands on the issues. When a person crosses the line with Aaron, there is no mistaking it. Converse to the governor, Aaron may add a curse word or two to his vocabulary when someone strikes a nerve. They may even each other out. Maybe by design, since the governor always emphasizes a balanced approach.

Aaron may frequently serve the role of enforcer and protector, but the governor is quick to point out that he gets to see a side of him few get to see. "Aaron has heart and compassion few people outside the office get to witness. He truly loves and cares about people. It is humbling to see him emotional when discussing issues critical to the well-being of all Missourians," Governor Parson spoke of Aaron.

Aaron frequently serves as the liaison between the legislators and the lobbyists and the governor. He serves a similar role in the leadership of the governor's cabinet. Almost everything that gets to the governor moves through Aaron. Governor Parson recited Aaron's "go to" phrase saying, "Don't come to me with a problem, unless you have a solution."

When the governor approached Aaron about his potential interest in being his chief of staff, the governor realized quickly he was being interviewed by Aaron. Aaron did not need a job; if he was to take the position it would be because he wanted to make a positive difference for Missouri. Aaron wanted to know if the governor's plan was to be slow and controlled or was to swing for the fences and be big and bold. The governor looked Aaron directly in the eyes and responded, "Let's go big and bold." It was the right answer. As they say, the rest is history!

Governor Parson will forever be the fifty-seventh governor of the Great State of Missouri, but at the end of 2024, his first chapter as life after governor will be written. One thing he will never forget are those who walked beside him in his administration every step of the way. To the governor, Aaron and Kelli did not treat their time on the governor's team as a job but rather a calling. The steadfast loyalty and dedication of Aaron and Kelli to him and Missouri will be forever etched into the mind of G57.

Governor Parson was briefed by Kelli Jones, his communications director at the time, for the media avail following the 2021 Missouri Bicentennial Inauguration.

Governor Parson laughed with Chief of Staff Aaron Willard after the 2021 Missouri Bicentennial Inauguration.

APPENDIX

MICHAEL L. PARSON
LIFETIME ELECTION RECORD

General Election: November 3, 2020
Governor (3692 of 3692 Precincts Reported)

Mike Parson	**Republican**	**1,720,202**	**57.1%**
Nicole Galloway	Democratic	1,225,771	40.7%
Rik Combs	Libertarian	49,067	1.6%
Jerome Howard Bauer	Green	17,234	0.6%
Arnie C. (AC) Dienoff	Write-in	4	0.0%
Theo (Ted) Brown Sr.	Write-in	5	0.0%
Martin Lindstedt	Write-in	4	0.0%

Total Votes 3,012,287

Primary Election: August 4, 2020
Governor (3575 of 3575 Precincts Reported)

Raleigh Ritter	Republican	27,264	4.0%
Mike Parson	**Republican**	**511,566**	**74.9%**
James W. (Jim) Neely	Republican	59,514	8.7%
Saundra McDowell	Republican	84,412	12.4%
Party Total 682,756			
Nicole Galloway	Democratic	455,203	84.6%
Jimmie Matthews	Democratic	20,586	3.8%
Antoin Johnson	Democratic	20,254	3.8%
Eric Morrison	Democratic	32,403	6.0%
Robin John Daniel Van Quaethem	Democratic	9,481	1.8%
Party Total 537,927			
Rik Combs	Libertarian	4,171	100.0%
Party Total 4,171			
Jerome Howard Bauer	Green	862	100.0%
Party Total 862			

Total Votes 1,225,716

MICHAEL L. PARSON
LIFETIME ELECTION RECORD

General Election: November 8, 2016
Lieutenant Governor (3237 of 3237 Precincts Reported)

Russ Carnahan	Democratic	1,168,947	42.3%
Mike Parson	**Republican**	**1,459,392**	**52.8%**
Steven R. Hedrick	Libertarian	69,253	2.5%
Jennifer Leach	Green	66,490	2.4%
Jake Wilburn	Write-in	87	0.0%

Total Votes 2,764,169

Primary Election: August 2, 2016
Lieutenant Governor (3214 of 3214 Precincts Reported)

Winston Apple	Democratic	38,372	12.0%
Russ Carnahan	Democratic	243,157	75.9%
Tommie Pierson Sr.	Democratic	38,700	12.1%
Party Total 320,229			
Arnie C. (AC) Dienoff	Republican	29,872	4.6%
Bev Randles	Republican	282,134	43.9%
Mike Parson	**Republican**	**331,367**	**51.5%**
Party Total 643,373			
Steven R. Hedrick	Libertarian	3,507	100.0%
Party Total 3,507			

Total Votes 967,109

General Election: November 4, 2014
State Senator District 28 (110 of 110 Precincts Reported)

Mike Parson	**Republican**	**34,573**	**100.0%**

Total Votes 34,573

APPENDIX 299

MICHAEL L. PARSON
LIFETIME ELECTION RECORD

Primary Election: August 5, 2014

State Senator District 28 (120 of 120 Precincts Reported)

Mike Parson	Republican	**27,014**	**100.0%**
Party Total 27,014			

Total Votes 27,014

General Election: November 2, 2010

State Senator District 28 (151 of 151 Precincts Reported)

Parson, Mike	**REP**	**47,380**	**83.7%**
Hatfield, Bennie B.	CST	9,213	16.3%

Total Votes 56,593

Primary Election: August 3, 2010

State Senator District 28 (151 of 151 Precincts Reported)

Wilson, Larry D.	REP	9,590	31.3%
Emery, Ed	REP	6,533	21.3%
Parson, Mike	**REP**	**14,518**	**47.4%**
Hatfield, Bennie B.	CST	107	100.0%

Total Votes 30,748

General Election: November 4, 2008

State Representative District 133 (27 of 27 Precincts Reported)

Parson, Mike	**REP**	**14,325**	**100.0%**

Total Votes 14,325

MICHAEL L. PARSON
LIFETIME ELECTION RECORD

Primary Election: August 5, 2008

State Representative District 133 (27 of 27 Precincts Reported)

| **Parson, Mike** | **REP** | **10,831** | **100.0%** |

Total Votes 10,831

General Election: November 7, 2006

State Representative District 133 (27 of 27 Precincts Reported)

| **Parson, Mike** | **REP** | **10,831** | **100.0%** |

Total Votes 10,831

Primary Election: August 8, 2006

State Representative District 133 (27 of 27 Precincts Reported)

| **Parson, Mike** | **REP** | **3,876** | **100.0%** |

Total Votes 3,876

General Election: November 2, 2004

State Representative District 133 (31 of 31 Precincts Reported)

Pankey, Marvalene	DEM	3,197	20.8%
Parson, Mike	**REP**	**11,471**	**74.7%**
Watson, F. Troy	LIB	689	4.5%

Total Votes 15,357

MICHAEL L. PARSON
LIFETIME ELECTION RECORD

Primary Election: August 3, 2004

State Representative District 133 (31 of 31 Precincts Reported)

Pankey, Marvalene	DEM	1,966	100.0%
Stark, Tom	REP	2,017	25.7%
Alexander, Sam	REP	2,225	28.3%
Parson, Mike	**REP**	**3,464**	**44.1%**
Harman, Mike	REP	152	1.9%
Watson, Jesse O.	LIB	30	100.0%

Total Votes 9,854

General Election: November 7, 2000

Polk County Sheriff

Michael L. Parson	**REP**	**8,116**	**100.0%**

Total Votes 8,116

Primary Election: August 8, 2000

Polk County Sheriff

Michael L. Parson	**REP**	**3,178**	**100.0%**

Total Votes 3,178

General Election: November 5, 1996

Polk County Sheriff

Michael L. Parson	**REP**	**7,183**	**100.0%**

Total Votes 7,183

MICHAEL L. PARSON
LIFETIME ELECTION RECORD

Primary Election: August 6, 1996

Polk County Sheriff

Michael L. Parson	REP	2,551	100.0%

Total Votes 2,551

General Election: November 3, 1992

Polk County Sheriff

Michael L. Parson	REP	1,602	100.0%

Total Votes 1,602

Primary Election: August 4, 1992

Polk County Sheriff

Roy Harms	REP	841	22.64%
Larry L. Wollard	REP	1,308	35.22%
Michael L. Parson	REP	1,565	42.14%

Total Votes 3,714

About the Author

Dr. James K. (Jim) Jones spent thirty-one years in Missouri public education. Dr. Jones finished his educational career serving nineteen years as superintendent of the Blair Oaks R-II School District located just south and east of Jefferson City. Before taking the helm as superintendent, he served as secondary principal at Blair Oaks High School and Middle School for four years. Prior to moving to the Blair Oaks R-II School District, he spent eight years in north-central Missouri as a secondary mathematics instructor and coach in the Marceline R-V School District. Dr. Jones graduated from Monroe City High School in northeast Missouri. He received his bachelor's degree from William Jewell College, his master's degree from William Woods University, his specialist degree from Saint Louis University, and his doctorate from Saint Louis University.

With this book being his first ever publication, Dr. Jones will never profess himself as an accomplished author, but he is an experienced storyteller. It's relatively certain that students, athletes, parents, teachers, or administrators he has worked with over the years would say they had to endure the storytelling feature that accompanies Dr. Jones. He has been humbled by this opportunity and the significant responsibility it demands. His intent is to pass the blessings he has received in this process on to all readers.

Dr. Jones and his wife, Kelli, live in Jefferson City, Missouri, and have four daughters and one grandson. Their daughters are Sara (Caleb) Bischoff of Jefferson City and twin sister Alyson (Cory) Epperson of Springfield; Emilee Jones of Overland Park, Kansas; and Kayla Jones (fiancé Garrett Francis) of Columbia. Their grandson Carter Bischoff will soon be joined by a brother or sister.